RELIGION, IDEOLOGY, AND HEIDEGGER'S
CONCEPT OF FALLING

American Academy of Religion
Academy Series

edited by
Carl A. Raschke

Number 54

Religion, Ideology, and Heidegger's
Concept of Falling
by
Gregory Tropea

Gregory Tropea

Religion, Ideology, and Heidegger's Concept of Falling

Scholars Press
Atlanta, Georgia

Religion, Ideology, and
Heidegger's Concept of Falling

by
Gregory Tropea

© 1987
American Academy of Religion

Library of Congress Cataloging in Publication Data

Tropea, Gregory.
   Religion, ideology, and Heidegger's concept of falling.

   (AAR academy series ; no. 54)
   1. Heidegger, Martin, 1889–1976—Religion.
2. Religion—Philosophy. 3. Ideology. I. Title
II. Series: American Academy of Religion academy
series ; no. 54.
B3279.H49T67 1987   200'.1   86-17685
ISBN 1-55540-041-8 (alk. paper)
ISBN 1-55540-042-6 (pbk. : alk. paper)

Printed in the United States of America
on acid-free paper

Dedicated to
The Hon. Elim I.L. Yen

CONTENTS

Acknowledgements

Many teachers and friends have had a hand in shaping this project. Among them are Prof. Stanley Hopper, who introduced me to *Being and Time*, Prof. Huston Smith, who brought the notion of tradition alive, Prof. James Wiggins, who thematized narrative, Prof. Michael Novak, who brought the polemics of religion and ideology into practical focus, Prof. Gabriel Vahanian, who transformed my understanding of technology, and especially Prof. Charles Winquist, whose incisive comments on the first draft and encouragement in the final stages of this project have given me a far better sense of the place and direction of my work. To all of these teachers and to others in the Department of Religion at Syracuse who have provided years of stimulating conversation, I owe many thanks.

Prof. David L. Miller, advisor for the dissertation, has been relentless in carving away everything that does not feel like work and careful to preserve everything that does. One cannot ask for more than to have a teacher so dedicated to the *tao* of thinking.

Through changes upon changes, Ko-Ko Yen Tropea has patiently endured the demands of this project on our family life and still provided encouragement at the times it was needed most. This document and several related works-in-progress benefit from a steadiness of resolve that would have been impossible without her faith in the way we have chosen.

Preface

The Being-free of beings for the call of Being, the *Bhagavad-Gita* teaches, is the purpose of all true work. It is the justification I would claim for inviting readers to work through this lightly edited version of my Syracuse University doctoral dissertation.

Though changes have been made in view of the wider readership this text is expected to have, there have been no substantive additions and most technical points have been left intact. These latter include notes on translations of Heidegger's works which are in every case intended to supplement the work of the translators, not to find fault with their very significant acheivements. I have restricted such notes to problems which would affect the course of thinking the questions of the text.

For the push to go back into this material to reduce the depart-ment-specificity that characterized its life as a dissertation, I am indebted to one whose aim is true, Charles Winquist. For the fine-tuning of focus reflected in the changed title of the work, I thank Carl Raschke, under whose series-editorship this book appears. If my work at points falls short of the appropriate ideals, it is not for want of able critics; sooner or later it has to come down to the writer's hand. In polishing the rough edges of the original, the aim has mostly been to avoid inflicting certain of my own wounds unnecessarily upon those who are already so wounded that they would have reason to engage this text.

G.M.T.

But where danger is, grows
The saving power also.

— *Hölderlin*

Why do you look at the speck of sawdust in your brother's eye,
with never a thought for the great plank in your own?
— *Matthew 7:3*

Preface to the Dissertation

Working at Cross-Purposes?
Religion and Ideology in Terms of Heidegger's Concept of Falling

Neither in the dark compulsions buried by materialism nor in the sensible rationalizations that shine forth with unworldly luster in the filtered light of idealism do we seek the meanings of religion and ideology. No desirable perspective is gained in a view through the lens of an objectivistic metaphysics to either "the thing itself" or its close relative, "the thing in its world." The meanings of religion and ideology as *existential facts* are first raised to consciousness when consciousness opens itself to the possibility of an engagement of beings in *uncertain terms*. An element of uncertainty is both integral to all signification and prerequisite to all thinking.

Semantic uncertainty is generally avoided in linguistic performance the way potholes in the road are avoided in driving, but just as potholes bring the road to presence for drivers, so semantic uncertainty brings to presence both the signifier and its possibilities of meaning for speakers and hearers. With uncertainty of meaning comes interruption of its flow, a phenomenon of the kind of irregularity in the surface of the semantic highway that challenges the inevitability of the way.

Because problems do not arise unless something is being put to the test, a search into the possibilities of meaning cannot be an objectivistic, thematic survey of one's own uncertainties, and still less can it be a finger-pointing exercise directed at perceived deficiencies in others' understandings; it can only proceed authentically through an actual attempt to achieve conscious certainty, and that entails not only some kind of logical coherence but also a sense of rootedness in the economy of factical pressures and resistances. Only in this mode, pursuing a veridically smooth flow of meaning, can an actual irregularity of consciousness occur that is worthy of extended observation and exegesis.

The search for certainty concerning the meaning of a signifier may be provisionally identified with the kind of phenomenological project that seeks the essence of the signified thing itself, but the search for the meaning of a signifier cannot stop with the results of phenomenology or else the thinking of meaning is condemned to mechanical repetition of what has already been achieved. Still less can a true search be satisfied with the presupposition-laden shorthand of traditional, formulaic definitions. A phenomenological search does have value in exposing the topography of subjective certainty (and the intentional reductions that are part of phenomenological study are an important component of the search), but, as Heidegger found when he thought through the initial stages of the problem that motivated *Being and Time*, the great value of such an undertaking appears after consciousness has been surveyed and the impulse to closure and conclusion has asserted itself. The vision that is so complete as to tempt one to satisfaction is the legitimate starting point for polemics. It is in resisting the impulse to closure and eschewing the appearance of knowledge that the first chance of entering the realm of uncertainty appears. An investigation which begins at the edges of the realm of uncertainty proceeds by rules which are different from those of phenomenology.

The first step in a post-phenomenological inquiry is to supplement the recognition that what is signified always remains partially concealed with the further recognition that a signifier has possibilities which exceed those of the signified itself, essentially due to the amplified metaphorical and metonymic properties of abstractions. If the possibilities of significant abstractions in thinking are limited either to codification of the appearances of the moment or to conservative reifications of semi-critical phenomenology, then meaning goes around in uninteresting circles. In both cases, the cataloguing of what-has-been replaces the understanding of what is becoming. In both cases, history of ideas becomes a reactionary, antiquarian enterprise. Certainty is circular but uncertainty breaks up the circular flow of meaning. The places at which breaks and discontinuities occur, we call changes. Changes make possible the experience of the becoming of beings. Meaning is experienced as such when it breaks, that is, changes. The limit to how far beyond certainty one may proceed in the investigation of meaning is determined by changes that are factically taking place in the history of ideas and in the phenomenal world.

Investigation of ideas of religion and ideology does call for a certain amount of antiquarian attention, but that does not in any way diminish the need for synchronic critical inquiry, since religion and ideology are also always *essentially* not yet fully understood. Critical inquiry calls for attention to apparent breaks and changes in the factical being of signifiers, especially as revealed in the structures of their possible semantic environments. Such phenomena of interruption and incompleteness, when they appear, are not at first amenable to being surveyed transcendentally and catalogued thematically; they are only revealed partially as virtually raw data at the conclusion of a systematic search for certainty. A second order inquiry, critical interpretation, carries on once gaps and breaks call attention to themselves. In the discussion which follows, we intend to see how this two-step operation works.

Materialists can be satisfied in advance and on their own terms concerning the theoretical possibility of such phenomena by the observable changes that have occurred and will continue to occur in the material basis. Idealists can see how conscious understandings have come and gone, each making its own contribution, but none ever permanently grasping the totality of its object, *even when that object is itself purely a product of consciousness.* Neither of these two ways of coming to terms with abstractions (as consequences of material relations or as independently subsisting realities) dominates the present study, however. Instead, religion and ideology, as uncertain givens, are to be observed breaking in upon each other as existential challenges to the Being of human beings. As the terms of the challenges become clearer, so do the being of religion and the being of ideology.

The idea that religion and ideology challenge each other is surely not new. What is new in this procedure is a glimpse of how ideology belongs with religion in a positive as well as a negative way. In other terminology, ideology is revealed as a necessary station on the way to both damnation and salvation.

In addition to a theological justification for holding the ideas of religion and ideology in relationship, there is also a methodological reason, albeit a negative one, that shows its value especially as the phenomenological data thins out. It has to do with difficulties attendant on studying a signifier by simply breaking it down on one's own terms and into one's own terms, which are subsequently projected onto the idea as knowledge.

On its own (which is to say, on our own), the signifier is as a wild, elusive butterfly whose flittings can be followed and maybe even brought to a halt (at the risk of killing it), but never unerringly predicted, never known in advance beyond the principled uncertainty of calculated probabilities. Moreover, in the event that reason succeeds in reducing the idea to its own pre-given terms (closure of phenomenological inquiry), pinning the idea itself down as a butterfly in a collection, the essence of the idea is then as absent in the rationale as the Being of the (murdered) butterfly is in the assembly of insect bodies. The only breaks in the flittings of the butterfly that preserve its integrity are those which occur when the butterfly responds in its own way to a call in its own world.

Ideas of religion and ideology already are entities in a world; they do not need to be pinned down by finalizing definitions any more than butterflies need to be put in collections; multiplication of such Procrustean definitions only introduces supplementary and unnecessary possibilities into the Being of an idea, just as the invention of the butterfly collection introduces a new and unnecessary set of possibilities to the Being of the butterfly. The benign view of definitions suggests that they are something like innocent emanations of the thing itself while other, more critical views understand definitions as repressions of various kinds. The decision to exchange understanding that comes through participation in the ensemble of beings for understanding that comes through objectification of beings effects the most radical repression.

We feel the charm of the butterfly in its flittings about and brief engagements in the world. This charm is for many the predominant reality of the butterfly; when it is violated to turn the butterfly into a specimen, the butterfly becomes something that is merely colorful or interesting. The longer such interest is sustained, the further we are from the charm of the fluttering butterfly. We forget what attracted us to the butterfly in the first place. As a constant, the dead butterfly presences less and less of the charming Being of the butterfly and more and more of the alien Being of the insect. As a constant, the dead metaphor, untimely killed in order to display its definition, presences less and less of its original force. At times, the search for the original force of a word assumes the appearance of etymology, as in some of the later essays of Heidegger. If such attempts to recover original force are (mis)construed as actual etymologies, however, the results may scandalize philologists as much as they excite philosophers. What is important is that they do not leave words for dead.

Alive, the butterfly comes and goes. It engages with other butterflies and makes more butterflies. Its self-revelation is intermittent. Yet in
this intermittence, we sense no danger to the Being of the butterfly; on
the contrary, intermittence affirms the Being of the butterfly. The
intermittent revealing and concealing of itself is part of the Being of the
butterfly; we discover just how much a part of the Being of the butterfly
this intermittency is only after the butterfly has been caught and pinned
to a board. Similarly, we have already seen what linguistic analysis does
to language and we know what one-sidedness does to human beings. In
response to the attempt to force the butterfly to reveal itself constantly,
one-sidedly, the butterfly itself retreats into near total concealment and
ceases to venture butterflies into a future which denies the Being of
butterflies. It withholds its most precious gift: delight. It confronts us
then with its anatomical otherness, but only after it has already been
reduced to anatomy in the act of collecting.

The movement of thinking is worth charting. A certain reduction
has already occurred at the moment we identify the butterfly as such. We
may choose to stop at that level of reduction or move on to some other
level of reduction. This is a decision that is allowed by the Being of the
butterfly in cooperation with the Being of human beings. Whether we
ignore butterflies, take passing notice of them, enjoy them fluttering
about, pin them to boards, monitor their movements systematically, or
study their physiology, we are behaving in ways that presuppose a
certain grasp of the Being of butterflies. Typically, our grasp of the Being
of butterflies is sufficient unto our purposes, so much so that if we think
about it, we might even think that we could give a fair general account
of what we do not know about butterflies. That can only happen in the
presence of a prior grasp of the imagined totality of a thing.

But what if we try to begin with the assumption that our grasp of
butterflies is insufficient, that we do not know what a butterfly is? Is the
next thing to take a butterfly apart and look inside to find out what it is?
Is it to pin the butterfly to a board and stare at it? These operations surely
will not help us to understand why butterflies can be charming, yet the
charm of butterflies might very well be what is most important to us
about them. Whatever may be the best way to find out what the
butterfly is, it probably is not forcing the butterfly into a constant
revelation of what can be constant in itself, because what can be constant
in a butterfly surely does not constitute the vitality of its essence.

If I am charmed by the butterfly and tempted to catch it and
mount it in a collection, what in the world will stop me? As I turn over
the likely possibilities for the future of the butterfly, I may remember
what other butterflies in collections are like or imagine what the butterfly

in question would be like. If I like the thought of the butterfly in a collection, I may proceed to try to catch it and pin it down. If I do not like that thought, I find some other way to enjoy the butterfly. If I had liked the idea of religion as it could be pinned down, I would have attempted that, but after completing this study, I know I do not like this kind of idea because it is not true to the Being of religion. Moreover, it is not true to the Being of human beings in any way that I can responsibly imagine. The pinning down of religion that can be observed is perpetrated by totalizing ideologies which will be shown to be essentially antagonistic to the Being of religion even as they are essentially included in the Being of religion. The reason why it is important to demonstrate the essential uncertainty of religion as signifier is to give the term its full potential to resist definitive *inclusion* in the self-serving lexicon of any ideology.

As with butterflies, so with signifiers: they can be pinned down or left free to make engagements where they will. Pinned down, we still call them "words," but at that point, they are more truthfully spoken of as sub-parts of an encompassing ideology which forces presentation of a limited group of their most marketable characteristics. In uncertainty, signifiers are themselves in their moving from engagement to engagement in the world. To catch them in mid-flight and force an engagement is an act of violence. To catch sight of a word in engagement and not totalize the engagement is the beginning of letting the idea be.

The ideas of "religion" and "ideology" have been engaged with each other since before this project began. Though the discourse of the inquiry might be said to be "about" religion and ideology, it never defines these terms as a way of trying to reveal the forces they represent; it defines only some differences between them, for these are what appear in factical engagements, and it defines its own fundamental ontology as well as is practicable. The way these differences and ontological claims are defined, it appears that religion and ideology are inextricably bound up with each other. Imagining how this is so is the step into uncertainty that is taken at this juncture. Imagining how this is not so is the step that awaits the reader after the step about to be taken.

Sometimes they say, "Watch your step." Other times they say, "Don't fall." But the danger remains.

SECTION ONE

What looks like a digression is in fact the actual proper
movement on the way by which the neighborhood is deter-
mined. And that is nearness.

— *Martin Heidegger*
"The Nature of Language"

I. Method and Metatheory

Conflict and struggle come to dominate existence when apparently incompatible and inflexible purposes and symbol systems are thrown into contact and competition with each other. In situations of being-at-odds, there is reason to value understandings of self, other, and situation which promise to increase appreciation of the complexities of presence and foster awareness of the potential depth of the logics of difference, thereby conditioning impulses to violent exclusion and coercion. One way of favoring the development of a disposition toward appreciating or at least admitting the possibility of logics of difference calls for attention to the fundamental understandings and experiences that inform cultures and communities as ways of being in the world.

This formal study of two ontic fundamentals, religion and ideology, commences with an empowering observation of an aspect of change. We begin with the category of change because at whatever depth, the study of change is the study of existence. In this case we observe that cultures and communities come into being and inexorably develop upon the ecstatic initiatives of human beings, beings who exist as historical facts in the mode of Being-there (Dasein). The founding and renovating initiatives that are presented in history to history, which all cultures formally have in common, are properly called "ecstatic" because it is only by stepping outside their own historical-factical what-is that human beings (necessarily) participate in the creation of what-is-to-be. Of special interest for this study are the ecstasies that eventuate in socio-cultural creativity; *mutatis mutandis*, such ecstasies anticipate the irreducible differences which challenge understanding.

The essentially ecstatic creative initiatives that proximally guide human beings in the construction of their cultures and communities can be seen as uniting pasts and futures in venturing projections of presence into absence. It is both formally and really possible that productive ecstatic initiatives occur according to what we might call "natural laws,"[1] but the precise specifications of these laws (if there are such laws) are not at issue here, only the formal precondition of all such cosmological orderings is; this formal precondition should hold essentially that Dasein's constituting initiatives always come into being when situations somehow call for them.[2] Though this study attempts to deal with what cultural initiatives essentially are, it does not seek to investigate the mechanics of their appearance (the "somehow"); in order to keep the essential in view, we focus on the question of the significance of what appears when cultural initiatives are at work and new possibilities of consciousness and anaesthesia come into being. Any such focus, when pitched on the level of the ontological question (as an explicitly linguistic issue) injects a pause precisely at the point where uncritical judgement (the conservative calculation of common sense) rushes to emplace a stock evaluation.

The ecstatic, historical initiatives of human beings not only bring cultures and communities into being, they also cooperate with the multifarious initiatives of other kinds of beings to constitute the existence of all human beings as Dasein, whether factical human individuals choose to recognize it case-by-case or not. While other kinds of beings (those which apparently do not have the Being of Dasein, at least in the sense that Heidegger understands Dasein in his writings) receive only fleeting thematic attention in our look at the dyadic complex of religion and ideology, it will be obvious that they are never far from human concern. Still, they are never as close to Dasein ontologically as other beings which do have the Being of Dasein, even though they may come to presence ontically as closer.[3] The relationships that obtain among beings with the Being of Dasein and other beings form a multiplex whole that is unique to each individual, a perpetually unfinished totality that is developed through religion and ideology and mediated in theology. As Heidegger characterizes human existence in *Being and Time*: Being-there (Dasein) is also Being-with (Mitsein).[4] It is precisely because of this integral element of Being-with in the structure of Dasein that the ecstatic constituting initiatives of cultures and communities are of any interest at all and are, in fact, of vital interest for reasons ranging from the strategic to the aesthetic.

It is of the essence of human beings to exist, claims Heidegger in his partially-thought interpretation of these traditional categories in *Being and Time*;[5] this existence, which *as the existence of Dasein* is always thoroughly symbolically motivated by both religion and ideology (in a relationship of dynamic succession, not synchronic complementarity), can be revealingly and usefully fictionalized as a unified complex of cooperating (*mitarbeitend*) initiatives that originate in diverse corners of creation. Factically, an actual complex of cooperating initiatives that motivates and thus actively constitutes human existence may appear as coordinated progress, as a historical movement that leads ever onward and upward toward some ideal. By contrast, though, this formal unity may also appear in less obviously coherent and productive manifestations, as in the instance of discord. Discord occurs as a phenomenon in the event of divergent constituting initiatives of Dasein. Underlying the thought of progress and discord for Heidegger is a primal *polemos*, though this concept does not emerge until the 1935 lecture, *Einführung in die Metaphysik*.[6]

In Dasein's Being as Mitsein, the polemical discord of distinct initiatives may appear publicly as the phenomena of conflict or controversy, but it may also appear as ambivalence or as psychopathology. The reason why any of these ontic phenomena should be analyzed ontologically as grounded in polemically discordant initiatives lies in the catholicity of ontology and in the essentially polemical nature of discord itself. Discord, as a complex being-at-odds, can be imagined on the one hand as a force preventing decision, while on the other, it can as well be imagined as the necessary reality that, often concealed, acausally underlies all phenomena of absence of decision. Either way, the situation is existentially the same because it is structurally the same: no decision (no movement of being) occurs and the dynamics of change are unaffected. Note, however, that in an actual situation, the addition of a factical observer compelled to make interpretations would make an ontical difference, necessarily changing the mix of possibilities available for appropriation or rejection. One who pursues the religion/ideology problematic is liable at any time to become just such an observer. Note also that the thematizing of conflict and discord, as found in the sciences of crisis management and conflict resolution, carries with it an agenda to obscure all aspects of discord which work against restoration of tranquility; the choice to employ such techniques is always an existential decision for a specific possibility from among the inventory of discordant initiatives and a de-legitimation of all the impulses which may have come to expression as the "reasons" for the problem.

Discord appears as the preventing of decision when the situation presents too many confusing possibilities upon which Dasein can project itself. It then comes to presence as distracted preoccupation with the exigencies of the present or as vacillating indecision. Such preoccupation can only be authentically overcome by decision for a true occupation and such indecision can only be authentically resolved by Dasein's own resoluteness. In the moment of indecision, however, Dasein's own ontological possibility of resoluteness is factically concealed by the presence of possibilities already at hand in the world.

In contrast to its appearance as that which prevents decision, discord can appear as the absence of decision either on the part of an individual, in the case of an "internal" ontical conflict of unrecognized existential import, or among individuals, when an individual conflict has been projected onto others or when the conflicting initiatives structurally include more than one individual. In that case, discord appears deceptively as a virtually gratuitous freedom from the necessity of decision. For Heidegger, decision (*Ent-scheidung*) signifies a closing of the space that separates beings with the Being of Dasein and the reality of the *polemos*, the factical dynamic of revealing and concealing in which beings come to presence in a ceaselessly changing *chiaroscuro*. Both confusion and freedom from necessity are marks of inauthenticity, loss of self, in the ontology of *Being and Time*.

To show the significance of decision and resoluteness for the human being sketched in *Being and Time*, we propose to consider the *polemos* of revealing and concealing as essentially linked to another of Heidegger's concepts, **falling**, in this way: falling, as the difference between a Dasein which existentially grasps both its There and its Being and a Dasein which is oblivious to them, is the ontological basis for the most radical polemical discord, namely, the revealing and concealing of the truth of Being. The polemical flux, in which not only other beings come to presence (always) inconstantly, but Dasein itself as well, renders instantly untruthful every decision (authentic or not) which is grounded in presence, leaving Dasein with but two real choices: to keep its own counsel and attempt to refrain from all decision grounded in presence, or to attempt (as in the name of pragmatism) to force decisions which are grounded in presence. The refraining (not from all decision, just decision grounded in presence), we will say, is characteristic of religiously motivated behavior and the forcing will be analyzed to be characteristic of ideologically-determined behavior. Dasein's own continual modal alternation between preserving authentic, resolute existence and falling into the inauthentic lostness of "taking someone else's word for it" determines that all decision, whether grounded in presence or not, will always be questionable by the lights of one disposition of Dasein or another. Then, as soon as a decision is questioned, a space must be opened between observer and observed, thus destroying the matter-of-factness of the decision. Dasein is thus fated to be engaged in a perpetual destruction (or deconstruction) and reconstruction of itself.

It is the not uncommon phenomenon of an absence of decision, which is to say the hidden or revealed presence of an open question (or,

still truer to the language of this study, the fact of existential distance),
that calls for an ontological investigation of fundamental personal and
cultural initiatives, for it is through these often obscure initiatives that
human beings come to co-create the conditions of a reality in which none
is truly independent of the other. Ontological investigation, in bringing
to light hints of the extent of what is at stake in specific modes of
personal and cultural development, also brings the observer existentially
closer to what is observed, ideally reducing perceived distance to the
vanishing point. From perspectives located both inside the Heideggerian
corpus and (nominally) outside it, these minimal facts may be taken to
constitute a sufficient preliminary motivation for our central thesis that
**Heidegger's concept of "falling" articulates a fundamental
principle which ontologically unifies "religion" and "ideology" as the complementary existential moments of Dasein
and which, by implication, unifies the phenomena of actual
religions and ideologies.** That there obtain fundamentally discordant personal and cultural initiatives competing in the world is
empirically beyond question; that this irreconcilable discord appears to
be **essentially** existential, at least if we think along the path on which
Heidegger set out, may justify or even demand inclusion of an explicitly
ontological dimension in *any* critical analysis which tries to interpret it.

Existential discord may be able to occur in a number of ways but
only one way comes under active consideration in these pages, namely,
the discord that is brought into being through what Heidegger perhaps
disingenuously calls "falling," a state-of-Being peculiar to Dasein which
occurs as the condition of trusting acceptance of available public initiatives which are then appropriated and projected into the future as one's
own true existential initiatives. In the case at hand, in which both Dasein
as Mitsein (i.e., Dasein in the mode of necessarily-being-in-relationship)
and Dasein as that type of being which ontologically grasps itself for
what it is (i.e., Dasein in its existential solitude) turn out to be at issue,
we find an apparently irreconcilably divided self working at cross-
purposes but in spite of all appearances, we never, never reify the
division even as we repeatedly accentuate the facts of existential discord.
Thus it is that distinct existential initiatives of Dasein can and must be
imagined essentially as unified (and imagined without recourse to
premature assertions of identity), even though the emerging reality is a
perpetually disruptive unification in discord.

Perhaps one of the most public symptoms of this discord has been
the so-called science-religion debate, which has been at most points over
the centuries little more than a conflict of vested interests, being then an
exercise in ideological competition more than anything else; that it is

possible for an authentic expression of existential discord to be projected as a social reality and then degenerate into something like pretentious squabbling over territory is more an indication of the empirical realities of falling than of the essential structure of the matter. It is characteristic of fallen Dasein to lose sight of itself and get caught up in a metonymically-determined competition of claims and counter-claims, but this is only one of the strategies available to fallen Dasein for preservation of the psychic anaesthesia that is the consequence (and not the cause of) existential oblivion.

Logically, the public discord which is created by the kind of essentially obscurantist rhetoric that one finds in the science-religion debate need not have eventuated out of an existential-ontological complexity in Dasein, but the specific proposal of existential complexity that Heidegger presents in *Being and Time* shows itself as having a perhaps unintended explanatory power, namely, the power of a meta-narrative, in being able to illuminate and provisionally ground *the disagreement itself* with regard to the most significant parts of the altercation. As our discussion of religion and ideology proceeds, it will become apparent why it is important to maintain an intentionality which is drawn to specific kinds of difference; in approaches to conflicts such as this, Heidegger's concept of falling marks the terms of essential difference and in so doing directs intentionality toward those questions in which the potential gains upon prevailing of one interest are of a generically different character than the potential gains of the other. Unlike the conflicts of classical Marxism, these would be matters that in a sense lie half inside and half outside the scope of ideological construction, and because the potential gains that are riding on resolution of the projected *essential* conflict necessarily acquire their respective meanings within incommensurable logical systems, the real issues are difficult to bring into the open, much less resolve. The difference marked by falling determines that in every case essential issues must at some level challenge all parties involved; in the case of the science-religion debate both "sides" are challenged because the essential question has more to do with the integration of science and religion rather than the much-publicized and apparently more entertaining "confrontation" of science and religion.

Given the factor of surface conflict of interest linked with deep incommensurability of implicit goals, certain issues become virtually impossible for reasonable people to discuss in public terms. The origins of conflicts become virtually lost as signifier replaces displaced signifier in the search for a common language that can never be except as final lie. Further, negotiation which presumes that some kind of synthesis of any faithful remnant of initial positions will be satisfactory only obscures the terms of *existential* conflict that is playing itself out. It is simply naive to expect the ramified energies of the psyche to cooperate in a sham resolution whose guiding principles include the repression of primal force through relentless refinements of signification, undeclared bracketing of ultimacy, and avoidance of the possibility of exhaustion. Naive negotiation thus creates a smokescreen of imperfectly realized signifiers whose power is not to convince, but to irritate.

By way of contrast, it is characteristic of purely ideological disputes truly to admit of solution without remainder by syllogistically reasoned discussion; a dispute becomes purely ideological, and ceases to be a matter of existential discord, assuming it ever was one, whenever continuation of polemical discourse presumes a possibility of agreement on a question of metaphysical essence where before there was no such presumption. In addition, it is characteristic of all ideological disputes that they are predicated on desire to approach or avoid outcomes which have been reductively calculated in advance. Other kinds of indications of discourse functioning at the level of ideology can, like these, be assembled on the basis of a fundamental ontology from either *ad hoc* or formal critiques and theories of ideology in various genres.[7] The validity of principles of identification such as these is not a matter of inherent accuracy, but consists essentially in their fidelity to the functioning regional ontology of which they are necessarily possible elaborations.

A theory of ideology consonant with the thinking of Heidegger remains to be fully developed, but it promises to include on internal grounds several features reminiscent of Marxian and Freudian theory. It will contain some variant of the classical notion that ideology is a construction whose purpose is concealment of the realities of domination dependence, and repression, economic and otherwise. Also, in pursuing Heidegger's way, it will analyse ideology essentially such that the construction of concealments will be seen as belonging to the Being of ideology and, further, it will seek to open the phenomena of ideology to both ontical and ontological investigation. It can be expected to insist on the viability of its conceptions of truth and the discovery of truth insofar as it incorporates the sense of *alētheia* that Heidegger attempted to communicate. As this study's ontological observations of what is generally called ideology unfold to replace programmatic capsule-definitions, one aspect of the beginning of a critical theory of ideology emerges as the essence of the science-religion debate shows itself through the problematics of technology to be a question of ideology and religion.

Because ontological investigation is only meaningful with regard to what is of existential import, its scope is thematically more limited than scientific investigation and it is methodologically different at least in that it always gives credence, even if not allegiance, to its initial conceptions. What for science is a hypothesis to be tested has as its structural analogue in ontology an incomplete but inviolate given. This is not to say that science is violent while ontology is non-violent, which is a trivial truth at best, since every science is the consequence of an ontology just as all theoretical language is consequent upon an ontology. The problem lies in obscurity of the nature of theory in general. Theoretical language, even the sort of critical theoretical language that attempts self-consciousness, is always violent, always manipulative, always seeking to introduce novelty that fits its own program; Marx and Freud are perfect examples. The only way to develop a theory of ideology that is properly reflexive, that is, which includes itself, is to accept one's own participation in a consciousness that is somehow false (if only for all that is forcibly concealed) and accept the violence and the contradictions inherent in the critical theoretical techniques of expanding and reordering the linguistic universe.

With all of these qualifications, this inquiry into the essential relationship of religion and ideology seems best read as a critical theoretical document. What this means substantively to the work being undertaken is suggested in three contrasts between critical theory and scientific theory proposed by Raymond Geuss in *The Idea of a Critical Theory*.[8] First, he points out, scientific theories as "instrumental reason" have manipulation of the external world as their goal, while critical theories strive for creation of a state of awareness in which hidden coercions and one's own true interests are revealed. While Heidegger does not explicitly pursue a thoroughgoing program to this end, he does make progress toward it; on this basis, his writings can be construed as a foundational contribution to a critical theory. The second point Geuss proposes is that scientific theories are objectifying (in the formal sense that they refer to objects different from themselves), while " . . . a critical theory is itself always a part of the object-domain which it describes; critical theories are always in part about themselves."[9] This condition would appear to be met by any theory grounded in Heidegger's ontological work. The third point Geuss makes is that while experimental verification is sufficient support for scientific theories, critical theories must additionally give account of themselves as elements of the realities they propose. In the chapter on technology below, for example, theory as such appears as a component of ideology and the contradiction that theory in general (as technique) introduces into Being is revealed as ontologically coherent and essential to the dynamics of Dasein's venturing.

An apparent advantage of the critical theory that is developed in these pages, then, is that it does not seem to require a privileged position for itself with respect to consciousness. It does, however, explicitly require a consciousness prepared to grasp the difference between what we might term existential freedom and domination. Since false consciousness in Heideggerian thinking is a matter of concealment rather than outright disagreement[10] and since concealment is a given for finite beings, a Heideggerian critical theory is inherently capable of a higher degree of reflexivity than any theory employing a correspondence theory of truth, a device which is diabolically powerful and forces any thought eventually into rigid orthodoxy and dogmatism.

As the argument unfolds in these pages, the constant play of contradictory initiatives can be kept in mind as the guarantee against an inflated estimation of one's own epistemology as well as thinking's best effort to avoid the kinds of coercion that certain strains of "Marxist" self-assurance have tortured the world with for so many decades. An observation of Heraclitus speaks to subject matter at hand: "Out of discord comes the fairest harmony."[11] The discord implied in the dynamics falling remains concealed until the initiatives that formally constitute it can be both joined to and distinguished from one another at a level other than a mere *ad hoc* linkage of terminology. This is not an impossible task. An eventual unifying principle is always near and waiting to be brought out into the open in the construction of a somehow more original, more primordial, less contingent pretext. Such a pretext functions as a "transcendent why" that appears in every case categorically to exceed and include *both* of any two ontically (and as well, perhaps foremost, ontologically) discordant initiatives. While ontically discordant initiatives may each be ecstatic or not, only one of any pair of ontologically discordant initiatives can be ecstatic. For this reason, it is only when we speak of ontologically discordant initiatives that the unification investigated in these pages is properly invoked. Purely ontic discord, in agreement on the (always opaque) terms of conflict, can be seen as unified by conventional linguistic analysis, which excludes the possibility of the ecstatic from the outset.

The proximate origin of any given ecstatic historical initiative is to be recognized as a replacement position, deceptively located at some remove from a significant break in an economy of pressures and resistances. This proximate origin, which may be ventured without really risking the originary ecstasy, always asserts itself in the present and calls for some action in the present, which " . . . is defined by the 'in-order-to'."[12] The transcendent why must be defined ontologically. Although Dasein's ultimate factical "why" may remain hidden,[13] there is always a finite (and ontically absolute) "in-order-to" which is equiprimordial with every authentic or inauthentic presencing.[14] Surface (ontical) discord, underlaid by a deeper (existential) discord, grounded in a yet deeper (ontological) unification is the structure of Being that occurs when ontologically distinct initiatives, each with its own present "in-order-to," seek to function in the field of the same transcendent why. Ontological discord occurs whenever decisions that are grounded in presence, namely ideological decisions, seek to exclude those which are not, namely religious decisions, and vice-versa. This seeking to exclude is ontologically determined. It will proceed.

A distinction is suggested in the title of this study between religion and ideology as two recognizable elements that are supposed to be somehow connected in a significant way by Heidegger's concept of falling. Though this linking concept is presented as relevant to a distinction that in fact has already been made and is now explicitly being made questionable, the reasons for proposing this particular relationship between religion and ideology and, beyond that, the appropriateness of "falling" as a third term that relates to each of the others are obscure at this point, since no explicit indication of their difference beyond the juxtaposition of terms has been provided. The aim is to propose an understanding of an *essential* difference that separates religion and ideology, a difference that may well be archetypal for all of the analyzable differences that occur as small twists and compound fractures in language and society. We are not concerned to catalogue phenomenal differences; essential difference can only come into view if ontological elements are introduced and coherently ordered. The two terms set in opposition in the title are already superabundantly rich in traditional associations; their linkage is anticipated as early as Plato's discussion of the relationship of religion and state in the *Laws*, so a variety of historically precedented reasons could be brought together to justify both their linkage and the making of a distinction between them. Unless those reasons also happen to be ontologically grounded in a non-*ad hoc* way, however, they must presuppose exactly what has already been projected to be in question, namely, understandings of religion and ideology which somehow require a distinction to be made between them.

It was just this type of problem that Heidegger had in mind when he set out to formulate a fundamental ontology. What he achieved in *Being and Time* does not, by his own estimate, complete the work of fundamental ontology, but it is the most comprehensive attempt so far, and while he did not succeed in his aim of definitively clarifying the meaning of Being,[15] he did propose a number of significant theses concerning human beings in a powerful, if timeless, narrative. In promulgating fundamental ontology as the eternal structure " . . . from which alone all other ontologies can take their rise,"[16] Heidegger sought to provide a possible beginning which was claimed to be typologically unlike all other points of departure for the making of distinctions.[17] The existential analytic, which claims to be a true beginning, still admits that its theme, Dasein, has already been grasped beforehand pre-ontologically.

Any distinction between religion and ideology that can be independently motivated in terms of an ontology like Heidegger's has the advantage of compatibility with all other work done in those terms as well as a more explicit understanding of its own premises. Theoretically, its epistemological status should be clearer than that of a distinction made without reference to fundamental ontology, but as yet, the basic epistemological status of fundamental ontology itself has not been clarified. If a distinction between any two initiatives of Dasein can be made on the fictionalizing assumption that the fundamental ontology can be taken as fundamental, then there is reason to believe that the ontology will provide a sufficient transcendent why which encompasses the two initiatives. (The concept of "falling" is related to the problematic of the transcendent why by way of the ontologically given "in-order-to.") With this provision that Heidegger's ontology be fictionalized as fundamental (with no more warrant than the force of its language), an analysis of the religion/ideology problematic that was structured according to the title of our project would be independently established as relevant to both of the designated existential initiatives on the basis of the synchronic narrative of the existential analytic. Though the existential analytic of *Being and Time* did not fully satisfy Heidegger's plans for a fundamental ontology, it can still work as a regional ontology of human existence which is virtually fundamental for this project. The Gödellian metaphor, which saliently echoes a point of Vedanta metaphysics, has moderated this era's sense of the fundamental such that our project proceeds without even a trace of nostalgia for the bold confidence of the early Heidegger that the fundamental would yield its secrets in a process of direct interrogation.

Distinctions between religion and ideology based on *ad hoc* definitions of the terms are actually thinly-disguised attempts to restrict what the terms mean in order to use the results ideologically-technologically, that is, in order to achieve an already-specified goal. For reasons that are detailed in the discussion of technology, it is both impossible and undesirable to avoid completely the ideological-technological use of intellectual results, but it should still be both possible and desirable to avoid the **exclusively** ideological-technological use of the results of thinking. In every case, the fundamental meaning of the work definitely becomes a question of the "in-order-to" of the intellectual undertaking, specifically whether the research of the project has been conducted in order to encounter ideas or entities that have presence or in order to hold them at a distance and obscure them. Further, it must be asked, assuming the overt intention of the work is to encounter ideas or entities that have presence, if such relationship as can be discerned is to be understood wholly or mostly in terms of that presence, or if there are other bases of relationship imaginable. In short, does Dasein's understanding of beings reach beyond the metaphysics of presence or doesn't it?

In the making of the distinctions that are necessary when presence itself becomes an issue, the in-order-to of the impulse to decide (that is, in fact, the impulse to determine a relationship) ontically takes precedence over the transcendent why of the initiatives in question and tries to determine the outcome of the inquiry in advance in such a way that the future is closed off for the sake of the present. In Heideggerian terms, this preponderance of presence in the existential dynamics of Dasein is given with the structure of care, and in particular with its component of falling. Further, such a presence-oriented making of distinctions for technological purposes entails that the transcendent why of the initiatives, that for the sake of which they come into being in the (so to speak) first place, get lost as the initiatives *qua* phenomena are defined as already pressed into the service of whatever ideological-technological impulse had moved to distinguish them. Even starting with the virtually clean slate of a fictionalized fundamental ontology, there is no pristine beginning.

Thus, *ad hoc* definitions of questionable terms only cause the question of the difference between them to be transposed into another key, into a questioning of the transcendent why of the impulse to distinguish. Since any transcendent why can be seen as originally fictional, it follows then that decisions which are predicated upon it are themselves essentially fictional also. The issue of distinctions easily becomes one of the adequacy of the transcendent why of the making of a particular distinction, which would be an issue for a future existential ethics.[18]

Distinctions which arise out of the technological impulse alone can have no status except as the calculated elaborations of ideologically predetermined positions. The aim of this categorization is not to contend that all technologically-inspired *ad hoc* definitions of religion and ideology (among other things) are necessarily totally and unredeemably wrong, only that they proximally appeal to the hidden assumptions of the individual for their validation. When definitions are decided in this way, any basis is as legitimate as any other; but when critical understanding is the goal, as it arguably is in the modern university, then self-critical thinking is the place to begin. Distinctions that begin and end in the conditioned opinions of the individual, no matter how "right" or "wrong" they are, exit the conversation precisely because of their intractable (but illusory) autonomy. When distinctions are made in terms that are originally public, they may be less novel, less striking, and less entertaining, but their structures are more open to view. In this case, it is the structure of a distinction between religion and ideology that comes into view and, along with it, aspects of religion and ideology. This coming into view of the Being of religion and ideology, which looks as though it could be the purpose of the discussion, is actually an **effect** of inquiring into what is already the case and not the product of an effort of prescriptive definition.

The question that motivates this study is in fact not the metaphysical/technological one — "What is the difference between religion and ideology?" — but rather a variant of the ontological one, in this case framed: "Why distinguish between religion and ideology?" Still, in order to respond creatively and accessibly, we proceed technologically.

G. Spencer-Brown suggests the essential logic behind the proposed separation of religion from ideology in a general way in *Laws of Form*: "There can be no distinction without motive, and there can be no motive unless contents are seen to differ in value."[19] It is already given in the lexicon of our language that religion and ideology as generic phenomena are seen to differ in value for the purposes of Dasein as Mitsein. The phenomena of religion and ideology that Mitsein sees and wants to distinguish originate in Dasein; the logic of the distinction which is given in language remains obscure, however, without representation of Dasein's prior ontological transcendent why. Moreover, is only because of a transcendent why that differences in value have meaning.

It appears, then, that distinctions between religion and ideology which grow out of *ad hoc* definitions of the terms in question are not viable in the same ways as those interpretations of their meanings which appropriate an ontologically-given transcendent why as their proximate origin. In addition, the uncritical acceptance of the opaque motivations that lie behind *ad hoc* distinctions simply places one into a different realm of discourse from conversations that begin with and proceed in terms of an explicit transcendent why. Thus, what is needed for the distinction between religion and ideology to go beyond vapid agreements to disagree is a conscious step beyond mere definitions of "religion" and "ideology" into the **ontology** of religion-and-ideology. This step presupposes both preliminary ontologies of religion and ideology and some kind of fundamental ontology.

Willard Quine suggests in an article, "Ontology and Ideology Revisited," that we are justified in attributing something like our own understandings of ideas and entities to others if they react to them in distinctive and unique ways. Further, these understandings, according to Quine, constitute for all intents and purposes the ideology of the individual. For Quine, there is an intimate and formal connection between ontology and ideology which obtains in theoretically formalizable values. Thus he writes, "To be, I have persistently maintained, is to be the value of a variable."[20] Quine's analytic ontology is not intended to be metaphysically prescriptive, but allows its content (its account of presence) to be derived from ideologies, which he defines as " . . . one's stock of simple and complex terms or predicates."[21] If we accept this way of beginning, then definition of the study's substantive terms in advance is methodologically excluded, and establishing the meaning of "religion" and "ideology" clearly becomes a hermeneutic exercise.

Two points emerge out of Quine's definitions: if there has already been coherent conversation which makes use of the terms "religion" and "ideology," then the entities that the terms signify can be taken to have existence and it is not necessary to worry the question of whether or not there is such a thing as religion or ideology; second, ontologies of these entities categorically belong to our ideologies. Though the sense of the word "ideology" will not remain focused in the way Quine's definition projects it, its basic implications that ideology determines ontology and that linguistic competence determines ideology will not be challenged; if a challenge were to be constructed, it would be a matter for linguistic theory. We content ourselves for now that facts of usage sufficiently demonstrate at least the psycho-linguistic reality of the existence and difference of the much-defined "religion" and "ideology."[22]

While the fact of the difference between "religion" and "ideology" is reasonably easy to discern and accept, the reason why the difference is meaningful, which must be the origin of any difference in value between them, is not illuminated by the kind of rigorously delimited *ex post facto* ontology of entities that Quine favors. One possible basis for determining and articulating the difference in value between "ideology" and "religion" that is posited here at the outset is an updated variant of the fundamental ontology that Heidegger introduced in *Being and Time*. While the motivations of his self-proclaimed fundamental ontology are themselves less than transparent, the ontology as it stands is at least an attempt at explicit description of categories and dynamics which cannot be entirely co-opted by either of the terms in question. By virtue of this apparent independence, Heidegger's work provides a questionable, but nonetheless serviceable, picture of the transcendent why of religion and ideology, namely, **human being**. Insofar as the fundamental ontology we work through speaks truthfully, the difference between religion and ideology predicated upon it has value and how one conceives religion and ideology "makes a difference"; without this particular ontology, of course, the specific difference in value projected here disappears and so does the proximate motive for the distinction that is being projected. Other ("traditonal") distinctions between religion and ideology remain untouched in this discussion, but only because they are being engaged here negatively, as beside-the-point, instead of positively, point-by-point.

Notes

¹ As some traditional beliefs, such as Oriental yin-yang philosophy, and several major contemporary models, among them Ervin Laszlo's interpretation of systems theory and B.F. Skinner's behavioral psychology, have it.

² The distinction between formal and real possibilities is taken from Herbert Marcuse's 1936 essay, "The Concept of Essence" (in *Negations*, trans. J.J. Shapiro. Boston: Beacon Press, 1968.) Marcuse traces the idea back to Hegel's *Wissenschaft der Logik*, in which formal possibilities are logical propositions which are bounded only by the law of non-contradiction, while real possibilities are presented in a sub-class of propositions which must take actual contingencies into account. Whether one arrives at a consideration of immediate existence by the consideration of real possibilities, as Hegel seems to suggest, remains in question. Less questionable is Marcuse's intent in quoting Hegel. He wants to arrive at the point where he can write, "Real possibility exists. Therefore it can be known as such by theory, and as it is known it can be taken up by the practice for which theory is the guide and be transformed into reality." (p. 82) The real possibility of cosmic order can not be considered critically, however, if beings happen to remain metaphysically opaque, as Heidegger would claim they did for Hegel and Marcuse. Leaving aside the materialist/idealist epistemological dispute, the fact remains that working with the real possibilities (and what they are in principle for present purposes emerges below) is the ultimate point of this study. We might note at this point also that one feature Hegel admired in realistic metaphysics, namely, the taking seriously of the given, is preserved in our outlook.

[3] The contrast of one's own feelings about a pet or a cherished keepsake with one's feelings about certain other (especially unattractive) people may make this point at the ontical level. As I write this, there is a sensationalist newspaper on display in the local supermarket announcing that four out of ten people surveyed prefer their cars to their mates. Whatever the method and results of this "survey," the point is that ontical proximity does not necessarily mirror ontological proximity. An informal argument for a category of ontological proximity unfolds below, in the discussion of falling.

[4] See for example the discussion of destiny in Martin Heidegger, *Sein und Zeit*. Tübingen: Neomarius, 1927, pp. 384-385 (*Sein und Zeit* henceforward given as SZ); *Being and Time*. New York: Harper and Row, 1962, p. 436 (*Being and Time* henceforward given as BT).

[5] "The 'essence' of Dasein lies in its existence." SZ, p. 42; BT, p. 67.

[6] Published as *Einführung in die Metaphysik* in 1953 by Niemeyer, Tübingen.

[7] In the preliminary remarks of an essay, "Nietzsche's Concept of Ideology," (*Theory and Society*, Vol. 13, No. 4 [July 1984], pp. 541-565.) Mark Warren summarizes several widely-held thoughts on ideology in the tradition of the Frankfurt School. He writes, "The outlines of a critical theory of ideology with roots in Marx and Freud are now relatively clear. Its essential aspects can be summarized in the following claims. First, ideological forms of consciousness, whether social or individual, conceal essential aspects of social and political reality. Second, the concealing attributes of ideology are not accidental (that is, ideologies are not simply 'errors'), but relate systematically to some set of social, psychological, and cognitive interests within a determinate historical context. Third, because ideologies relate systematically to interests and historical realities, they can be criticized so as to provide knowledge about these interests and realities."

[8] Raymond Geuss, *The Idea of a Critical Theory*. Cambridge: Cambridge University Press, 1981.

[9] Op. cit., p. 55.

[10] "Nature loves to hide," Heraclitus is reported to have said. See "Heraclitus," *The Presocratics*, tr. and ed. P. Wheelwright. New York: Odyssey Press, 1966, frg. 17 (D-K 123), p. 70.

[11] Op. cit., frg. 98 (D-K 8), p. 77.

[12] SZ, p. 365; BT, p. 416. Heidegger also notes that presencing (making present) first structures the encounter with any entity that has presence (SZ, p. 326; BT, p. 374). This is the primary authentic in-order-to of the present.

¹³ SZ, p. 276; BT, p. 321.

¹⁴ "Presencing" is the word we will use to represent the Heidegger's German *terminus technicus, gegenwärtigen,* which Macquarrie and Robinson translate as "making present." It includes creating the present (which Heidegger analyzes to be one of the three aspects of temporalizing), coming-to-presence, and bringing-to-presence. While "making present" is a justifiable translation of *gegenwärtigen,* it lacks the inherent agentive ambiguity of the German (in which two beings are equiprimordially *gegenwärtig*), a feature which retains its prominence in the later Heidegger corpus as indications continue to suggest that overtly one-sided (or "logocentric") interpretations of *gegenwärtigen* and related terms are to be avoided. Also to be registered in this connection is Heidegger's explanation (SZ, p. 338; BT, p. 388) that he uses the term *gegenwärtigen* by itself to denote inauthentic, visionless, irresolute presencing. Authentic presencing is characterized as the "moment of vision" (*Augenblick*). For Heidegger, both authentic and inauthentic presencings are pursuits of Dasein, but Dasein is always located in its equiprimordially constituted world, which must also participate.

¹⁵ SZ, p. 11; BT, p. 31.

¹⁶ SZ, p. 13; BT, p. 34.

¹⁷ That Heidegger's fundamental ontology may not be as unique an alternative as Heidegger himself characterizes it to be is suggested by variants of process philosophy. Robert C. Neville, to cite a recent example, proposes a kind of process philosophy, and not Heidegger's fundamental ontology, as the kind of general background or framework that philosophical theology needs to be adequate to both Eastern and Western religious experience. See Robert C. Neville, *The Tao and the Daimon: Segments of a Religious Inquiry.* Albany, N.Y.: State University of New York Press, 1982.

¹⁸ The close relationship between ethics and aesthetics would be clearly demonstrated in fundamental issues.

¹⁹ G. Spencer-Brown, *Laws of Form.* New York: Julian Press, 1972, p. 1.

²⁰ Willard Quine, "Ontology and Ideology Revisited," *The Journal of Philosophy,* Vol. LXXX, No. 9 (Sept. 1983), p. 499.

²¹ Op. cit., p. 501.

²² We are reminded of Rudolf Otto's response to this issue as he opened a discourse which presupposed meaningfulness of the concept of numinosity in *The Idea of the Holy* (tr. John W. Harvey. London: Oxford University Press, 1928): "The reader is invited to direct his mind to a moment of deeply-felt religious experience, as little as possible qualified by other forms of consciousness. Whoever cannot do this,

whoever knows no such moments in his experience, is requested to read no further . . . ." (p. 8) Otto is not being exclusivistic, just responding in the only honest way to a deficiency of linguistic competence; he is closing off as best he can the possible creation of a sham understanding of his theme. It will be claimed below that it is a tendency of ideological Dasein to collect just such understandings to create the illusion of knowledge.

A poor workman always blames his tools.

— *Popular saying*

II. Religion as Something Present-at-hand

In *Being and Time*, Heidegger focuses on the properties of existent beings, mostly those which have the kind of Being of Dasein, but he also is drawn by the logic of his inquiry to survey entities which do not have the kind of Being of Dasein, especially insofar as these latter have the Being of equipment. The intention in the remarks on equipment is to give a general, non-metaphysical account of situationally equipmental entities as their existence is determined by the existence of Dasein, and to this end, he proceeds to survey equipment not as it is in itself, but as it is experienced by concernful Dasein in its involvements with the world. A sense of the Being of equipment is relevant to the problematic of the relationship of religion and ideology because both religion and ideology are slated to be thematically treated as equipment in this essay.

Within the framework of *Being and Time*, equipment in the world of Dasein is conceived as liable to be experienced in one of two modes, as present-at-hand and as ready-to-hand. That equipment can be related to Dasein in these two ways meets the first epistemological problem of how religion and ideology as questions could come to our attention in the first place; it happens that *religion's* presence-at-hand called attention to the problem in this case, but, one suspects, on the other side of the world *ideology* could perform in much the same way. Regardless of whether the equipmental nature of religion or of ideology is discerned first, the next step should reveal that the problem is larger than just a single term. Before getting into the specific dynamics of the tension that appears to obtain between religion and ideology, let us consider what it means to say that religion and ideology can have the Being of equipment.

"The kind of Being which equipment possesses — in which it manifests itself in its own right — we call '*readiness-to-hand*'."[1] It is the nature of equipment that it be put to use, Heidegger claims, and it is only in being put to use that equipment can realize itself as being ready-to-hand. Readiness-to-hand, which is not simply usability (but which includes usability), is primarily a relationship of equipment to Dasein in which the equipment functions unobtrusively. "Unobtrusiveness" is not just an arbitrary matter of taste; it belongs categorically to the Being of equipment. Dasein itself is the origin of the Being of equipment; it is, in other words, the referential center for "equipment." Citing as an example the hammer, which he imagines showing itself most genuinely as hammer when it is being put to its intended use (in this case, hammering), Heidegger demonstrates that an experience of the readiness-to-hand of equipment is one that virtually any entity with the Being of Dasein will have had, with the lone possible exception of the "primitive man."[2] We are expected to be able to identify readily and understand without rigorous explanation what he is talking about here. Because this element of readiness-to-hand is constitutive of the Being of a hammmer (which is being understood ontologically as equipment whose reason-to-be is hammering), it is the case that any given hammer is "more of a hammer" when it is being put to use than when it is just lying around. The hammer, which is ontologically defined as a tool, was never intended just to lie around and thus it cannot fulfill itself as equipment by manifesting itself as a tool when it is not at work.

It is significant for the religion/ideology problematic that a necessity to be at work pervades the Being of the tool (as tool) as far as Dasein is concerned. If, as I am explicitly contending in this study, actual religions and ideologies can be beneficially and truthfully imagined as symbolic equipment, or tools essentially-metaphorically like the hammer, but of a different order, then they would be subject to the same basic conditions as more tangible tools; in this case, there is an implication that it is an ontological necessity, arising out of their existentially- and culturally-determined natures, for both religions and ideologies to be put into practice. When they cannot be put into practice readily, then they are bound to come to presence as problems. When religions and ideologies cannot be put into practice at all, they come to presence as curiosities.

The hammer's Being as hammer is determined in this ontology by its primarily equipmental nature. The nature of equipment, for its part, appears on closer analysis to be ontologically defined for Heidegger in the equipment's having an unquestionable reason to be as it is. This reason to be is the equipment's "towards-which."[3] The towards-which of something is defined for Heidegger by the specific involvement of the item of equipment within the primordially-given totality of involvements that makes up the worldhood of the world. As Heidegger construes it, the "towards-which" is essentially the understood purpose, or serviceability, of a thing, but this purpose is not limited to Dasein's concernfully anticipated tasks at hand for which the tool might be used;

the tool is ultimately brought into play for the purpose of the presencing of the Present (a category of temporality) itself. At this point, the difficulties with relationships grounded in presence (mentioned in the previous unit) appear, though Heidegger does not really make the point forcefully until "The Origin of the Work of Art." In that essay, he observes,

> Earth. . . shatters every attempt to penetrate into it. It causes every merely calculating importunity upon it to turn into a destruction. This destruction may herald itself under the appearance of mastery and of progress in the form of the technical-scientific objectivation of nature, but this mastery nevertheless remains an impotence of will. The earth appears openly cleared as itself only when it is perceived and preserved as that which is by nature undisclosable, that which shrinks from every disclosure and constantly keeps itself closed up.[4]

Not all beings retreat into themselves in the same way as the earth (shrinking from every disclosure), but all do conceal themselves in the *polemos* of revealing/concealing. Also, not all beings have the unique power of the earth to destroy inappropriate, calculated projections, but all do defeat them even if it is by the conservation in retreat of all that does not fit the calculation, as in the example of the butterfly collection. How Dasein presences the Present depends upon a recognition of the fact of concealment and how this fact limits relationship, even with equipment that is present-at-hand.

For Heidegger, these limits are apparent as he writes *Being and Time*, but they are sublimated from the standpoint of Dasein to an absolutized towards-which. Ultimately, Dasein does not desire to get involved with other entities (especially including those with the Being of equipment) for their own sakes, but for its own sake. It seems that the "correctness" of Dasein's various involvements is not the paramount issue in relationships from every standpoint in Dasein's repertoire; Dasein is portrayed by Heidegger as likely to attempt whatever suits its mood, no matter how importunate it may be. He writes:

> But the totality of involvements itself goes back ultimately to a "towards-which" in which there is *no* further involvement: this "towards-which" is not an entity with the kind of Being that belongs to what is ready-to-hand within a world; it is rather an entity whose Being is defined as Being-in-the-world, and to whose state of Being, worldhood itself belongs . . . . The primary 'towards-which' is a for-the-sake-of-which. But the 'for-the-sake-of' always pertains to

> the Being of *Dasein*, for which, in its Being, that very Being
> is essentially an *issue*.[5]

After locating the ready-to-hand within a prior (always already obtain-ing) matrix of involvements, Heidegger can be observed in this passage continuing the thinking of the "towards-which" with the two observa-tions that: 1) the towards-which is ultimately to be analyzed in terms of a "for-the-sake-of-which," and 2) the for-the-sake-of-which pertains exclusively to Dasein. In these observations, the transcendent why of the ecstatic initiatives of religion and ideology can be glimpsed as Dasein itself. The passage cited above continues on to remind the reader that Dasein's Being is the only authentic "for-the-sake-of-which" in the ontology. The decisive mark of inauthenticity, conversely, would be a complex of "towards-which" and "for-the-sake-of-which" that ulti-mately led consciousness elsewhere than the sense and thinking of the Being of Dasein. In falling, Dasein is oriented toward such an elsewhere. Therein lies perhaps the most important aspect of the tension between religion and ideology: the always-open question of the orientation of Dasein.

The tension between religion and ideology occurs at any point where Dasein's being is at stake. In one sense, these points are scattered flashes of mood, but in another they are everywhere. Ninian Smart explains:

> For if we take religion in its widest sense to mean the
> response to our cosmic and personal environment, then
> indeed at the heart of religion lies a kind of quest for
> identity: and so too at the heart of secular worldviews there
> lies a reflection about what the identity of the human being
> consists in. [6]

This ontological reflection is not a casual, "aesthetic" speculation; it poses possibilities that must be thought in every phenomenology of religion or ideology, not to mention every sociology and anthropology whose students allow themselves to be addressed by implications of their work. Shifting his mode of discourse but preserving categorial relation-ships, Smart continues:

> But whether we speak of religions or ideologies, we speak of
> identity and location: for human beings are restless without
> placement and a sure feeling of who and what they are. [7]

When the tools which Dasein uses become present-at-hand, it means not only that the tools themselves have somehow become problematical, it is also a sure indication that the focus of the tools, in this case, the being of

Dasein, is itself already in need of attention. Thus, "the spiritual crisis of our age," shorn of all sensationalism, presents itself not only as a danger to consciousness, but also as an opportunity for it as the Being of Dasein presents itself as an issue which we are hard pressed to ignore.

Indeed, we do not ignore the problem of the Being of Dasein even if there is little explicit recognition. The difficulty in selecting the right tool persists. When the problem first arose, it appeared that the tools of the past could be used, but as the Kantian project demonstrated, elements did not mesh satisfactorily; something was missing or perhaps something was excessive. More radically, it may be that something important was being closed off, something like the consciousness of what we are calling the dynamics of religion and ideology.

If the dynamics of religion and ideology are raised to consciousness and kept in consciousness, then choices and changes are forced again and again. For Dasein to evade its choices when they are clearly presented requires a conscious act of betrayal of the possibility of truth. Events of the possibility of betrayal, when they occur, may be forgotten or they may be incorporated into the ritual repetitions of Dasein's personal or community liturgies of self-identification. Such liturgies may appear as religion but they need not be realized in the forms associated with institutional piety.

As the thinking of the modern age has progressed, it has seemed less and less likely that reconstructions of the past will yield a religious tool for this age that does what the religion of the past could do in the sense of providing a secure ordering of existence. Mircea Eliade speaks for the traditional conception of religion:

> The manifestation of the sacred ontologically founds the world. In the homogeneous and infinite expanse, in which no point of reference is possible and hence no *orientation* can be established, the hierophany reveals an absolute fixed point, a center. [8]

If one holds to a traditional conception such as this, religion will appear as a defective tool when no sense of center is forthcoming from religious practice. This is just what has happened, as, for example, Eliot describes it. Definitions of religion that only look back to the past have become exercises in nostalgia.

The need to define "religion" has not disappeared or been defined into oblivion because of difficulties with the sense of center. It has been redirected toward the future. Consonant with this shift, the impulse to define religion no longer expresses itself with the certainty of an account of what has already happened; instead there has arisen the questioning attitude appropriate to uncertainty in the face of the veiled not-yet. This age witnesses the advent of the open definition of religion. Writing in the *Journal of the American Academy of Religion*, Richard W. Comstock gives an idea of what this is:

> An open definition is a process of continuous interrogation rather than a definite answer provided in advance of the empirical investigation that it initiates. It is a point of departure, not a conclusion. [9]

The open definition institutionalizes religion's presence-at-hand and projects it into the future.

The "for-the-sake-of-which" reaches beyond presencing in the Present to relate especially significantly to Dasein's temporalizing of the future, that is, the making of the future as an integral aspect of Dasein's own understanding of its own being in time. Since temporality is given as the ontological meaning of care by Heidegger in *Being and Time* (i.e. temporality is that upon which the possibility of care is conceived), and since care includes falling (a phenomenon of presence) in its structure, there surfaces at this point a hint of the close relationship of presencing (of the Present) and anticipation (of the future) in the religion-ideology problematic. This link becomes more explicit as religions and ideologies are analyzed below as ways of tying together past, present, and future, though that function does not exhaust the Being of religion and ideology by any means.

It seems to be that, with respect to the logical possibility of being ready-to-hand at least, the primary difference between those entities which have the Being of equipment and those which have the Being of Dasein lies in equipment's having a purpose which is always acceptably defined by the absolute, factical structure of involvements and ontology of another being (which always has the Being of Dasein), even when that structure of involvements is in question. It is the case in the ontology of *Being and Time* that Dasein's structure of involvements is given with its "there" and that the givenness of involvements is a primary ontological fact for Dasein. In other words, Heidegger is saying that the ontology of Dasein is given; what is not given is Dasein's own understanding of that ontology.

In theory, Dasein's factical structure of involvements faithfully reflects the fullest range of its ontological possibilities when it exists in the mode of authenticity, but Dasein is also always driven to compile a record of attempts to deviate from its highest truth when it is fallen and existing in the mode of inauthenticity. The deviation occurs when Dasein passes off responsibility for its involvements to another or to the group.

Dasein's own factical structure of involvements (as differentiated from its inviolate ontological structure of involvements) is not decided for it by another except in the case of Dasein's losing itself in the "they," which occurs in falling; this is how falling places Dasein into inauthenticity.

Even in falling, the structure of involvements which Dasein may accept from the "they" is still ambiguous in a sense, because although the inauthentic, public structure of involvements that is given by the "they" specifies a great deal of Dasein's existence with promises of something like authenticity, and although it imperiously determines that certain phenomena shall be of "decisive" importance to Dasein, the complex of ersatz involvements foisted upon a colluding Dasein by the "they" will never allow Dasein to dwell authentically on a particular task (as, for example, a hammer can do). Rather, the demand will be that fallen Dasein hop, skip, and jump from occasion to empty occasion, as it were, never being able to "do justice" to the demands which have been made by the "they." On the one hand, the "they" demands a commitment as absolute as the authentic self, but on the other, it demands constant attention to the shifting themes of public interest, whose constant flux tends to arrest attention before authentic involvement can take place. And then, in the event that authentic involvement with one of the themes given by the "they" does take place (as could occur, for example, through a mood shift), the structure of involvements given by the "they" will already have been dissipated by the power of authentic vision, which sees deconstructively through the manipulation.

The apparently unilateral determination of Dasein's factical structure of involvement according to the dictates of the "they" is never authentic for Heidegger in any case because by definition it is not truly one's own; even though resolute Dasein takes up its factical possibilities from among those available to the public, it charts its own course and thus differs from fallen Dasein, which does not chart a course of its own. Authenticity then, can not be discerned through appearances of "independence" and "originality" whose great distinction is simply distinction itself. The difference of authenticity is independent of appearance, which in a sense makes the authentic more purely one's own. What is formally one's own (i.e. that which does not originate outside one's own existential imperatives) is Dasein's Being as a thrown projection which comes into existence and endures (however intermittently) in existence without subordinating itself to the spurious initiatives and validations of the "they." Entities with Dasein's kind of Being (i.e. thrown) are thus ontologically excluded from authentic existence (i.e., sense of self in this context) as beings which are potentially ready-to-hand (and, by implication, from that presence-at-hand which derives from readiness-to-hand) according to Heidegger.[10] One cannot place oneself at the disposal of the "they" and desire to be recognizably useful except as fallen Dasein. This insight does not originate with Heidegger, of course, as it is found, for example, close to the surface of the Taoist doctrines of *wu wei*, or non-action, and personal uselessness, which, in the Chinese tradition, function to complement and criticize the unrelieved intensity of ritual responsibility which logically accompanies Confucianism's absolutization of social relations. This tension is part of what Heidegger means when he says that Dasein's Being is an issue for it. As he sees it in a key passage of *Being and Time*,

> Dasein is an entity for which, in its Being, that Being is an issue. The phrase 'is an issue' has been made plain in the state-of-Being of understanding — of understanding as self-projective Being towards its ownmost potentiality-for-Being. This potentiality is that for the sake of which any Dasein is as it is. In each case Dasein has already compared itself, in its Being, with a possibility of itself. Being free *for* one's ownmost potentiality-for-Being, and therewith for the possibility of authenticity and inauthenticity, is shown, with a primordial, elemental concreteness, in anxiety. But onto-logically, Being toward one's ownmost potentiality-for-Being means that in each case Dasein is already *ahead* of itself in its Being.[11]

For Dasein to be true to itself, and this is the essence of authenticity for Heidegger, its potentiality-for-Being cannot be circumscribed by another. Coming into its own potentiality-for-Being is, we might say, both the right and the responsibility of Dasein.

What is factically ready-to-hand or present-at-hand is either equipment which is intended for the use of entities with the Being of Dasein or else it is some virtually independent existent object given in the world. Equipment as such is thus always already included in an "in-order-to." The in-order-to, as was noted above, is what gives presencing its distinctive motivation and its particular kind of priority in contrast to the other temporal ecstases of having-been and anticipation. Our conclusion is that equipment exists for the (temporally conditioned) purpose of presencing the Present in Heidegger's ontology. One thing this means is that as equipment, religion cannot exist exclusively for the hereafter.

Heidegger observes in the course of his analysis of equipment that when something is ready-to-hand, it is not grasped thematically. Onti-cally, this means that the user of the hammer does not think of the hammer as a hammer when working. The user of the hammer is supposed to be thinking about the work. All workers with hammers know what happens when one uses a hammer without keeping one's mind on the work. Explaining further, Heidegger writes:

> That with which our everyday dealings proximally dwell is not the tools themselves. On the contrary, that with which we concern ourselves primarily is the work — that which is to be produced at the time; and this is accordingly ready-to-hand too. The work bears with it that referential totality within which the equipment is encountered. [12]

In this way of thinking, that which is made or repaired with tools is proximally intended to assume a place which already exists in the referential totality. On the way to this placement, tools are employed in work. Ultimately, this work is for the sake of Dasein itself, or, in plainer language, for the sake of being human. Moreover, when equipment is being put to use toward some end, that equipment itself " . . . must withdraw in order to be ready-to-hand." [13] That which is actually in use as equipment does not present itself as an issue, does not obscure Dasein's Being as an issue for it.

When the ready-to-hand is functioning properly (as it was intended), it is grasped only circumspectively (so that one knows what to do with it), not thematically. [14] In the event of equipment which is ready-to-hand, however, the object which previously functioned as equipment may become something obtrusive and thus present-at-hand. Unlike that which is ready-to-hand, the present-at-hand can (and, in fact, must) be considered thematically. It is easy under these circumstances for presence to obliterate the fact of concealment. This amplification of the power of presence, Heidegger asserts, is the relational modality of scientific investigation to what is thematically investigated. Such investigation structures a relationship to things in which Dasein takes up the present-at-hand and gives some kind of thematic account of a segment of it. Although not every understanding of the present-at-hand is scientific, it is, for Heidegger, "theoretical." [15] We interpret the term to be a cipher for "coercive" as Heidegger uses it in this context.

The class of objects which are present-at-hand is basically defined by the way Dasein pays attention; it is thus not limited to non-functioning pieces of equipment conspicuously waiting to be restored to readiness-to-hand. Things in the world that are encountered and only looked at theoretically are also included. Between the ready-to-hand and the present-at-hand there is an important ontological discontinuity such that they are not just "flip-sides" of each other; though together they account for all entities (other than those with the Being of Dasein, Heidegger claims) present in Dasein's world, the complementarity between the ready-to-hand and the present-at-hand is not a simple division of territory in that one and the same entity may, without any special alteration on itself, move freely from one category to the other. The raggedness of the distinction is pointed out by Heidegger in a brief discussion of the case of animals, which he sees as having the potential of being themselves as equipment or not (as far as Dasein is concerned).

The possible constitution of the classes of the ready-to-hand and present-at-hand is being examined because it has a bearing on how the phenomena of religion and ideology may be understood. With regard to the presence-at-hand of religion, which is the issue of the moment, this may mean, among other things, that for the phenomena of religion to shift from being present-at-hand to being ready-to-hand does not necessarily call for a "reform" of religions. It may just as well be that Dasein's understanding of religion is in need of reform, even though a case can be made that Dasein alone constructed religion in the first place. Of additional interest is the reliable coincidence of ideology (or what may be analyzed as notational variants) as a presence-at-hand with religion as present-at-hand; this phenomenon is exemplified in the predicament which finds succinct statement in the God/Caesar pericope in Matthew 22.

We find the Archimedian point of the readiness-to-hand/presence-at-hand question for the religion-ideology problematic far away from uncertainties concerning the ontological status of the animal population, in which some of the edges of the *Being and Time* framework begin to be visible. It is another, fundamentally different class of the ready-to-hand which shows itself as most relevant to this problematic, namely, the class of signs. The sign's importance for this ontology of the difference between religion and ideology derives not only from the current interest in semiotic analysis, but also from the internal evidence of its being treated as a pivotal datum in *Being and Time*, where Heidegger devotes a sub-part (I.3,17) to discussion of several attributes of the sign as equipment which is ready-to-hand. Signs, he explains there, " . . . in the first instance, are themselves items of equipment whose specific character consists in *showing* or *indicating*."[16] As equipment, signs are endowed with an intended function, which is basically to direct Dasein to be on its way in a certain way. In Heidegger's ontology, "Dasein is always somehow directed and on its way . . . "[17] and the sign merely influences this given, showing Dasein some factical way. The sign appears to be ready-to-hand for a somewhat more abstract purpose than the production or repair of some article that itself will become ready-to-hand. The purpose of the sign in directing Dasein within its structure of involvements is both the essence of the sign's readiness-to-hand as equipment and the basis of the possibility of religion's being present-at-hand in this time.

Heidegger thinks the sign in *Being and Time* especially in terms of reference, but not in the narrowest sense; a sign may "stand for" a thing or it may orient Dasein in relation to things in the world which are present-at-hand or, implicitly, ready-to-hand. Either way, and this is important for the thinking of religions and ideologies as sign/symbol systems, the pre-condition of the sign is the worldhood of the world, namely, the structure of Dasein's involvements. This structure of involvements comes into being through Dasein's grasp of itself in its factical situation and is perpetuated through Dasein's projection of itself onto certain factical possibilities.

Dasein's factical situation is disclosed in its state-of-mind, which constantly wants to remind a self-evading Dasein of its thrownness,[18] and in its various moods, which, whatever else may be said about them, do not give anything like an objective picture of the situation as Dasein finds itself in a succession of very different dispositions.[19] The references of the sign, then, because of the shifting of Dasein's understanding of its world, must also shift. With this shift in references, Dasein's orientation to the ready-to-hand and present-at-hand has to become questionable. "It is precisely when we see the 'world' unsteadily and fitfully in accordance with our moods, that the ready-to-hand shows itself in its specific worldhood, which is never the same from day to day."[20]

Because the referential totality of the sign shifts with every change of mood, the sign is not even reliable in principle as equipment; a fixed intention thus cannot be programmatically brought to fruition if the function of its mediator (in this case, the sign) is unpredictable, unless some kind of "wild-card" factor is part of the original intention. Further, unless the "wild-card" factor is part of the original intention of the sign as equipment (which would make the sign's "reference" a problematical concept indeed), any "product" or effect of the sign as equipment would clearly be suspect with regard to its fulfilling the intention which lies behind the equipment. In short, the sign itself, as equipment, is always problematical and tends to obtrude as a question precisely when dependability is most desired. In Dasein's day-to-day experience with signs, ontically satisfactory results may conceal the fact, but the sign is still inherently present-at-hand. More precisely, the sign is ontologically present-at-hand.

What holds true for a single sign also holds true for a group of signs or, in a compound way, for an entire symbol system. Natural language, especially as it appears in a codification or in directions, can be reduced to a group of such signs. Such appears to be true in analytic philosophy, for example, though this extremely reductive classification by no means exhausts the possibilities of natural language. The problem of indeterminacy is no less acute with designated subsets of natural language and is only covered up by theoretical devices, such as binary formalisms. The placement of natural language into the category of equipment may at first look like a dubious and troublesome reduction which does not mesh entirely well with the temper of the later Heidegger, but 1) in the framework of *Being and Time*, which remains valid for the later Heidegger in most particulars, the possibility of the reduction exists, and 2) the reduction may allow some aspect of the problem to be seen that otherwise would be hidden. It is not indicated in Heidegger's ontology or in other of his writings that entertaining the theoretical possibility of natural language as equipment entails the irrevocable factical reduction of language to equipment. When natural language is intended as equipment, however, it needs to be considered as such. This means that whenever language is intentionally put to use as a collection of signs with an intended purpose (an overt towards-which), then the language itself becomes present-at-hand. This is the ontological origin of critical analysis.

Critical analysis of language arose as the hallmark of a significant intellectual movement in nineteenth-century biblical scholarship. Exegesis had been going on since the church fathers, of course, but what was a trickle of non-orthodox intepretation in the seventeenth century and a stream of philosophical commentary in the eighteenth became a torrent of philological research in the nineteenth. This fashion in the sphere of religion could only have occurred if the language of the Bible had become present-at-hand. The alternative would be for the language of the Bible to be ready-to-hand, which there is reason to believe it was for earlier ages. This is not to say that the Bible was somehow easier to understand for our more remote ancestors, only that their sense of where the important difficulties lay was obviously different from that which held sway among the learned commentators of the recent past. Sufficient evidence of this difference is that the sacred text of the religion suddenly appeared to be unserviceable without thorough philological analysis.

Heidegger notes in "The Origin of the Work of Art" that the material of the equipment is taken into the service of the piece of equipment. In this service, he writes, "It disappears in serviceability."[21] The language of religion did anything but disappear during the age of classical philology. No longer ready-to-hand but still felt to be important, first the symbols of the Christian symbol system and later the symbols of others became objects of present concern; the relationship of Dasein to religious symbols (language) then became understood as a technical question which demanded resolution in terms of the public Present. In religion's presence-at-hand, then, is the origin of the academic study of religion, whose beginnings in philology do not appear at all accidental.

Given this background, the extensive analysis that has been generated around the phenomenon of religion becomes more than a monumental testament to the unfathomable depth of the concerns addressed by religions. It also gives some positive insight within the framework of our fundamental ontology into a possibility of the Being of the object of this extensive attention. If "religion" can be phenomenologically reduced so that it is thought of philosophically as equipment which has become present-at-hand (if only because equipment inherently tends to become present-at-hand), then as equipment (however deficient), all religions would categorically have a purpose. This purpose would necessarily have to do with presencing and anticipation, because that is generally the case with equipment and Dasein's sense of the towards-which. If this is so, it offers an ontological basis for the heavy futural emphasis that can be observed in the world's religions.

There is a speculative possibility that merits turning over at this juncture, and that is the question of whether religion is a human universal, whatever "religion" is. There is no question that signs are human universals and no question that symbol systems are human universals, but for the symbol systems that are generally called religions, there is no consensus. It is not necessary to specify what religion is in order to see that if it appears universally, the question then becomes whether it is only accidentally a universal or whether it is equiprimordial with that Dasein which is specifically human (or all possible Daseins, for that matter). This cannot be argued from empirical ontical data, no matter how carefully compiled. To get at this question, one must ask whether there is some ontologically-given purpose to the phenomena that have typically been called "religion" that would be part of the essential constitution of Dasein.

It would apparently inscribe a circle of the smallest radius to ask what ontologically-given purpose religion as equipment might have for Dasein and then answer with a proposal taken straight from the ontology. The logic might be acceptable, but the language appears to run the risk of sterility from inbreeding. On the other hand, since all analysis and critique of religion as either concept or phenomenon necessarily carries with it either an implicit or explicit ontology of religion, any such proposal comes down to the existential axioms of an ontology in the end. Why should the answer of an either explicit or *de facto* adversarial ontology be preferred over one generated by the ontology of explicit choice? At this point, questions about the ontology of an entity resolve into a question of the adequacy of the ontology. This is both a philosophical and a political issue. To avoid it is simply to make an unconscious or intended conservative ideological choice, to choose uncritical reification of existing structures of understanding, to foreclose the possibility of ontological inquiry in favor of metaphysical convenience.

The priority that is being given in development of our fragment of a critical theory to a thematically focused interpretation of the existential analytic of *Being and Time* and the hermeneutic work that followed it suggests that any other (especially regional) ontology which is subsequently introduced into the discussion be at least readily addressable in its language and preferably overtly compatible with the framework. This restriction appears at first blush likely to help keep our logic orderly, though at the price of reducing the very useful breaks and stops that alien material forces upon discourse. Free selection of an example of critical analysis of the (implicitly present-at-hand) phenomenon of religion, which could easily entail the importation into the discussion of an incompatible fundamental ontological structure, can thus no longer be entertained as a neutral, innocent way of extending the conversation. It risks violating the internal logic of those elements in the existential analytic whose integrity is required by the unalterable condition of the priority of fundamental ontology that Heidegger insisted upon. If, however, Heidegger was right in claiming that his ontology is the basis for all future regional ontologies, then the formal issue of addressability is null for this problematic since the ontology would always provide a valid critical standpoint. The compatibility issue remains, however, being focused on first principles, specifically, the need to avoid concealing them. This is the same as the need to avoid turning discourse into the kind of calculative word-vomit that characterizes all varieties of interest-peddling upon encounter with the indigestibility of the primal and the virulence of its uncanniness.

Any randomly selected analysis or critique of "religion" is evidence that something which an engaged commentator felt deserved to be called "religion" had once made itself present-at-hand. The fact of the engagement in terms of "religion" is what matters for purposes of seeing how religion is present-at-hand at the time of the writing. The engagement itself is significant as a fact because it could only have taken place on the basis of a functioning ontology of religion. As we understand Heidegger's sense of fundamental ontology, the critical commentator's choice of vocabulary (in this case, "religion") does not guarantee the prospect of productive conversation, but it does at least provide an occasion for the fundamental ontology to found an interpretation of the meaning of the phenomenon. The work of thinkers outside the orbit of Heidegger's fundamental ontology presents problems and opportunities similar to those encountered in trying to talk with a self-assured exponent of another culture: the angles can be interesting but a sustained exchange is difficult or even impossible. The need to lay out issues in the attempt at bringing this material to language remains none the less. We attempt not to let interest in essential or incidental semantic differences, which make the point of religion's presence-at-hand, become the sustained focus of attention.

The choice of potential conversation partners on the topic of religion is great. The vast store of analysis and criticism already produced allows virtually any disposition of Dasein to find somewhere a sympathetic resonance or even a detailed exposition. For the fundamental ontology with which this discussion has concerned itself, finding some compatible conversation partners eventually comes to pass in brief encounters below with Paul Tillich and Mircea Eliade, among others. Before engaging them, however, a "false start" should prove useful to discover some negative possibilities.

There are a number of kinds of false starts that could be made, but some kinds of analysis promise to be more revealing of the contours of a functioning ontology of religion than others. This is more a matter of style than anything else, since every discussion of religion entails a functioning ontology. Theoretical treatments, such as statistical studies, "purely descriptive" sociological or anthropological accounts, and also sympathetic surveys, such as Huston Smith's *The Religions of Man*,[22] together comprise the broadly defined genre that is being called analysis. While ontological issues are not absent from these kinds of analysis, the emphasis tends to be on the phenomenal and for this reason, working far enough back into the foundations to engage a work of this type would entail too long a digression for this space. The perennial paradigmatic example of accounts of religion, William James's *The Varieties of Religious Experience*,[23] which has remained a reference of choice for its forthright approach to the broad issues of its topic, occupies for our purposes a sort of middle ground in the field and exemplifies the genre of analysis as it shades into criticism.

Critical exposition focused on issues of definition and factical possibilities of the theme offers both the easiest engagement on the ontological/metaphysical level and, once there, the sharpest polemics. Sidney Hook's polemic, *The Quest for Being*,[24] which was, in fact, selected at random from a list of publications including essays on religion by Reinhold Niebuhr, Walter Kaufmann, Sigmund Freud, Huston Smith, and others, provides the case-in-point for a brief look at one of the recently popular modes of religion's presence-at-hand. Some of the key issues for both religion and ideology in communities of faith emerge as Hook seeks to cast light on differences between traditional religion and his humanistic version of the American Dream.

The Quest for Being instantiates several points about religion's presence-at-hand which reflect well the ontical experience of presence-at-hand sketched in a general way in *Being and Time*. One of Hook's main themes is that favorite of anti-clericalists, the existence of God. Throughout his book, whose chapters span more than twenty-five years of thinking, Hook is concerned about the vast potential for mischief, especially political mischief, that he perceives to be inherent in organized religion and superstition. As we may frequently observe, the phenomenon of religion's presence-at-hand tends to carry with it a heavy political component. It is common for writers to be so impressed with this aspect of the phenomenon of religion that they use the language of political theory to speak of religion. The most recent major example that comes to mind is Ninian Smart's infelicitous distinction between religious and secular ideologies in *Beyond Ideology*. In that instance of division without remainder, Smart apparently was using "ideology" in much the same way as Otto Rank was when he spoke of religious sensibility as "spiritual ideology."[25] The coincidence of terminology is not what is important; the fact that "ideology" normally belongs to the universe of political theoretical discourse is.

To illustrate the problem as it strikes him, Hook cites examples of the anti-humanistic and anti-democratic actions and writings of the Roman Catholic Church which clash with his own historical-political outlook, analyzes arguments for the existence of God which (as he interprets them) run counter to the logic he lives by, argues against the notion of a dialectic of being and non-being which Tillich seems to have gotten mostly from Heidegger (though Hook does not concern himself to comment on Tillich's sources), restates the overdrawn hypothesis of ineluctable opposition between superstitious religion and technology, publicly wonders about Reinhold Niebuhr's grasp of basic logic, and directly accuses large sectors of humanity with a "failure of nerve" in an essay featuring that phrase. These discussions are obviously not simple accounts of objective phenomena, but are records of instances in which religion has appeared as an interloping obstruction to what Hook understands as the good. Flowing from a primary vision which is far removed from traditional religiosity, Hook's discourse proximally originates in an idea of liberalism " . . . as an intellectual temper, as faith in intelligence, as a tradition of the free market in the world of ideas . . . ."[26] It is by virtue of his liberal ideology that Hook can see religion as present-at-hand; and if the enabling intellectual tool were not liberalism, it would be some other ideology.

What is of interest in thinking the religion-ideology problematic is not the details of the particular stands that Hook takes himself; it is, rather, the themes he has chosen. He would not have chosen these specific themes, our ontology suggests, unless he was forced to by (not necessarily material) circumstances. It is circumstances which have led Hook and the many circumspect others who write on the theme of religion to turn their thinking toward fundamentally important topics such as the Being of God, the development of technology, the coexistence of religion and politics, and the relationship of religion and ethics. With the exception of the last, these same themes show up prominently in Heidegger's works, which are not supposed to be about religion. They are all themes which can shed light on the meaning of the formal relationship of religion and ideology that is presented in the course of this study. Though development of these themes could flesh out the meaning of this formal relationship, it would not of itself encourage the observer to attain an essential grasp of that relationship; the observer of phenomena is thus left at the level of first-order contemplation of issues with questions of why these themes come together and why they remain distinct. One way of understanding the confluence of interests is to posit a formal ontological basis for the relationship of religion and ideology as the pre-condition of these themes as such. The same hypothesis will account for their difference, but only with the actual laying out of that basis does anything like a reason why for the relationship emerge.

In the essay, "The New Failure of Nerve," Hook brings the practical aspect of this problematic to the fore in a pragmatic way. He writes:

> The social principles of Christianity have had almost two thousand years in which to order the world on a moral basis. It is not likely that anything new can be discovered from its principles or that its social gospel will succeed better in eliminating war, social distress, and intense factional strife than it did during the historical periods in which religious institutions enjoyed chief authority. [27]

It is in passages of this sort that writers in both modern and pre-modern eras have brought religion's presence-at-hand into a readily recognizable and problematical focus. In Hook's case, these thoughts lead him to make a sharp and presupposition-laden distinction between choices made on the basis of an allegedly illusory knowledge of religion and choices made on the basis of that true, or at least conventionally epistemologically legitimate, knowledge which he understands to be the product of the (rational) intellect. If this way of conceiving the role of religion and the nature of a community of faith were to hold, there would be little question that the primary function of religion was to soothe the emotions of *homo technologicus*. The fact that Hook's comments and those of others in a similar vein are regarded as cogent is evidence enough that religion is present-at-hand in the way Hook describes and, it would seem, that ontologies of religion like Hook's function at present. Whether such ontologies are held by secularized writers such as Hook or institutions such as the Roman Catholic Church (as Hook demonstrated was the case in the forties, when he was writing), they are always inadequate because of an arbitrary (ontologically opaque) absolutizing of a polarity of faith and reason.

The essential feature that the humanistic critiques of religion such as Hook's and Walter Kaufmann's appear to have in common is that their criticisms of religion are predominantly aimed at religion conceived as ideology — as a phenomenon that is not only in the world, but of the world. Even the discussions of God tend to assume a political focus at one point or another, probably since the abuses of the medieval church's temporal authority present such a large and dramatic thesis. It is necessary to avoid simply reducing both religion and ideology to politics in general critical analysis, though, for that represents a premature narrowing of the concepts.

At this juncture, with both "religion" and "ideology" in whatever condition language has delivered them, there is a necessary obscurity to the contention that critiques of religion are often targeted on religion as ideology, rather than on what we might call religion itself, despite this claim's intuitive plausibility. Were it to remain at this level, the thinking of "religion" would never get beyond irreducible opinion. Its possibilities of clarification and of fictional factuality (no oxymoron) lie in pursuing something like a phenomenological investigation of religion and ideology to yield, directly or indirectly, an ontology that projects both religion and ideology; only on the basis of such an ontology, grounded in an accepted fundamental ontology to bind its elements, can the kind of distinction proposed above be meaningful, going beyond mere provocation to fund conversation by providing both a beginning and a public language.

It is not quite enough for purposes of conversation merely to establish the presence-at-hand of one phenomenon that we agree to call "religion" and another that we agree to call "ideology," though it comes close to what is needed. The real need is to lay out these terms in a way that is as transparent as possible with reference to the fundamental ontology that we take to undergird them. This need is for a language that can flow in its own terms, being able to carry on without calling attention to itself by continual preoccupation with translation. Only with the achievement of a language which can flow in its own terms does it become possible to break the flow creatively, rather than reactionarily. It is the difference between the possibility of *anamnesis* of the existentially archaic and the certainty of distraction into the incidentally present.

Though the claim has been made that what is criticized in essays such as Hook's is religion construed as ideology, the engagements of religion that have occurred in these pieces have been of much wider scope than just problematics of ideology. Virtually all aspects of religion have been opened to question, examination, and analysis. While the critical theory of ideology that develops in this and subsequent chapters may reveal why ideology provides the beginning for critiques of religion (and, incidentally, why materialism may well be the ultimate ideology), it is precisely the relationship of ideology to religion that is the problem, so a more general beginning that provides a basis for locating ideology in relation to religion is indicated. Several sources contribute to this picture.

Paul Tillich was one of the first theologians to attempt to integrate the insights of Heidegger into the work of theology. The terminology and arguments of *Being and Time* are sprinkled throughout his post-Marxist work, sometimes attributed and sometimes not. Tillich was always more overtly politically concerned than Heidegger, and, since Heidegger had very little to say about political theory, his influence on Tillich is scarcely to be discerned beyond occasional terminological borrowings when topics in this area come up. In a recorded conversation late in his career, Tillich was engaged by his interlocutors on the subject of the nature of religion and some of his remarks have a bearing on understanding the dynamics of religion's presence-at-hand. His observations are more indicative than ontologically definitive, however, since there remains at the forefront of Tillich's comments the fact of his own formulaic definition of religion as point of departure. What we see in his remarks, whose vocabulary is precisely placed within the purview of our problematic, are two place-holders, namely "religion" and "ideology," which still stand as questions for the ontology of religion that Tillich never developed explicitly outside the framework of his theology.

Early in the conversation, Tillich makes it clear that his understanding of religion is a broad, generic one.

> If religion is defined as a state of 'being grasped by an
> ultimate concern' — which is also my definition of faith —

> then we must distinguish between this as a universal or
> large concept from our usual smaller concept of religion
> which supposes an organized group with its clergy, scrip-
> tures, and dogma, by which a set of symbols for the ulti-
> mate concern is accepted and cultivated in life and
> thought.[28]

When we speak of religion's presence-at-hand, it is both impossible and undesirable to exclude the phenomena of the "smaller concept of religion," for these are the material basis of religion's presence. They are the pretext of any discussion of religion and they are also its nominal end. Tillich, however, has a larger interest, the cultural place of religion and its secular facsimiles.

When imagining the relationship of religion and culture, Tillich remains mindful of the fact of secularity. Perhaps as a consequence of his early Marxist phase, he formulated something like an opposition between religion and ideology, though it was not a relationship of absolute exclusion; a person could live according to a particular religious faith and still participate in ideologies, or what Tillich termed "quasi-religions."[29]

What separated true religion from superficially similar phenomena for Tillich was the factor of finitude; Tillich believed that if ultimacy was attributed to the finite, the result could only be deep disappointment in the long run. Tillich never doubted the legitimacy of the secular as such, but he also never doubted the divide between it and true religion. Even as he observed the waxing of the ideological in the Protestant tradition, he avoided the convenient humanistic conflation of religion and ideology into mentalistic homogeneity; he analyzed it to be a case of religious ideas functioning ideologically. Tillich would not want either the origins or the transcendence of religious ideas to be lost or denied because of the trivial appearance of ideology, for that would spell the end of the possibility of religion properly so called. As he once wrote of ideology, "All human consciousness suffers from this fatal tendency."[30]

Though Tillich had apparently satisfied himself that he was sufficiently aware of the difference between a true religion and a pretender, he was not so sanguine about popular culture. Coming out of the experience of the rise of Nazi Germany, he had reason to believe that even the most thoughtful people can easily become confused on this question. As he stated it in the conversation mentioned above,

> It is possible for this secular or profane reality to express
> ultimate concern, and so we have the concept of quasi-
> religion. But of course these quasi-religions must come

under the same criticism as the religions proper. They have their own danger, namely, complete secularization and emptiness, while the religions proper, the religions in the narrower sense, are subject to the danger of what I call demonization, which occurs when particular symbols and ideas are absolutized and become idols themselves.[31]

Religion's presence-at-hand for Tillich can be seen from this excerpt to be a two-part proposition. In addition to the possibility of dysfunction ("demonization"), there is also the chance that superficial patterns of religion will be replicated to create quasi-religions.

In the case of the presence-at-hand of quasi-religions, it is religion (inauthentically copied) that provides the material basis for the presence of the quasi-religion. Moreover, it is when ideologies become quasi-religions (and that happens as soon as they are put into practice) that they can both function as religions and become present-at-hand in the same way as religions. Until presence-at-hand occurs, there is no way to thematize something, but when presence-at-hand does take place, then the quality of the thematization becomes important. Thus, Tillich noted, there is a need for us to take cognizance of the dynamics of " . . . ideologies, such as nationalism or socialism which claim the loyalty or veneration of their followers with the intensity sometimes of the theistic religions."[32] The concern to point up differences between religion proper and its imitators, as well as his insistence that there is a need to distinguish meaningfully between them, make Tillich a figure of note in the history of religion's presence-at-hand. Even though he did not really make full use of an explicit ontological ground, Tillich believed that theology and ontology sometimes mixed and that he had an adequate foundation for his distinctions. It remains, however, to find an ontological reason why Tillich's distinctions between religion proper and apparently similar phenomena should matter to human beings for any reason other than to avoid an unpleasant feeling of emptiness or to satisfy some vaguely defined "highest aspirations of humanity."[33]

A significant element which belongs at the beginning of any thinking of "religion" must be the possibility of no religion at all. It can mean either the willful banishment of phenomena of religiosity from life or the imperceptible forgetfulness that concludes in a monolithic secularity — it does not matter. Either way, such appears to have been one of the uppermost features of religion as present-at-hand for Mircea Eliade as he was writing *The Sacred and the Profane*. In the introduction to that book, he explains,

> Our chief concern . . . will be . . . to show in what ways
> religious man attempts to remain as long as possible in a
> sacred universe, and hence what his total experience of life
> proves to be in comparison with the experience of the man
> without religious feeling, of the man who lives, or wishes to
> live, in a desacralized world. It should be said at once that
> the *completely* profane world, the wholly desacralized cos-
> mos, is a recent discovery in the history of the human
> spirit.[34]

The idea of the wholly desacralized cosmos is recognizable, of course, as
an intentionally constructed antithesis of the wholly sacral cosmos of
traditional societies. Eliade's language here raises the dialectical problem
of how something that has been "desacralized" could ever be "completely profane," but the mental reality which informs this assumed
primacy of a sense of the sacred in Eliade's report is, at this stage anyway,
more an empirical question for the psychology of religion than the
opening thought of an investigation of religion itself.

There are two points in Eliade's statement of purpose above that
are of special interest to the thinking of the religion-ideology
problematic. The first is the idea that there is a tendency to want to stay
in the sacred universe as long as possible and the second is the fact that a
completely desacralized world has been imagined at all. In both cases,
assuming Eliade is reporting accurately, the reason **why** the phenomena
reported should occur is anything but clear. This "why" becomes the
question of the hour once *The Sacred and the Profane* has drawn to a
close. Eliade knows this and, at the conclusion of his study, he both
ventures an explanation for what he has observed and speculates on how
the next step in working through his problematic will be taken. He
knows it will not be through amassing more evidence to support further
the points he has already made, but rather will come to pass in attempts
to get behind his data. At the close of his discussion, Eliade contributes a
proposal that allows the questionable phenomena of wanting to remain
in the sacred universe and the imagination of a desacralized world to be
tentatively interpreted in essentially mythological terms. At the same
time, he anticipates the necessity of a critical theory as he suggests how a
parallel version of the myth might be achieved in some other language.

> From one point of view it could be said that in the case of
> those moderns who proclaim that they are nonreligious,
> religion and mythology are eclipsed in the darkness of their
> unconscious — which means too that in such men the pos-
> sibility of reintegrating a religious vision of life lies at great
> depth. Or, from the Christian point of view, it could be said

that nonreligion is equivalent to a new "fall" of man — in other words, that nonreligious man has lost the capacity to live religion consciously, and hence to understand and assume it; but that, in his deepest being, he still retains a memory of it, as, after the first "fall," his ancestor, the primordial man, retained intelligence enough to rediscover the traces of God that are visible in the world. After the first "fall," the religious sense descended to the level of the "divided consciousness"; now, after the second, it has fallen even further, into the depths of the unconscious; it has been forgotten. Here the considerations of the historian of religions end. Here begins the realm of problems proper to the philosopher, the psychologist, and even the theologian.[35]

Eliade's story bears witness to the presence-at-hand of religion. The forgetfulness that he speaks of in this passage is exactly on target as a primary factor in the presence-at-hand of religion. To return to the equipment metaphor, a breakdown of the equipment is not the only way for equipment to become present-at-hand; it could also become present-at-hand if the equipment is durable and remains as an observable relic even after the way of using it has become lost.

Relics typically receive a quality of attention far beyond what was accorded them in their time of being ready-to-hand; they may not only help us recall what has been, they may remind us to embark on the project of recall in the first place if we are receptive to the relic *qua* relic. Language, which can be both the most ephemeral and durable of materials, provides a sufficient material basis for imagining religion's presence-at-hand as originating in forgetfulness, specifically in a forgetfulness of Dasein. But is it so that the origin of this forgetfulness of the Being of religion is of the same order as the origin of the divided consciousness that is said to precede it?

As the meaning of the Heideggerian ontology for the issue of religion and ideology unfolds, there will be reason to construe divided consciousness as characteristic of natural Dasein, while the forgetfulness that Eliade notes will appear as the consequence of a fateful tension which has always been present, but which has intensified comparatively recently in the history of consciousness. A detailed account of the dynamics of this intensification presupposes an ontological foundation which has not yet been adequately laid out. The reading of an existing ontological foundation (Heidegger's) in a way that exposes the structure and meaning of this tension is the task given by our thesis, whose larger purpose is to ground future examinations of the interplay of religion and ideology in history.

Notes

¹ SZ, p. 69; BT, p. 98.

² SZ, p. 82; BT, p. 113.

³ SZ, p. 84; BT, p. 116.

⁴ Martin Heidegger, "Der Ursprung des Kunstwerkes," *Holzwege.* Frankfurt/M: Klostermann, 1972, p. 36 (henceforward UK); "The Origin of the Work of Art," *Poetry, Language, Thought,* tr. Albert Hofstadter. New York: Harper and Row, 1971, p. 47 (henceforward OWA).

⁵ SZ, ibid.; BT, pp. 116-117.

⁶ Ninian Smart, *Beyond Ideology: Religion and the Future of Western Civilization.* San Francisco: Harper and Row, 1981, p. 13.

⁷ Op. cit., p. 26.

⁸ Mircea Eliade, *The Sacred and the Profane,* tr. W.R. Trask. New York: Harcourt, Brace and World, Inc., 1959, p. 21.

⁹ Richard W. Comstock, "Toward Open Definitions of Religion," *Journal of the American Academy of Religion,* Vol. LII, No. 3, p. 510.

¹⁰ Heidegger claims early in *Being and Time* (SZ, p. 45; BT, p. 71) that ". . . any entity is either a '*who*' (existence) or a '*what*' (presence-at-hand in the broadest sense)." These designations do not of themselves explain their origins and thus cannot be taken for granted. While many differences between entities which have the kind of Being of Dasein and those which do not are detailed in the ontology, the analysis begins at a point where Dasein is already a "who" and any entity of another type is already a "what." The assumption seems to be that any "who" is a Dasein and any Dasein is a "who." It is, moreover, by no means self-evident that every Dasein factically must take every other Dasein as a "who," especially given the phenomenon of technology, which raises the possibility of the use of other, factical beings of the type of Dasein as equipment. These phenomena do not seem convincingly excluded by definition alone, unless a distinction is made between Dasein and the body through which it may come to presence. While there is nothing essentially corporeal about Dasein in this framework, which thus leaves open the possibility of the body as equipment, as long as Dasein and body are factically coeval, Heidegger's implicit conditions on relationships among beings with the Being of Dasein would appear to constitute the basis of an ethics. Also, unless "who-ness" is identified with Dasein *a priori*, in which case the vacuity of the tautology obtains, it has not been made explicit what that term is saying ontologically in *Being and Time*.

¹¹ SZ, p. 191; BT, p. 236.

¹² SZ, pp. 69-70; BT, p. 99. Grammatically, Heidegger treats "the work" as an entity, rather than an activity.

¹³ SZ, p. 69; BT, ibid.

¹⁴ There is a distinctly conservative bias in this idea. Tools which are being put to ideologically-determined use (which is how tools are mostly used) by one interest will be anything but ready-to-hand for an antithetical interest. That a user of a tool could (must?) experience such a conflict is not ruled out by Heidegger, but the fact that this kind of conflict is not entertained as a feature of the world seems to be a a break in the carrying out of the assigned tasks of the limitation of the ontology. The schema in which things either work properly or do not suggests a categorical assimilation of understanding to a pure form of whatever happens to be the dominant ideology.

¹⁵ In theoretical understanding, things have a uniformity which Heidegger attributes to the dim understanding one has of what is merely present-at-hand and no more (SZ, p. 138; BT, p. 177). The understanding of things merely present-at-hand must be different from the understanding of the formerly ready-to-hand which becomes present-at-hand through a deficiency of serviceability. In any case, "theoretical" does not have only the meaning of "formal scientific theory."

¹⁶ SZ, p. 77; BT, p. 108. The italicized words in the passage are renderings of the German *zeigen* and *anzeigen*. They deserve attention, considering the importance of the *zeig-* root for Heidegger. Also, an exception to the characterization of signs as equipment exists in the phenomenon of signs in the primitive world, Heidegger claims four pages later.

¹⁷ SZ, p. 79; BT, p. 110.

¹⁸ SZ, pp. 134ff.; BT, pp. 173ff. and SZ, p. 276; BT, p. 321.

¹⁹ SZ, p. 134; BT, p. 173.

²⁰ SZ, p. 138; BT, p. 177.

²¹ UK, pp. 34-35; translation mine. Hofstadter's translation, OWA, p. 46, contains an error. Heidegger has, "Er verschwindet in der Dienlichkeit." Hofstadter renders the dative "der" as an accusative of motion to get, "It disappears into usefulness."

²² Huston Smith, *The Religions of Man*. New York: Harper and Row, 1958.

²³ William James, *The Varieties of Religious Expeience*. New York: New American Library, 1958.

²⁴ Sidney Hook, *The Quest for Being*. New York: Delta, 1934-1961.

²⁵ Otto Rank, *The Myth of the Birth of the Hero*, tr. C.F. Atkinson. New York: Vintage, 1932 (1959), p. 183.

[26] Hook, p. 74.

[27] Hook, p. 81.

[28] Paul Tillich, *Ultimate Concern: Tillich in Dialogue*, ed. D. Mackenzie Brown. New York: Harper and Row, 1965, p. 4.

[29] Op. cit., p. 30.

[30] Paul Tillich, "The Attack of Dialectical Materialism on Christianity," *The Student World*, No. 31, p. 121; quoted in Terence M. O'Keeffe, "Ideology and the Protestant Principle," *Journal of the American Academy of Religion*, Vol. LI, No. 2 (June, 1983), p. 299.

[31] Tillich, *Ultimate Concern*, p. 30.

[32] Ibid.

[33] Op. cit., p. 71.

[34] Eliade, p. 13.

[35] Op. cit., p. 213.

Man's being consists primarily of his existence in economic sociological, and political situations, upon whose reality everything else depends; perhaps, even, it is only through the reality of these situations that everything else becomes real.

— *Karl Jaspers*

The state of the outer world does not merely correspond to the general state of men's souls; it also in a sense depends on that state, since man himself is the pontiff of the outer world.

— *Abu Bakr Siraj Ed-din*

III. Historical Episodes of Religion as Problem

Among the first records of human culture and thought that we have, there is evidence of religious concern. Whether one looks at fragments of discourse of Presocratic philosophers, ancient Near Eastern monuments, early Chinese oracle bones, or pre-historical American Indian ruins, the history of our race universally shows signs of what is generally called religion, that diverse body of thoughts and practices people have developed over the centuries to bring themselves aright with the conditions of existence and maintain themselves under these conditions in the best way possible. While in typical traditional societies the manifestations of religion seem to be virtually as sacred as cultic divinities themselves, there exist also early records of attempts at defining or criticizing religion, as in Plato's *Laws*[1] or Lucretius's De Rerum Natura. The Bible, to cite a sacred text which presents in itself both sides of this tension, records the Hebrews' experience of their religion as the central fact of cultural identity. It also records their experience of religion as problem and chronicles their attempts to "solve" the problem along with the consequences of their consistently ill-fated solutions. Religion as problem thus appears to be as old as awareness of religion; in the ontology being developed, it yields a tautology to articulate this observation as the proposition that religion as problem is coextensive with awareness of religion.

While the problem of religion is demonstrably old, its history appears to have taken a decisive turn around the time of the Enlightenment in Europe. The Enlightenment itself does not constitute the turn precisely, but can be seen more appropriately as a manifestation of it. As Frank Manuel traces this movement in his preface to *The Changing of the Gods*,

> Self-conscious exploration of religious behavior has been a perennial theme of Western culture. In many respects the eighteenth century interpretations were elaborations, made forceful with contemporary empirical data, of insights that had already found embryonic expression in the writings of the ancient Greeks and Romans and the Church Fathers. [2]

The Enlightenment was a time when it could be important for a Locke to write *The Reasonableness of Christianity as delivered in the scriptures* or a Wolff to formulate a philosophy of religion in systematic, logical argument or a Kant to write *Religion within the Limits of Reason alone*. It was also a time, however, when a William Law needed to write *A Serious Call to a Devout and Holy Life* and a Zinzendorf needed to compose ecstatic paeans to the blood and wounds of Christ. Theodore M. Greene presents one side of the Enlightenment in his extensive introduction to Kant's *Religion within the Limits of Reason alone*:

> In it we see the Renaissance working itself out through the agencies of its scientific and philosophical discoveries . . . . It was essentially revolutionary, directed against tradition. The positive force at its core was a determined assertion of the freedom of the individual — freedom in affairs social and political, intellectual and religious. This spirit expressed itself most emphatically in a new and extravagant belief in the power of reason. Faith in the old presuppositions and authorities, for so long considered valid beyond question, gave way to a spirit of criticism . . . . reason claimed to be autonomous and set itself up as the unique court of appeal . . . . To strictly religious values the age was for the most part blind. [3]

In Greene's observations, several significant features of the period of the Enlightenment are brought out. First, the connection of the Enlightenment with the Renaissance makes the point that we are setting up the seventeenth and eighteenth centuries as the temporal locus of a major cultural discontinuity. There are reasons why the period of the Enlightenment is radically different from what went before, but two earlier periods, classical antiquity and the Renaissance, contributed much of the original basis for Enlightenment innovations. The fact that pagan culture and the philosophies that grew with it appeared viable after one-and-a-half or two millennia was liberating to the mind, but this alone did not sufficiently determine the leap made in the Enlightenment; the new mechanical technology growing out of the age's scientific progress, which was, in turn, proximally traceable to the Renaissance, also played a major role in the development of Enlightenment culture. The nature of this technology is not an agreed-upon datum.

Jacques Ellul suggests the decisive difference between the Renaissance and the Enlightenment is to be found in the decay of Renaissance humanism. This humanism, he claims, was the curb on an emerging impulse for man's being in the world to be understood (even if still subconsciously) as technique because it encouraged resistance to the leveling action of technique on the individual. For Ellul, the expansion of the role of technique in civilization is the most serious challenge facing humanity today and, in his analysis, there was a major turning point in the history of technique in the Industrial Revolution. No materialist, he does not propose to interpret the dramatic mechanization of production that occurred with the Industrial Revolution as the primary conditioning factor in the dramatic shift in consciousness that he is attempting to describe and explain in *The Technological Society*. As he frames the issue, "It is preposterous that a specialist such as Lewis Mumford can write that he has found the various modes of exploiting energy the key to the evolution of technique and the moving force behind its transformations."[4] For Ellul, it was the unprecedented development of the technical way of being in the world that made the Industrial Revolution's progress in energy use and mechanization possible. Ellul is thus providing an explanation for what Greene observes, but we are inclined to wonder how much of an explanation it really is.

If one says that technique is autonomous, then it is necessary to explicate what feature or features in the Being of technique grant the necessity or possibility of autonomy. Ellul's assertions may be provocative and they may be revealing, but they do not constitute an ontology; in a sense Ellul's work may be read as a sustained call to an ontological reflection that he himself undertakes only implicitly. In the ontology of this study, the autonomy of technique appears to be no such thing; technique will be shown below as an expression of the basic ideological compulsion: the denial of alterity through its overcoming-in-principle or through direction of attention away from the intractable.

Let us entertain the thought that in ancient times, prior to the advent of sophisticated mechanical technology and the trend to urbanization, the ideological impulses of fallen Dasein operated on a mythological level, *exactly where the religious impulse was located*. As William Irwin Thompson argues in *The Time Falling Bodies Take to Light*,[5] mythology re-presents understandings of the structures of publicness. Insofar as this is the case, one would expect to find in mythology not only religious energies coming to expression, but also the proto-technological, ideological impulses that would pre-figure the technological thesis of the current age. The distinction between religion and ideology, recent as it is, may not have been able to come clear at the phenomenal level until the natural (read polyvalent) language of earlier mythology gave way to the univocity of technical formalisms. Clear or obscure, the *polemos* of religion and ideology would be represented in stories of struggle and domination, of which we find many in the world's mythologies. It happens that the language of technology, that peculiar anti-poetry which reveals only what is permitted in advance to be seen, has developed in such a way as to force into view the disjunction between what admits of technological manipulation and what does not. In doing so, technological language, especially since the Enlightenment, has shifted the scene of the *polemos* from the epic past to the material present, a present which is dominated by the metaphor of the machine; the machine is recognizable as the ideological metaphor *par excellence*. The power of the machine as machine and the machine as metaphor have been significant in the history of ideology and thus in the history of religion as problem. With a focus on the machine, it becomes justified to trace the proximate beginnings of the dramatic Enlightenment turn in the history of religion as problem back to Renaissance innovations.

To accept the continuation of the Renaissance progress in mechanical engineering as the primary interpretive key for explaining the accelerated industrial development of the Enlightenment is to focus on only part of the picture, however, as Ellul's disparagement of Mumford suggests. While Ellul idealistically concentrates on the power of the mental discipline of technique, Mumford materialistically stresses the power of the physical environment. He does not really conclude very far away from Ellul in practical terms when he writes, "In projecting one side of the human personality into the concrete forms of the machine, we have created an independent environment that has reacted upon every other side of the personality."[6] Mumford clearly knows that the discontinuity of the period is not to be ignored; the technological explosion in the second half of the eighteenth century is an important datum to consider in assessing the way Enlightenment culture interacted with traditional culture.

For Karl Marx, who saw how technology could be the catalyst for thinking which would challenge and supercede the palliative mythologies that disguised or otherwise defended industrial culture's structures of domination, industrialization was the mechanism of alienation that crystalized inequities and created the consciousness of the proletariat.

With this consciousness, the parasitism of the exploitative classes and the ideologies with which this parasitism was justified would be exposed and eliminated in the inevitable transformations of history. The expected emancipation of the workers that Marx publicized was a stage in human cultural evolution that could not be reached until the engines of capitalism had run long enough for a dialectical countermovement (namely, socialism) to have been engendered. As the production and reproduction of reality in industrial society altered objective material conditions, the basis for revolution grew more powerful. What Marx did not take very seriously was that, by the time he and Engels got together, the revolution had already happened and they were recapitulating the past rather than projecting the future.

What makes Marx interesting as a figure in the history of religion-as-problem is not so much his revolutionary vision as his revolutionary blindness. As many others did, Marx saw the great changes that were taking place in his time; unlike many others, he devoted massive amounts of energy to trying to understand them. One of the fruits of this effort was his theory of dialectical materialism. This theory, in totalizing the material plane of existence, developed a theoretical basis for taking the changes in living and working conditions of the time more seriously than any other contemporaneous conceptual framework. That was Marx's vision. His blindness lay in believing that the proletarian classes would use their consciousness of social parasitism to reject it; instead they set about developing their own techniques of parasitism.

The real action in the eighteenth century, which Marx did not see, was not with the proletariat, which should not be very surprising in itself. It was in the dominant classes, where a variety of collapses were occurring. It was not only the French Revolution which signaled collapse in the upper classes, it was the work of philosophers who were justifying ways of being in the world that were not beholden to the existing structures of domination. The proclamation of reason as the court of last appeal was not only directed against superstition, but also against all unreasonable social orders. Hegel's ideas about Napoleon notwithstanding, the philosophers and entrepreneurs of Continental Europe and England were steadily building up an inventory of ways to think and live that did not presuppose the realities of the class structure of the Old World.

In Germany, the Pietistic movement also contributed to a revolution that Marx did not see. Dietrich Ritschl relates the mood of Pietism to its context:

> . . . theological enlightenment in its German form within
> the *Aufklarung* is *not* the opposite of pietism. August
> Hermann Francke and his pupil Graf Zinzendorf are no less
> children of the *Aufklarung* than Wolff or, later, J.F.
> Jerusalem and J.J. Spalding, or the great scholars S.J.
> Baumgarten and J.S. Semler. The Pietists, too, want to be
> "modern men." [7]

With its early emphasis on the plain spirituality of the common people, which broke down many distinctions between nobles and their subjects, Pietism virtually collapsed believers into a single class, at least for a while. This collapsing of classes was enthusiastically supported by a considerable number of titled German families, with the most obvious monument to their feelings being Francke's school at Halle (fl. early eighteenth century) and the roster of students who were sent there. Though Pietism later became an enervated orthodoxy, its effects were long-lasting.

One of these effects was the renewal of the Moravian Unity of the Brethren. Sometimes looked upon as one of the most extreme of the Pietistic sects, the eighteenth-century Moravians represent more than an extreme linear development of Pietism. They also merit historical interest for being an embodiment of a strikingly comprehensive antithesis of the ideals of the Enlightenment; they violated the existing social order by practicing common ownership of possessions, experimenting with destruction of both extended and nuclear family, ecstatic rituals, extravagant linguistic deviations from standard usage, and so on. Much of this behavior was uneasily countenanced by authorities in their area because their protector, Count Nicholaus von Zinzendorf, was a noble in comparatively good standing himself. But when Zinzendorf began publicly referring to himself as a little worm in the side-hole of Christ and publicizing other such expressions of abjection, the threat to order and decorum was just too much for Zinzendorf's conservative peers, and the group's affairs became almost fatally complicated by official interference and resistance.

Even at his most self-abasing, Zinzendorf was never inclined to act or allow himself to be perceived as "just folks," but the international spectacle of the Moravian experiment in social destruction, which constituted a radical religious challenge to ideology, was still an affront to the refined sensibilities of the nobility and a provocation to the German *literati*; references to it are sprinkled through the writings of Goethe, Novalis, Schleiermacher, Nietzsche, and many others. Perhaps because the Moravians created the purest form of their classless society in the American Colonies, Marx never noticed that an example of ownership of the means of production by the workers was already into its second century in the commercial center of Bethlehem, Pennsylvania and was, in fact, near to being abandoned in favor of private ownership and free enterprise as he was involving himself with the 1848 revolution.

The Moravians are not just interesting as non-violent social/economic revolutionaries; they are, as we have said, also significant for thinking the history of religion in the eighteenth century. During a time designated by the Moravians as the "Sifting Period," the revolution was being as intensely pursued in religious practice as in social affairs. As Jörn Reichel observes, "Thus, the Sifting Period (1743-1750) is to be understood as a challenge and at the same time as a dynamic-prophetic reaction of lay theology and individual piety of the heart to Pietism's impious striving for sanctification, to the rigid moralism of the Enlightenment, and to an orthodox Christianity fixated in dogmatism."[8] In short, there was a kind of religious awakening occurring in the German and American Moravian communities that was in some sense destructive, an awakening which had a distinctive emphasis. As often occurs in Christian religious awakenings, this one had a strong component of the awareness of death in it, but unlike most others, this awareness was not expressed in terms of judgement, afterlife, etc. It took the form of intense, occasionally quasi-erotic meditations on the blood and wounds of Christ. Given the cultural context in which this aberration in revivals occurred, it can be seen that the carnal imagery was not without justification.

William Irwin Thompson once liked to talk about the stages an idea passes through in its lifetime. It begins with the crazies, Thompson said, and then is picked up in turn by savants, then scholars, then pedants. In the history of religion, Sifting Period Moravians certainly qualify as crazies, but what was their idea and who were the savants who picked it up? At the time of the Sifting Period, the energy in literature was draining out of the Neo-Classical movement and into the *Sturm und Dränger*, whose writings reached an apogee of shock effect in the cannibalism scene of Gerstenberg's *Ugolino*. As a reaction to the Classical theorists' austere emphasis on form and contemplation of the eternal priniciples of beauty, the *Sturm und Drang* style makes dialectical sense. But making dialectical sense to give coherence to a history of German literature is not what these people were doing; they were out to recapture human existence, whose unpredictabilities and ragged edges were being glossed over by the style of the times in both literature and religion. The extremely abject, physical presentations of the body's sufferings and death by both the *Sturm und Dränger* and the Sifting Period Moravians were part of a last, desperate attempt to keep the body in symbolic existence before the finalization of the shift in consciousness that Ellul interprets as a development of technique. For Christian theology, this is a high point of metonymic incarnational thinking and, for the Moravians at least, the period in their five hundred-year history of most intense Christological emphasis.

The initiatives of the *Sturm und Dränger* eventually evolved into the Romantic movement in Germany, typified by Friedrich, Freiherr von Hardenberg — Novalis. If there was a savant who transmuted the energies of the *Sturm und Drang*, it was he. The story of Novalis has a prominent place in the history of German literature, but it is also meaningful in the history of German religion. Novalis, as it happens, was born into a family of Moravians about a generation after the Sifting Period had run its course. By his time, many Sifting Period documents had been suppressed by the pragmatic August Gottlieb Spangenberg, Zinzendorf's successor as leader of the renewed church, so Novalis was reared in the quiet piety that was typical of post-Sifting Period Moravians. Complaining that Protestantism had made a religion out of philology, Hardenberg converted to Roman Catholicism in search of the true faith. His polemic, *Christianity or Europe*, represents his vehement rejection of all divergence from the medieval Church. That work, the testimony of a frenzied spirit, was itself suppressed until twenty-five years after his death, a correspondence with the fate of some of Zinzendorf's writings that reflects the spirit of the times. Consonant with his reaction to that spirit, Novalis did not relent in his search for the one true faith; on his deathbed, he was reading the works of another relentless searcher, Zinzendorf.

The point of these glimpses into German history is to present a picture of religion *in extremis*. The extremity in this period is not so overtly manifested as in the days of the persecutions, but it is the more difficult for religion to overcome spiritually because of that. The outward manifestation of this difficulty was the eloquently articulated religiosity of a Zinzendorf or a Novalis, a religiosity not quite acceptable in a larger society that was doing the work of the Industrial Revolution and busy forming new opinions about the religion of its ancestors.

Much more in sympathy with the dominant spirit of his times was Immanuel Kant. Though Heine's famous sketch of Kant speaks of the philosopher's world-crushing thoughts, his description of Kant's legendary punctuality suggests a man perfectly at home with the time-clock mentality that would be ushered in by the Industrial Revolution. The widely-circulated story of how Kant's neighbors could set their clocks according to his walks is a fitting piece of an extended metaphor which includes not only the element of Kant's mechanical life-rhythms but also the portent of the influence of the kind of ideas that came to expression in Kant's work. Heine says the people of Königsberg could not suspect from looking at the diminutive philosopher how radical his thoughts were, but in fact, the world that was crushed in the *Critique of Pure Reason* was one that the philosophes had been dismantling for half a century and which was about to be virtually processed out of existence in the new factories of England.

While Kant is today most appreciated in theological and critical theoretical circles for his strict limitations on metaphysical thinking, there is another aspect of his thought that is especially apposite for this discussion, namely his consideration of good and evil as dual aspects of human nature in the late work, *Religion within the Limits of Reason alone*. Even before writing this last major essay, Kant had already established a pattern of thinking by imagining dualistic constructions that resolved into an uncomfortable unity, as he speculates in the early pages of the *Critique of Judgement* and as can be seen in his analysis of the cosmological antinomies in the *Critique of Pure Reason*. Though the domains of the phenomenal and noumenal were theoretically distinct for him, and science and religion were essentially independent of each other, it remains undeniable that they are unified in the lives of real people; it was the problematic of this unity that brought the conflict of empiricism and reason to Kant's attention in the first place. The unity that he imagines, then, is not an essential one, but rather a factual one whose structure Kant experiences in a moment of discovery. That Kant's own psychological makeup eventuated in works with curious lacunae does not detract from his own reported experience of having thought his problems through as far as possible, thereby discovering something true about reality in his time.

In his treatment of good and evil, Kant presents human beings as being born with an innate sense of good. This innate sense of good does not rule in life, however, since it is opposed by an impulse to elevate what Kant (prejudicially) calls "lower incentives"[9] to an improperly high place in the inventory of maxims. These maxims Kant speaks of appear at this point best classed as ideology according to current usage of the word, but for Kant they were the stuff of moral understanding, which he imagined as being central to religion. In what appears to be basically a traditional Christian schema, Kant describes the difference between good and evil in terms of a fall, the effect of which is a corruption of the predisposition to good with which people are born.

With regard to evil, Kant was a guarded optimist. He writes, "For man, therefore, who despite a corrupted heart yet possesses a good will, there remains hope of a return to the good from which he has strayed."[10]

It is especially noteworthy in the present context that Kant imagines this corruption to be virtually equiprimordial with the good. He does not choose to speculate about the absolute origins of evil but he does note in an ontological observation that the possibility of evil is the condition of freedom, and by the time he writes *Religion within the Limits of Reason alone*, Kant is convinced of the necessity of freedom. Without freedom, he argues, there is no point in speaking of good and evil; since we possess an intuition of good, however, as well as a sense of evil, it is also justified to speak of freedom. Given this freedom, one is also given the possibility of actualizing the innate good of humanity in the living of a virtuous life, which Kant imagined as a struggle that one must constantly work hard to win.

The general, practical import of what Kant says is not very different from what the Christian tradition had been saying before him, but Kant felt compelled to justify an interpretation of the moral-social ideals of religion on independent grounds. In carrying out this project, Kant was doing his duty to his society, something which was very important to him. He saw the challenge to social stability that was forming in his age as the old onto-theology began to break down. A personally pious individual, Kant strove to preserve the wider validity of his religious intuitions by deriving them in the modern idiom of reasoned argument. His philosophical postulation of a fall as part of the logical constitution of man marks a decisive shift in the history of religion from the mythological framework of traditional religion to the technological framework that was coming together in Kant's age. Though Kant did not intend his philosophical writings to be used in biblical exegesis, he could not honestly have ignored the fact that his explanation of a fall would make more sense to the pragmatic bourgeois consensus in the Age of Reason than the supernaturalistic scriptural narrative.

Walter Kaufmann has written in his *Critique of Religion and Philosophy*, "Historically, it has been religion above all that has awakened and cultivated men's ontological interest and raised the sights of the mass of men to some idea at least of a higher level of being."[11] Kant's way of realizing this general principle in his own work was not direct sermonizing, but it was no less an overt religious undertaking. As he explained in *Lectures on Philosophical Theology*,[12] knowledge of the highest being was the province of theology. The kind of knowledge that Kant felt was possible for theology (*theologia ectypa*) was knowledge of the part of God that lies in human nature. This knowledge, he asserted, could be applied to morality, and the result would be religion. Rational theology may not be able to describe the Being of God, but it can contemplate human nature. For holding such views, Kant has been described as advocating "a religion of pure reason."[13] Rudolf Otto, in an introduction to one of Schleiermacher's early works, *On Religion: Speeches to its Cultured Despisers*, characterizes the religion drawn by Kantian philosophy as a complex of metaphysical speculation and moral rules. Otto, prophet of numinosity, was unimpressed by the results.

Religion is not totally subordinated to reason for Kant, but all that is supernatural is placed at one remove from everyday life in his thinking. His treatments of miracles, mysteries, and means of grace are good examples. In the manner of the Enlightenment, he recalls the problems that have arisen when a course of action was decided on the basis of an appeal to the unseen or the ineffable. Kant notes a certain disposition of reason to invent impressive constructs in order to compensate for its own deficiencies and observes that religion has not avoided this temptation as assiduously as it might have. In his judgement, "Reason does not dispute the possibility or the reality of the objects of these ideas; she simply cannot adopt them into her maxims of thought and action."[14] He consigns such phenomena to the periphery of religion without ever having to dispute articles of faith. This may be interpreted as a realistic intellectual modesty, but, after Heidegger, it may also be seen as a concealment of the Being of religion. This is a significant alternative reading in the history of religion's presence-at-hand.

What matters to Kant in this essay is religion as morality. It does not appear that he wants to reduce religion, but only present that aspect of it which can be accommodated by reason. Thus, Kant's Christ becomes at minimum the exemplar of the moral archetype which is present to reason, and whether or not one can explain the historical Jesus in other terms becomes almost incidental. Reason can work from the fact of this moral archetype, which becomes the sufficient basis for any understanding of Jesus as Christ, though (tellingly) the morality of the parables is not much clearer after Kant than it was before. In guiding the understanding of religion to some kind of least common denominator, Kant was not only making the possibility of religion more accessible to the people of his time, he was also fulfilling the new requirements of the ideological impulse; in minimizing precisely those aspects of religion, especially of Christianity, which constitute an unremitting challenge to convention, he was, in fact, doing a service to the emerging technological interests of his time. In what Jonathan Bennett calls "his obsession with *apparent* shape,"[15] Kant selects features of reality that owe but little to any religious *Weltanschauung* that does not happen to square with ordinary perceptions and rational extrapolations from sense data. Though Kant's system ultimately depends upon God for its anchor, and though such a system may be imagined as carrying on the tradition of

Anselm in its special appeal for the faithful, it is important to remember that the role of reason in human consciousness has undergone a significant change in the years intervening between Anselm and Kant. Whereas for Anselm, it is a source of delight that reason can accord with revelation, for Kant it becomes a virtual necessity that revelation accord with reason. Whatever the *sub rosa* forces that drive Kant, it remains important that on the surface, reason sets the agenda for reflection on religion in his writing; it does so, moreover, not in the mode of lonely iconoclasm but as the *ex post facto* articulation of the emerging order.

One of the most mordantly polemical commentators on these intellectual developments in European society was Friedrich Nietzsche, whose views on religion owe more to the writings of Kant than to those of Zinzendorf, but which sympathize with neither. Nietzsche had only a sketchy idea of Zinzendorf's Herrnhut, but he did not like what he saw, an apparent complacency which, in retrospect, it seems better to interpret as a spiritual exhaustion following the violence of the Sifting Period as opposed to the kind of somnolent equanimity that Nietzsche seems to project onto the community. Kant is a problem of a different order for Nietzsche. He accuses Kant of being overly committed to concepts of duty and morality under cover of rationality while at the same time being disposed to desert reason at any convenient time, as Nietzsche claims Kant does in inventing the concept of freedom in order to excuse God for the presence of evil in the world. Interestingly, Nietzsche also accuses Kant of being out of touch with history and blind to the reality of his time. It may well be that Kant did not participate in the full spectrum of revolutionary energies that were working themselves out in his era, but, on balance, it is more difficult to *exclude* Kant from the revolutionary ascendence of bourgeois values and attitudes that was externalized in the Industrial Revolution than it is to *include* him in that phenomenon.

Nietzsche desires to live in a different historical current from Kant. Though, like Kant, Nietzsche almost never mentions anything relating to industrialization or the problematic of technique, his thinking also presents a view of how religion has been a problem and how it can continue to be. The difference in temperament between Nietzsche and Kant does not alter the fact that claims and attractions of religion elicited responses from both that were intended for the ideal readers of their respective times and that both of these responses are characterized by rationalization of religion, though toward different ends.

In one of the fragments collected in *The Will to Power*, Nietzsche writes,

In the same way as today the uneducated man believes that anger is the cause of his being angry, spirit the cause of his thinking, soul the cause of his feeling — in short, just as there is still thoughtlessly posited a mass of psychological entities that are supposed to be causes — so, at a yet more naive stage, man explained precisely the same phenomena with the aid of psychological personal entities.

. . . The psychological logic is this: When a man is suddenly and overwhelmingly suffused with the *feeling of power* — and this is what happens with all great affects — it raises in him a doubt about his own person: he does not dare to think himself the cause of this astonishing feeling — and so he posits a stronger person, a divinity, to account for it. [16]

When Nietzsche analyzes the origin of religion in terms of power, he is speaking a language that is informed not only by the history of Western philosophy but also by the industrial and colonial experiences of his age. At the time he is writing (in an only apparently non-industrial location), the factories of Europe have come into full operation, the colonial empires dwarf the motherlands that control them, and the writings of Kierkegaard are making their way out of Denmark. Whether one chooses to agree with Nietzsche's provocative reduction of religion or not, and whether one additionally chooses to go along with Nietzsche's literal acceptance of the displacement of force that is represented in the ideological manipulation of the concept of suprasensible reality (to which he so strongly objects), the situation of religion in the industrial age appears in an interesting light if the surface of his analysis is read in conjunction with two other thoughts: from the future, Ellul's fundamental thesis that technique becomes the prime determinant of man's being in the world in the industrial age and, from the past, a different view of religion found in the writings of Schleiermacher. We also bear in mind this chapter's sub-thesis (which was inferred from the events represented above by the German anecdotal material) that the coming of the industrial age placed religion *in extremis*.

Nietzsche's account of the origin of religion is in some sense a negation of the usual psychologistic theses that religion originates in fear of natural phenomena or awe at the incalculable immensity of the universe. Ludwig Feuerbach's idea[17] that religion grows out of experience is generally interpreted as referring to the chronological or existential primacy of this "overpowering" realization in the genesis of religious consciousness. In the same thread of history, Schleiermacher's famous phrase, which defines religion as "a feeling of absolute dependence" is sometimes interpreted popularly in this way, though that is not what Schleiermacher seems to have had in mind.

Although Schleiermacher did place an unqualified feeling of dependence as the central fact of religious experience, he did not thereby define religion as a simple movement of depending-upon. To see how religion came to presence in his thinking, the importance he assigned to feeling must first be recognized. Schleiermacher connected "feeling" and "piety" so closely in this context that they became interchangeable. In his thinking, feeling was the faculty that stimulated knowing and doing. He imagined a kind of dialectic involving these terms. He writes:

> Life, then, is to be conceived as an alternation between an abiding-in-self (*Insichbleiben*) and a passing-beyond-self (*Aussichheraustreten*) on the part of the subject. The two forms of consciousness (Knowing and Feeling) constitute the abiding-in-self, while Doing proper is the passing-beyond-self. Thus far, then, Knowing and Feeling stand together in antithesis to Doing.[18]

That knowing and feeling should be distinguished in this way obviously had implications for an understanding of religion that was centered on feeling. Schleiermacher accordingly held that religion could have no warrant for claims that involved issues of objective knowledge. His philosophy of religion also removed conceptual thinking from the realm of normative possibility with regard to religious experience. In doing this, Schleiermacher sought not only to be true to his own experience, but to remove religion from areas where it would (un)necessarily come under attack by the increasingly imperialistic forces of science and reason. He did not anticipate anything like Nietzsche's genealogical method and its master trope, the metaphysics of power, however, perhaps because in his time religion was still being brought to presence following the Enlightenment agenda. Though Schleiermacher sought to free religion from the entanglements of disputed truth-claims, his own writings had to frustrate this intent by involving religion in truth-claims of an only slightly different type from those he was excluding and thereby directing more critical attention to religion as a problem, this time, however, as a problem of psychology instead of geology or physics or moral philosophy. In this sense, Schleiermacher prepared the way for Nietzsche, but his significance in the history of religion's presence-at-hand goes beyond this. His sense of self-consciousness bears distinct resemblances to the existential analytic that Heidegger was to develop a century later.

Knowing and feeling are not the only kinds of division that Schleiermacher imagines in the subject/self that one either abides in or passes beyond. The self-consciousness of this subject/self was in his view further divided into two constituting aspects, which he labeled *ein Sein* and *ein Irgendwiegewordensein*. These two aspects bespeak a present and a past respectively, but that structure of temporality does not convey Schleiermacher's most epochal thought: "In self-consciousness, there are only two elements: the one expresses the existence of the subject for itself, the other its co-existence with an other."[19] The other is important in Schleiermacher's thinking as that toward which we are free to comport ourselves in various ways. As something which originates outside oneself, he says, the other, posited as the condition of freedom, also occasions unconditioned dependence. Thus, Schleiermacher encourages his readers to consider the feeling of absolute dependence and the feeling of freedom as a unity. (There can be no feeling of absolute freedom since the feeling of freedom is conditioned by the fact of the other.) In imagining a psycho-temporal unity with roots in the writings of Schleiermacher, we come to a present which depends upon a freely-chosen past. This appears to be a rationale for something like the affects of Enlightenment Deism as well as the religion of the underivable (but not *sui generis*) self, to borrow part of an interpretation from Richard R. Niebuhr's *Schleiermacher on Christ and Religion*.[20]

In the history of religion-as-problem, Schleiermacher is an important figure partly because he almost takes for granted the logical limits imposed on religion by science, technology, and bourgeois ideology in the century before him, and partly because his understanding of the nature of religion depends so much upon the mix of the metaphysics of human existence and informal psychology that he develops. Schleiermacher's philosophical theology claims religion is essentially a relationship of a subject to an object, but the object has ceased to be an Absolute whose specific characteristics can be known empirically or intuited. For Schleiermacher, what can be known is one's own dependence, which affects one's relationship to everything in the world. On the basis of this knowledge, one is free to relate to and rely on the conditioning other in a way that feels appropriate, including realization of relationship through mediation. Faith then ceases to be belief in the empirical factuality of content-rich propositions construed as personal convictions and becomes instead an attitude of being in the world. If religion is imagined like this, then theology is certainly not to be cast as a natural science and involved in natural scientific disputes.

Despite its circumscribed role, religion was crucial to life for Schleiermacher. Specifically, it was a feeling, piety, which he analyzed as the stimulus for both knowing and doing. The feeling is a prime for him; it is the proximate beginning of self-consciousness. Schleiermacher seems to conceive of the dialectic of self-consciousness almost as the program of a cybernetic machine designed to perform a complex task. The machine begins operation when energized by a feeling, then surveys the situation to get relevant information (knowledge), and finally performs operations (doing) as long as the energy continues and the information is sufficient. With a few modifications, this structure would have little trouble being used as part of the psychological component of a philosophy of will.

Nietzsche's own philosophy of will and his interest in eliminating substantialistic metaphysical constructions of religion place him in closer proximity to Schleiermacher than the surfaces of their writings immediately suggest. The anti-cleric and the clergyman may have very different desires at work in their writings, but both write out of nearly the same presence-at-hand of religion and both write to a humanity which is no longer the humanity that was created in the opening pages of the Book of Genesis. In his perception of the integrity of the role of an other, Schleiermacher takes a step that is as decisive in the history of phenomenology of religion as Kant's was for the history of philosophical theology. In his questioning of the motives of religious man, Nietzsche generalizes Marx's critique of ideology to all values (including especially religious values) and thereby contributes to the groundwork for the thinking of religion as ideology.

In upending what he saw as platonistic essentialism and by locating reality in the here-and-now struggle, Nietzsche was able to justify his ontology-by-genealogy, and with the derivation-in-principle of all structures of reality through the principle of power, all values came to appear as tools of domination. Then, once Nietzsche was satisfied that he had sufficiently exposed values as devices of domination, any hierarchy of values had to collapse into an undifferentiated gallery of posturings; religious values came to appear to be constituted of the same stuff as any others, a view which is not without contemporary advocates. The word "ought" became meaningless for Nietzsche in this movement and evaluations of entities and thoughts became ideally situation-dependent. Both religion and ideology, insofar as they are structures of valuation, become mere vehicles for the self-serving construction and maintenance of illusory worlds whose real reason for being is the strengthening of oneself and the enhanced domination of others. Those who perpetuate such structures in the guise of disinterested philosophy, and here Nietzsche includes virtually every major figure in the two centuries of German intellectual history that preceded him, he calls in a word-play "mere

Schleiermachers,"[21] evoking not only the figure of the theologian but also the literal sense of the name, "maker of veils."

Religion comes to presence for Nietzsche as a nefarious tool used by the powerless to advance their interests at the expense of what he sees as healthy, noble, etc. It sucks the blood of the real world to feed the illegitimate projects of the so-called suprasensible realm, a phantasm Nietzsche analyzes to have been invested with more reality than life itself. This, he argues, is precisely backwards. In undertaking the reversal, Nietzsche does not have in mind a simple transferral of philosophical emphasis, he wants to eliminate the suprasensible as an alteritive term of the equation altogether. Once that is accomplished, he wants to eliminate the reactionary, ossifying influence of positivism as well. Nietzsche's specific agenda calls for a culture-wide recognition that there are no bare facts, only interpretations; the will to power is the central hermeneutic principle.

No method will yield to Nietzsche the truth of beings once and for all. Nietzsche himself does not desire to have the power to determine eternally the Being of the particular; he can only formulate the general in such a way that all particulars are explained in principle and also explained without recourse to a philosopher's god or God. Once God has become meaningless, beings are on their own and who or what they are becomes a matter of individual power. For Nietzsche, this ushered in the time when the strongest would be "(t)he most moderate; those who do not require any extreme articles of faith; those who not only concede but love a fair amount of accidents and nonsense; those who can think of man with a considerable reduction in his value without becoming small and weak on that account . . . ."[22] In this situation, beings are without their traditional, metaphysically-given essences, and reason is without its (also metaphysical) Kantian basis, and the significances of the moment are wide open to continuous revision, but the possibility of such continuous revision is precisely the condition of letting beings be. This is what Heidegger is speaking of in *What Is Called Thinking?* as he discusses a tree in bloom:

> When we think through what this is, that a tree in bloom presents itself to us so that we can come and stand face-to-face with it, the thing that matters first and foremost, and finally, is not to drop the tree in bloom, but for once let it stand where it stands. Why do we say "finally"? Because to this day, thought has never let the tree stand where it stands.[23]

One of Heidegger's great contributions to thinking was in finding new ways to show how coercively metaphysical preconceptions were working in this age which believes it has no taste for metaphysics. In this respect, he is not only the next step after Nietzsche, whose maximally general metaphysics of will was still, in Heidegger's view, an imposition on the Being of the tree, as well as on the Being of other beings, but he is also the anachronistic precondition of Husserl's work if Husserl's phenomenology is to be anything more than pseudo-scientific linguistic analysis in substance or significance. Heidegger's later ontological search for the lambent light of Being in the experience of poetry represents a qualitatively different approach to the question of the Being of beings, a re-discovery of a way he announced as meditative thinking, in contrast to the calculative thinking which is the basis of technology. Heidegger sees calculative thinking, which we link with ideology, as having dominated Western metaphysics and thus Western culture at least since the Enlightenment.

The non-metaphysical letting-be of beings, if indeed Heidegger actually has accomplished it, is the achievement of what Nietzsche appears to have set out to do. Nietzsche believed, it seems, that removing God as the ridgepole of idealism would be sufficient to eliminate theologistic metaphysics and that it would then be possible to argue the fact/interpretation question decisively against positivism to eliminate what he saw as a naive, empiricistic metaphysics. In reading Nietzsche, it is easy to agree with Heidegger that the real problem was onto-theological metaphysics and not the institution of religion that was the most obvious of its manifestations. Because religion was so obvious, however, it made an easy target and the clergy, as the acolytes of a cult of metaphysics (not to mention Kantians as the high priests), shared in guilt. For Nietzsche, religions had become mere power centers for the unfit.

Far more vital and true for Nietzsche was art. In *The Birth of Tragedy*, Nietzsche attributes to the artist much of what traditional religion has attributed the mystic and he virtually identifies the vitality of artistic experience with that of religious experience. Manfred Kaempfert, in his book about religious language in Nietzsche's writings, *Säkularisation und die neue Heiligkeit*, points out that Nietzsche was not untouched by the cult of the genius that had exercised such power over the art theories of the Romantic movement. If we may accept Otto Rank's plausible characterization of Romantic art as a private religion, the phenomenon of art would have been ripe for the kind of cathexis that Kaempfert observes in Nietzsche's writings. Kaempfert documents Nietzsche's own ambiguous feelings about the cult of genius, which centered on the cult-consciousness of Nietzsche's predecessors. In *The Will to Power* (215), for example, it is clear that the "type" of the genius is what Nietzsche propounded as the standard for humanity. Regarding the genius as exceptional, Nietzsche felt, was a sign of the degeneracy and nihilism of the culture he lived in.

In art, as Heidegger explains in his study on Nietzsche, the appearance of life is what is important, in contrast to the fixed reality of truth. Nietzsche appreciated and prized the erotic energy of phenomenal changes and felt that life was truly lived in full participation in the sensuous surface of the world. The vibrant intensities of art, which energetically illuminated the possibilities of the sensuous world and thus enriched life, stood radiantly in unmistakable contrast to the intense, "eternal" verities of institutional religion and platonistic metaphysical philosophy. In Nietzsche's estimation, the genius is the one who is spiritually strong enough to survive this flux without the support of a fixed reference. The contrast between the grand type of the genius and the crabbed type of the priest in the thought of Nietzsche is a stark one and it gives a clear sense of how religion was present-at-hand for him. Religion was present-at-hand for Nietzsche precisely as the concrescence of a fixated metaphysical determination of life. "Religion," as he perceived it, reduced the phenomena of the world so radically that life itself was eliminated.

Nietzsche does not participate in the emergence of the split between religion and ideology in the way that Kant did. It seems, however, that his perception of organized religion as power center has significant similarities to Marx's perceptions of the phenomenon, though these similar critiques obviously did not lead the two thinkers to many other points of substantive agreement.[24] For Nietzsche, religion comes to represent the life-denying claims of the suprasensible world, it is true, but that is not all there is to it. When Heidegger says Nietzsche is still thinking metaphysically, he indicates a way of reading Nietzsche such that the opposition between religion and art that Nietzsche constructs can be seen to have a direct bearing on understanding of the religion-ideology problematic.

Religion has traditionally had to do with a sense of life that transcends the categories of the five bodily senses. In the eighteenth century, implications of this sense of the suprasensible crystalized in the beginnings of the religion-science debate. As Nietzsche wrote, science had succeeded in moderating or discrediting a number of beliefs that had come to be a part of the traditional Christian cultural aggregate.[25] For those metaphysically inquisitive of the nineteenth century, Christianity did not offer the philosophical integrity that it had in earlier times. As the religion of Europe, it was the example of the type that was most before Nietzsche's eyes and it was not satisfactory to account for the vitality of beings that he cared to embrace. Indeed, religion could not even lead to an appreciation of the energies it could not explain. Religion was present-at-hand for Nietzsche because of these failings.

For many of those who found religion wanting, there were secular ideological alternatives to fill the various voids. As a rule, the alternatives that appropriated bits and pieces of religion's former place in the community offered highly reasonable arguments to justify their positions and avoided the appearance of revelation and mystery. The new alternatives to a vitiated and unattractive Christianity did not present themselves as alternative religions *per se*. Utopian socialisms, scientific socialism, scientism, free-market business, and so on were all possibilities that featured what Heidegger was later to call "calculative thinking." Nietzsche would never grant legitimacy to the absolutizing of the normal that seemed to animate such thinking. If he had a falling-out with religion, he was not about to fall into the kind of denial of life that was the final nihilistic outcome of religion's own internal dynamics taken to their apparent conclusion. He was not searching for the certitude of an ideology.

What Nietzsche in fact desired was just the opposite of perfection. By his own account, he found it in fleeting moments of art, though, as Heidegger claims, at the price of a calculated metaphysics of eternal imperfection. With this metaphysics, we note, Nietzsche achieved something like the sense of transcendence of death that the religious have enjoyed, but without the necessity of following one of the traditional ways of salvation. Moreover, he achieved this apparent independence of organized religion without falling into a fetishistic preoccupation with the specious logic of atheism or becoming dependent on an organized ideology. It was his appreciation of beings that was Nietzsche's undoing, claims Heidegger, forcing him into a grand scheme of permutations fueled by the will to power as fundamental principle or primal energy. We can see this occurring as a complex movement. In the first moment, religion's presence-at-hand caused Nietzsche to turn away from the ideal of perfection and turn toward the phenomenal play of becoming. Since it begins with an intentionality that directs attention to religion, this first moment is essentially religious, even if it manifests itself in a nominally anti-religious modality. This first moment is also where art becomes important. In the second moment, Nietzsche seeks to explain himself intelligibly, but the material comes to language in an assortment of metaphors that do not conform to the standards of his time especially well and he wonders if his writings even belong in print. He is driven to try to found his intuitions in the only way he knows how (metaphysically) and comes up with doctrines of eternal return and will to power that make sense in their own way.[26]

All ideologies make sense in their own ways, and the *de facto* ideology Nietzsche proposed, which can be a basis for a possible society if put into practice, differs from others only in the expanse of its cosmic scope. Thus, the second moment of Nietzsche's thought, which governs, for example, the metaphysical thinking of the will to power and the concept of eternal return, in which he lays out a logic which is meant to articulate his intuitions after the fact, appears to be ideological. **The basic reason why this second moment should be called ideological is that it founds a system of thought which is complete without an element of alterity.** As such, it represents a kind of retreat from Schleiermacher. It is an absolutizing of the world as given, as will be found in any ideology; there is just a disagreement about the terms of the given.

Heidegger's *Being and Time* is nothing if not an attempt to work with the terms of the given on a human scale. In this, the book is much more than a continuation of the conversation of the school of Husserlian phenomenology and more than the founding document of a fundamental ontology; it is also a response to Nietzsche. In a way intended to be more radical than the one Nietzsche chose, Heidegger asserts a primacy of becoming that goes beyond phenomenal description of processes of life to assert that becoming belongs to the essential constitution of human beings and does not need to be explained causally or genealogically. It is an important step away from the totalizations of calculated causality that Heidegger does not feel required to explain the universe genealogically in order to speak coherently of human beings and at the same time grant vitality to existence. It is also important that Heidegger chose a number of christianistic category names for the writing of *Being and Time*.

The theological-sounding language of *Being and Time* may be interpreted in a number of ways — as manifestation of the writer's inflated sense of self-importance, as a remnant of his discontinued theological education, as a call for help, as a provocation to theologians, as a sign of philosophy's continuing struggle with theology, as a first effort in a career dedicated to revitalizing language, etc. It is also possible to see in this language an indirect indication of religion's presence-at-hand. If the categories Heidegger chooses had been part of a healthy religious practice, they would have resisted appropriation of their names for any other purpose. As it was, a troubled Christian theology not only acquiesced in Heidegger's snatching of some of its key terms, certain influential circles were positively delighted about it, as the number of publications favorably connecting Heidegger and religion/theology attests. Yet in his own mind, Heidegger was not doing theology, if for no other reason than that he was not explicating a specific revelation. He was only engaging theologians in a dialogue which began with his insistence that philosophy could serve as a corrective to theology. This is not the kind of message theology historically enjoys. Why the embrace of Heidegger's work by theologians?

Perhaps seeing in the language of fundamental ontology a more fitting idiom for his interests than Marxism offered, Paul Tillich was one of the theologians who made most enthusiastic use of *Being and Time*. He did so for at least two explicit reasons. One was that he felt he detected in the material "hidden religious sources."[27] Another was that he felt there was some kind of "interpenetration of levels between theology and philosophy."[28] Thus, there are some indications that as he was writing his *Systematic Theology*, Tillich had the idea that philosophical treatises such as Heidegger's could be an actual part of the work of theology. It does not seem that Tillich and Heidegger were imagining the relationship of the disciplines in exactly the same way.

Heidegger was clear in his desire to keep ontology and theology generically distinct. He allowed them to meet in the constitution of metaphysics, but he did not think that the two disciplines had very much of substance to teach each other. Theology had its revelation to work from and ontology had the difference between Being and beings. They may ultimately converge, but finding the convergence through the one or the other entails traveling separate paths of being. Tillich wrote concerning his understanding of the distinction between them in the opening pages of the *Systematic Theology*, "Philosophy deals with the structure of being in itself; theology deals with the meaning of being for us."[29] Tillich's formulation is ambiguous as it stands, but the point is made that for Tillich there is a disjunction of tasks between philosophy and theology. Yet there remains none the less his apparent intuition that the cooperation of philosophy, especially as represented by Heideggerian thinking, and theology could be fruitful. Tillich's *Dynamics of Faith*[30] appears to be an example of how the cooperation was intended to be realized.

What Tillich seems to have been attempting when he used the language of ontology was a combination of theory of theology and philosophy of religion. In pursuing this work, which is one of the precursors of the discourse of the present project, Tillich made one assumption about Heidegger's ontology that Heidegger himself could could not sustain, namely that "being" could function metaphorically in a religious symbol system. This appears to be the step back into metaphysics that Heidegger was trying to avoid in his own thinking, but which does not pose a problem to Tillich. The reason it does not pose a problem to Tillich is that he may not really have been speaking ontologically at all, but rather in the genre of philosophical theology. Tillich's ontologistic language can be seen as part of an effort to legitimate (idiomatically, at least) his own religiously-determined structures of significance at a time when his own religion was present-at-hand and standing in need of decisive interpretation in new terms. Tillich's intellectual kinship with Bultmann shows up here, as well as his difference from Barth.

Though he made use of Heidegger's thought and taught the truth of becoming, Tillich still was not seeking to enter into a conversation with Nietzsche or develop a post-Nietzschean theology. In positing a "really real" (even if he could not speak about it objectively) that could be the supra-linguistic focus of one's ultimate concern, Tillich adroitly cleared the hurdles of idolatry, and by veiling the Being of the divine in an all-pervading sense of the holy, he effectively prevented anthropocentric operations of abstraction and reduction. Imagining ultimate concern as a possibility of being-in-the-world, Tillich appears to have something in common with Nietzsche. In dividing up existence between ultimacy and contingency in a way that looks similar to Heidegger's contrast between authenticity and inauthenticity, but has little to do with it (as comes clearer in the next chapter's account of the integration of authenticity and inauthenticity in *Being and Time*), Tillich reveals himself to be working from some variant of that traditional dualism which sees in fallen consciousness the aftermath of an expensive cosmic miscalculation. True or not, the employment of this logic places Tillich outside the affirmation of presence that animated Nietzsche. This is not to say that Tillich avoided every orientation to presence; the notion of ultimate concern calls forth the strongest possible sense of the metaphysics of presence in the Heideggerian vocabulary.

Unlike Tillich, Heidegger apparently did feel called upon to respond to the force of Nietzsche's challenge to religion. Heidegger's response logically could not come in the mode of theology, since in the event of religion's presence-at-hand, the basis of any theology that remained true to its warranting religion was already critically in question; since he understood theology to be a strictly religious undertaking, that is, one which presupposed a viable religious impulse, Heidegger was directed by the force of his own categories to look beyond religion for the thought that could renew the possibility of religion. He had no choice but to set to work in the genre of philosophy to formulate his answer to

Nietzsche. Heidegger's answer to Nietzsche was not a direct defense of religion, but something more subtle and at the same time more sweeping: a re-definition of fundamental categories in which he sought to imagine a human being that would be able to participate in the full range of this age's cultural phenomena and still be capable of religion in spite of all that had happened in science and philosophy.

This much he accomplished with the existential analytic of *Being and Time*. The post-Nietzschean human being that Heidegger constructed there is eminently suited to being an Augustine or a Mother Theresa or a Hitler. In the process of working through this thought toward the question of Being, Heidegger discovered the ontological difference and the underivability of Being. In the history of philosophy, that discovery may be momentous, but in the history of religion's presence-at-hand, the notion of the ontological difference is but a footnote to the reinvention of *homo religiosus*. This being, whose constitution occupies our attention in the next several chapters, is Heidegger's real contribution to theology, and not the warming over of theological terms for legitimation by secularization. The question now is what sort of being Heidegger imagined.

Notes

[1] Friedrich Solmsen makes an interesting point in his book *Plato's Theology* (Ithaca, NY: Cornell University Press, 1942): "But is it not rash to assume that the combination in one and the same work of two subjects like the State and religion, distinct or even heterogeneous as they may seem, is irrelevant for the understanding of Plato's thought on either of them? May it safely be left out of account, or treated as a mere literary device? The combination may seem to have little or no meaning for the modern reader and may yet indicate that the author felt a close and intrinsic connection between the two subjects." (p. 3)

[2] Frank Manuel, *The Changing of the Gods*. Hanover, NH: University Press of New England/Brown University Press, 1983, p. xiii.

[3] Theodore M. Greene, "The Historical Context and Religious Significance of Kant's *Religion*," *Religion within the Limits of Reason alone*, tr. T.M. Greene and H.H. Hudson. New York: Harper and Row, 1960, p. ix.

[4] Jacques Ellul, *The Technological Society*, tr. John Wilkinson. New York: Alfred A. Knopf, 1964, p. 42.

[5] William Irwin Thompson, *The Time Falling Bodies Take to Light*. New York: St. Martins, 1981.

[6] Lewis Mumford, *Technics and Civilization.* New York: Harcourt, Brace and World, 1934 (1962), p. 324.

[7] Dietrich Ritschl, "Johann Salomo Semler; The Rise of the Historical-Critical Method in Eighteenth-Century Theology on the Continent," *Introduction to Modernity,* Robert Mollenauer, ed. Austin: University of Texas Press, 1965, p.110.

[8] Jörn Reichel, *Dichtungstheorie und Sprache bei Zinzendorf.* Bad Homburg: Gehlen, 1969, p. 14, translation mine. Original: "So ist die Sichtungszeit (1743-1750) zu verstehen als Kampfansage an und zugleich als dynamisch-prophetische Reaktion der Laientheologie und individuellen Herzensfrömmigkeit auf das unfrohe Heiligungsstreben des Pietismus, auf den steifen Moralismus der Aufklärung und auf ein im Dogmatismus erstarrtes orthodoxes Christentum."

[9] Kant, *Religion within the Limits of Reason alone,* p. 39.

[10] Op. cit., p. 40.

[11] Walter Kaufmann, *Critique of Religion and Philosophy,* Garden City, N.Y.: Anchor/Doubleday, 1958, p. 442.

[12] Immanuel Kant, *Lectures on Philosophical Theology,* tr. A.W. Wood and G.M. Clark. Ithaca, NY: Cornell University Press, 1978.

[13] Allen W. Wood, *Kant's Rational Theology.* Ithaca, N.Y.: Cornell University Press, 1978, p. 16.

[14] Kant, *Religion within the Limits of Reason alone,* p. 48.

[15] Jonathan Bennett, *Kant's Dialectic.* Cambridge: Cambridge University Press, 1974.

[16] Friedrich Nietzsche, *The Will to Power,* tr. W. Kaufmann and R.J. Hollingdale. New York: Vintage Books, 1967, pp. 85-86.

[17] What we are calling "Feuerbach's idea" does not originate with him, but is represented by him. Much the same idea is found, for example in the lines of Lucretius:

> Fear holds dominion over mortality
> Only because, seeing in land and sky
> So much the cause whereof no wise they know
> Men think Divinities are working there.

(Titus Lucretius Carus, *Of the Nature of Things,* tr. W.E. Leonard. New York: E.P. Dutton & Co., 1921, p. 6.)

[18] Friedrich Schleiermacher, *The Christian Faith,* Vol. 1, ed. and tr. H.R. Mackintosh and J.S. Stewart. New York: Harper and Row, 1963, p. 8.

[19] Op. cit., p. 13.

[20] Richard R. Niebuhr, *Schleiermacher on Christ and Religion.* New York: Chas. Scribner's Sons, 1964, p. 181.

[21] Friedrich Nietzsche, *Grossoktavausgabe*, Vol. XV, p. 112, translated and quoted in Martin Heidegger, *Nietzsche*, Vol. 1, tr. D.F. Krell. San Francisco: Harper and Row, 1979, p. 206.

[22] Nietzsche, *The Will to Power*, p. 38.

[23] Martin Heidegger, *What Is Called Thinking?* tr. J. Glenn Gray. New York: Harper & Row, 1968, p. 44.

[24] Mark Warren agrees with Jürgen Habermas that Nietzsche seeks to destroy the rational ground on which the Marxian critique of ideology depends. What they do not see is that with destruction of all rational grounds, the possibility of ideology disappears. The Marxian critique would not only be impossible, it would be unnecessary in the first place. See Mark Warren, op. cit., pp. 541-565.

[25] As Karl Löwith observed, Nietzsche's transvaluation of the highest values merely completed devaluation of the highest values which was already underway. (See *Heidegger: Denker in dürftiger Zeit*. Göttingen: Vandenhoeck and Ruprecht, 1965; p. 95.)

[26] Alphonso Lingis provides an additional perspective on Nietzsche's metaphysics in an important essay "The Will to Power" (in *The New Nietzsche*, ed. David B. Allison. Cambridge, MA: MIT Press, 1977). He writes, "The will to power is not just power or force, but Will to Power: always will for more power. It is not an essence; it is neither structure, telos, nor meaning, but continual sublation of all telos, transgression of all ends. . . . It is the chaos. . . which precedes the forms and makes them possible as well as transitory. . . . If Being, then, is not a ground, but an abyss, chaos, there is consequently in Nietzsche a quite new, nonmetaphysical or transmetaphysical understanding of beings, of things." (p. 38) The point is an interesting one, with implications for metaphysics not unlike those Heisenberg's Uncertainty Principle has for electrons. Even given an always already acheived telos, a perpetually realized eschaton, a trace of the metaphysical remains in the ascription of a logos to history as the already of the present. The connection between this point and Nietzsche's use and non-use of the genealogical method belongs to another discussion.

[27] Paul Tillich, *Systematic Theology*, Vol. 2. Chicago: University of Chicago Press, 1951, p. 26.

[28] Op. cit., p. 30.

[29] Op. cit., Vol. 1, p. 22.

[30] Paul Tillich, *Dynamics of Faith*. New York: Harper and Row, 1957.

Theology must clearly and unambiguously represent "the Fall" as a symbol for the human situation universally, not as the story of an event that happened "once upon a time."
— Paul Tillich

People do not understand how that which is at variance with itself agrees with itself. There is a harmony in the bending back, as in the cases of the bow and the lyre.
— Heraclitus

IV. Heidegger's Concept of Falling, with Reference to Religion and Ideology

Our thesis is that Heidegger's concept of "falling" is a principle that ontologically unifies religion and ideology and also bears on understanding the phenomena of religions and ideologies. This unification is not a collapsing of religion and ideology into the theoretical oblivion of an explanatory "ur-phenomenon" and still less is it a claim that religion and ideology are basically one and the same; rather, this thesis of unification is a way of expressing a relationship of "religion" and "ideology" as names of **the two kinds of fundamental symbol systems** that are available to a Dasein which must use its own existence to come to terms with being in the world. The term "falling," which has been proposed as the conceptual glue that can bind these two types of symbol system together, suggests that the relationship of "religion" and "ideology" is not one of ontological equality, and that is accurate; though the Dasein of the Heidegger corpus will be shown to be in ontological need of both, religion and ideology are not on that account to be imagined as symmetrical elements in the constitution of its reality. The well-known fragment of Heraclitus quoted above provides us with a useful and appropriate mnemonic image for ordering the ontological abstractions which follow into a conceptualized unity-in-discord.

In *Being and Time*, there is a tension set up from the very beginning between two possible, mutually exclusive states (modes) of Being in which Dasein may exist, namely, the state of authenticity (*eigentlich sein*) and the state of inauthenticity (*uneigentlich sein*). In the ontology of *Being and Time*, authenticity and inauthenticity exhaust the formal dimension of Dasein in which they are located. Heidegger's opening remarks in the main body of the book focus on these two possibilities, specifically as belonging to the essential constitution of Dasein, thus defining them as formal possibilities that Dasein can and must choose to be. In authenticity, says Heidegger, Dasein chooses itself and wins itself, while in inauthenticity, Dasein chooses the public interpretations of the "they" and thereby loses itself. This asymmetry carries over into the regional ontologies of religion and ideology, which correlate with authenticity and inauthenticity, respectively.

Just because one of Dasein's two formal ontological possibilities entails a "winning" and the other a "losing" does not mean that Dasein is free simply to grasp its winning possibility in a moment of enlightenment and thus forever dispense with the possibility of losing itself. Salvation (which is not one of Heidegger's terms) works out differently, more dynamically, in the framework of *Being and Time*. Since the possibilities of winning or losing oneself are not choices like items on a menu but belong to the essential constitution of Dasein, the constant can never be authenticity or inauthenticity; **the only constant is choice**. The fact of the constant of choice is the ontological datum that makes it impossible for this study to be read as a simple advocacy of the way of religion to the exclusion of the way of ideology, even if one's reading of *Being and Time* emphasizes those parts of the ontology which valorize authenticity.

Dasein remains Dasein whether it factically exists in the mode of authenticity or inauthenticity. Whether it is resolutely living its "there" in a moment of vision or indulging in idle talk, Dasein neither rises so high nor descends so low that it is released from the fundamental ontological conditions of its existence. Heidegger makes it plain that while there is reason to give a certain (not absolute) priority to authenticity, it would be inaccurate to imagine an externalized division among factical entities with the Being of Dasein that cast inauthentic Dasein as a lesser class of being, the limitations of inauthenticity notwithstanding. In an important passage, he writes, " . . . the inauthenticity of Dasein does not signify any 'less' Being or any 'lower' degree of Being. Rather it is the case that even in its fullest concretion Dasein can be characterized by inauthenticity — when busy, when excited, when interested, when ready for enjoyment."[1] These readily recognizable features of normal existence that Heidegger catalogues as characteristic of the mode of inauthenticity make it clear that abandoning inauthenticity forever is not an option for human beings insofar as consciousness has to do with organization, anticipation, and desire. Even if it were an option, it would not be a very attractive one in the conventional economy of desire.

What allows inauthenticity to give authentic existence such stiff competition when existential choices are being made is its beckoning promise of enjoyability, no matter how one wants to define enjoyment. Even though lasting enjoyment can never really be delivered to match one's anticipations, hope apparently springs eternal that somehow "things will be different this time." This hope and the actions which follow from it give inauthentic existence many of the familiar features of daily life that Heidegger observes. Not contenting himself with observation of the first surface that appears, Heidegger describes and then exceeds the understandings of "everyday," unreflective consensuality as he develops concepts of "idle talk" and "curiosity," for example, that are closely connected with inauthenticity and, by implication, with ideology as we are construing it. Aspects of both ideology and religion can be illustrated out of Heidegger's descriptions of these phenomena.

Heidegger opens his thematic treatment of idle talk in a way that is characteristic of *Being and Time*'s discussions of inauthentic possibilities: "The expression 'idle talk' is not to be used here in a 'disparaging' signification."[2] He then proceeds into the first of several descriptions of idle talk, stressing the deficiency of understanding that attends its discourse. Heidegger writes in one of the most pointed of these explanations:

> And because this discoursing has lost its primary relationship-of-Being towards the entity talked about, or else has never achieved such a relationship, it does not communicate in such a way as to let this entity be appropriated in a primordial manner, but communicates rather by following the route of of *gossipping* and *passing the word along*. What is said-in-the-talk as such, spreads in wider circles and takes on an authoritative character. Things are so because one says so . . . .And indeed this idle talk is not confined to vocal gossip, but even spreads to what we write, where it takes the form of 'scribbling'. [3]

This passage is one of those in *Being and Time* that jumps out at the reader through its intensifying, tendentious language, but beyond its entertainment value, it is also important to the thinking of the nature of ideology. It is relevant to this problematic not because ideologies themselves are supposed to consist of "idle talk" and "scribbling," but rather because the discourse which is founded upon ideologies necessarily (that is, within our reconstruction of Heidegger's ontology) has this character since it must make sense to the public in the mode of the they-self. Ideological discourse must appear to deepen or extend understanding whether it changes public opinion or simply reinforces it by adding supporting logic or evidence.

The only ways this making public sense can be achieved are to manipulate what is already believed or to introduce novelty which somehow accords with the existing patterns of understanding. Even the phenomenon of replacement of scientific paradigms, a superficial exception to this rule, still follows the rule because the new paradigm, as a generalized theory, only gains currency when an existing paradigm can no longer accommodate all accepted data of observed reality; a new paradigm only comes to presence as "the way things are" because it already exists, even though in near-total concealment. Existing paradigms naturally resist replacement, but once a new paradigm establishes itself, it consolidates the field rapidly and becomes the conventional wisdom of the "they."

> Thus the "they" maintains itself factically in the averageness of that which belongs to it, of that which it regards as valid and that which it does not, and of that to which it grants success and that to which it denies it. In this averageness with which it prescribes what can and may be ventured, it keeps watch over everything exceptional that thrusts itself to the fore. Every kind of priority gets noiselessly suppressed. Overnight, everything that is primordial gets glossed over as something that has long been well known. Everything gained by a struggle becomes just something to be manipulated. Every secret loses its force.[4]

For Dasein, the collective understandings of the "they" are a pervasive fact in its existence as Mitsein. (Dasein always exists as Mitsein; we follow Heidegger in isolating aspects of Dasein to facilitate thematic treatment.) To press this point, Heidegger describes or alludes to the "they" and what "they" do at several junctures in *Being and Time*, filling out his construction in disparate terms such as "alongside everywhere,"[5] "stubborn dominion,"[6] *"nobody"*,[7] "not accessible,"[8] and "Self of everydayness."[9] He is adamant about the ontological necessity of the "they." In *Being and Time*'s main description of the "they," Heidegger leaves no doubt about this contention when he states,

> *The "they" is an existentiale; and as a primordial phenomenon, it belongs to Dasein's positive constitution.* . . . The Self of everyday Dasein is the *they-self*, which we distinguish from the *authentic Self* — that is, from the Self which has been taken hold of in its own way [eigens ergriffen]. As they-self, the particular Dasein has been *dispersed* into the "they" and must first find itself . . . .If Dasein is familiar

with itself as they-self, this means at the same time that the "they" itself prescribes that way of interpreting the world and Being-in-the-world which lies closest.[10]

There are several points that are made in this description of the "they" which not only help crystalize what Heidegger means when he speaks of "inauthentic Being," but also shed light on the mostly concealed Being of ideology as the **wisdom of the "they."**

First, in categorizing the "they" as an existentiale, Heidegger is cutting off the possibility of laying blame for the shallowness and various other difficulties of the "they" at someone else's doorstep. The "they," as an existentiale, is a first-person datum as much as it is the ostensible third-person phenomenon that is suggested by the grammar of the term. As this relates to ideology, it implies that the individual is always already predisposed to fall into the calculated interpretation of self and world that constitutes the ideological attitude in its sufficiency. In this focus, there is apparently little real advantage in the choice of one ideology over another, for all are presentations of the ever-changing face of the "they" and all function to circumscribe the attention of Dasein to itself either by providing reasonable answers to difficult questions or by directing attention away from such problem areas. In dimensions other than that of the formal structure of Dasein, however, there are ontically significant differences among ideologies; although all ideologies are totalizations of the finite, the terms of these totalizations vary considerably. Thematic treatment of the terms of ideological totalizations is a matter for anthropology and political philosophy, though a fundamental ontology is also a prerequisite for them as much as for this study, basically because it makes the foundations of their discourse as explicit as possible; that clarity is important not as food for the fantasy of the finally true foundation, of course, but as that which brings one closer to what is excluded and concealed in deception and delusion. The need for a fundamental ontology in sorting through ideological propositions shows up with special clarity in the problematics of ethics, where the main alternatives are axiomatic utilitarianism or the kind of contractual metaphysics John Rawls works from in his *Theory of Justice*,[11] both of which obscure, rather than overcome, the need for ontological considerations.

Second, in setting up a virtual dichotomy between the authentic self and the they-self, Heidegger is not thereby proposing a dualism of an intrinsically good nature and a corresponding evil nature. Much of what the they-self does is straightforwardly beneficial in certain situations, and even necessary for survival; also these two "selves" appear to be devoid of the kind of content to which notions of "good" and "evil" can meaningfully apply. If the they-self appears to be the origin of many problems, it also appears to be the solution to many others and, most important, it is ontologically the point of departure for Dasein's choice of authenticity. Were it not for the possibilities which the they-self is uniquely able to realize, inauthenticity would be outside the realm of possibility for Dasein. Without a factical, existential understanding of the false truth of inauthenticity, authenticity itself could have no meaning because **authenticity is not so much a state of grace as a state of _having chosen_**. It is well to note that this conception of authentic Dasein, which is faithful to the central insights of _Being and Time_, is thoroughly non-substantialistic.

Without the possibility of choice that first arises with the reality embodied in the they-self, the authentic self obviously would also be categorically excluded from reality. Though these two quasi-selves are always at odds, they logically need each other in their essence. Together, they constitute the complex ontological condition of the dialectical existence of Dasein.[12]

The third point Heidegger makes about the "they" in the passage above has to do with Dasein's dispersion in the "they" and the need for Dasein to find itself. Dasein's finding itself is complicated by the fact that the closest, readiest-to-hand tools with which it might carry out an interpretation of itself are those given by the "they." Left entirely to itself with only the opinions and methods of the "they" to guide it, Dasein would never leave the absolutized world of the they-self; but Dasein is not left to itself in this way, however, since it also carries the authentic self as part of its essential constitution. In the face of death, the possibility which Dasein always tries to evade by various strategies, the authentic self comes into its own as Dasein understands itself in terms of this ultimate possibility.

Both the they-self and the authentic self aim for their own optimal realizations in every case. The they-self, even though it is always already given over to the "they," imagines megalomaniacally that it is authentically pursuing its own interests. Because it understands itself in the terms given by the "they," which is the same thing as the moment's dominant ideology, the they-self begins and ends in the terms of its ideology as far as it knows and is so tranquilized by the sufficiency of its Being as mediated by one ideology or another that it does not seek further for additional knowledge unless that knowledge promises utility in bolstering its own prevailing views. The stronger those views appear to be, the more willing ideological Dasein is to seek to appropriate additional knowledge; the weaker an ideology is, the greater the tendency for the inherent delimiting violence of ideology to come to presence as "narrow-mindedness." Dasein as they-self always seeks the kinds of self-realization which are determined in advance as admissible by the ideology in precisely the ways that are allowed by the ideology.

The authentic self, also primarily interested in its own realization, does not fall for the totalization of the finite and the absolutizing of presence that characterize ideology. In seeking to claim itself from inauthenticity, authentic, resolute Dasein follows a way that is very different from the way of ideology. Specifically, the way of authentic Dasein is mediated by a kind of symbol system that is distinctively suited to the primary need of the authentic self to negate the impetus of ideology; this kind of symbol system is religion.

Cast in this light, some elements of both ideological and religious symbol systems can be projected as related to the interests that they serve. Where ideology maintains a primary awareness of the facts of life, religion appears contrariwise to maintain an awareness of what Heidegger calls Dasein's "ownmost possibility,"[13] namely, death. Where ideology grounds its sense of relationship among entities in presence, religion grounds its in absence. Where ideology functions to disperse Dasein's attention, religion seeks to concentrate it. Ideology's dispersion of attention, made urgent through the value bestowed by the "they" upon certain (always-changing) objects of public attention, is one of the most visible effects of fallen Dasein's life in the they-self; Heidegger discusses it in his remarks on curiosity.

Heidegger analyzes curiosity as belonging to the basic state of sight, and in particular, "the tendency towards seeing."[14] For Heidegger, "sight" is a synonym for self-knowledge and self-understanding; "sight" extends also to Dasein's appropriation of entities with which it has to do. Visual metaphors play a role in the discourse of both early and later Heidegger, though they become much more important after the project of *Being and Time*'s fundamental ontology had run its course and found its place simply as an existential analytic; the results of the analysis of curiosity do not figure prominently in the later thinking, but they do help relate the thinking of *Being and Time* to the theme of ideology.

Heidegger prominently cites Augustine's *Confessions* as he develops his understanding of curiosity. In Book X:30-35, Augustine discusses the triple temptations of the flesh and one of these is "the lust of the eyes."[15] Augustine himself associates this lust with curiosity, pointing out how people will not only exert themselves to see something pleasant, but also to see something which turns their stomachs and leaves them disturbed long afterward. This, suggests Augustine, is a kind of turning away from God, and he prays to be delivered from such temptations.

Like Augustine, Heidegger finds the category of curiosity useful for coming to terms with behavior as an expression of the way people are; the difference between their expositions is significant as they move along different paths beyond the theme of curious behavior and into the wider implications of the term.

The alternative to curiosity for Augustine is God; for Heidegger, who acknowledges his debt to Augustine, the alternative to curiosity is an authentic relationship with the entities that would otherwise become just the objects of curiosity. Heidegger is here closer to Augustine than the dissimilar surfaces of their discourse initially suggest. Though the function of divinities in the construction of authentic relationships among beings is not thematically discussed in Heidegger's work until some years later, it is negatively foreshadowed in the silence of *Being and Time*'s remarkable refusal to interpret both sides of Augustine's words, both the part dealing with the fallen condition of human beings and the other part. It must be on account of more than a gratuitous omission that Augustine could have moved Heidegger to an ontological discussion of curiosity but still could not get him to take explicit note of such a major theme as religion.[16]

With regard to curiosity, Heidegger stresses a quality of incessant movement in search of novelty. Curiosity prevents Dasein from developing anything like an authentic relationship with entities that are near or far. Curious Dasein is distracted Dasein for Heidegger, a mode of Being in which one flits from thing to thing, from affair to affair, without ever attaining any depth of relationship. Curious Dasein does not sense this lack of depth, however, and accumulates knowledge and experience in large, but always unsatisfying, quantities. Curious, fallen Dasein's only contentment lies in the illusion of having exhausted the objects of its momentary attention with the apparently profound, pre-given understandings of the "they." Writes Heidegger in summary, "Curiosity, for which nothing is closed off, and idle talk, for which there is nothing that is not understood, provide themselves (that is, the Dasein which is in this manner [dem so seienden Dasein]) with the guarantee of a 'life' which, supposedly, is genuinely 'lively'."[17] This is the enjoyment that inauthenticity promises and cannot deliver for long; it is the essence of all enjoyment for Dasein.

To see how curious Dasein is nonetheless an expression of essential Dasein requires a look at Heidegger's concept of "care." It is one of those fortuities of language that etymology makes the semantic connection between "care" (*Sorge*) and "curiosity" (*Neugier*) more transparent in the English translation than in the German in which these concepts were first publicly brought together as categories of an ontology. Both "care" and "curiosity" trace back to the Latin *cura*, a word that can be taken to mean much the same as the English "care." The basic idea of the Latin word has to do with a devotion of attention, and this is what Heidegger is trying to bring out when he speaks of care as the Being of Dasein. He points out that the kind of attention which occurs as care can manifest itself in two definite modalities, "anxious exertion" or "carefulness and devotedness."[18] This devotion of attention is not a simple looking-at something or other for Heidegger; it is how Dasein is itself, understands itself, and exists in the world. Curiosity is just one of the phenomena of care, which Heidegger imagines as having a tripartite structure that recapitulates the conventional ontic sense of time as past, present, and future, which Heidegger reconstructs in the course of his discussion. Curiosity belongs to the construct of falling, along with the phenomena of what are called in *Being and Time* "idle talk" and "ambiguity."[19]

To bring the concept of "falling" into a useful focus, it is necessary to situate it in some detail with respect to the structure of care as it is outlined in *Being and Time*. Heidegger states the importance of the concept of care to his existential analytic when he writes, "Dasein's Being reveals itself as *care*."[20] What he means by this formulation is not given overtly in the general semantics of the term "care." While a large part of *Being and Time* is devoted to providing an articulation of care, not every point bears on the question of how "care" and "falling" are related. Heidegger provides a schematic description at the beginning of Division Two of the book as he prepares to discuss the structure of death:

> The ontological signification of the expression "care" has been expressed in the 'definition': "ahead-of-itself-Being-already-in (the world) as Being-alongside entities which we encounter (within-the-world)". In this are expressed the fundamental characteristics of Dasein's Being: existence, in the "ahead-of-itself"; facticity, in the "Being-already-in"; falling, in the "Being-alongside".[21]

In this construction, "falling" is seen as one element in a tripartite division of care. Many consequences follow from this division, such as the temporalizing of existence into the ontical future, facticity into the ontical past, and falling into the ontical Present.[22]

The features that define the basic structure of falling, such that it can be the ontological basis of the Present, and such that the Present can be the existential meaning of falling,[23] are of special interest for the hypothesis of a deep connection between religion and ideology. In the first section of *Being and Time*, when Heidegger describes falling,

temporality does not figure prominently; already, however, the importance of presence in the Present is evident.

> To Dasein's state of being belongs *falling*. Proximally and
> for the most part Dasein is lost in its 'world'. Its under-
> standing, as a projection upon possibilities of Being, has
> diverted itself thither. Its absorption in the "they" signifies
> that it is dominated by the way things are publicly inter-
> preted. That which has been uncovered and disclosed stands
> in a mode in which it has been disguised and closed off by
> idle talk, curiosity, and ambiguity. Being towards entities
> has not been extinguished, but it has been uprooted. Enti-
> ties have not been completely hidden; they are precisely the
> sort of thing that has been uncovered, but at the same time
> they have been disguised. They show themselves, but in the
> mode of semblance. Likewise what has formerly been
> uncovered sinks back again, hidden and disguised. *Because
> Dasein is essentially falling, its state of Being is such that it
> is in 'untruth'*. [24]

Fallen Dasein's lostness in its world is the first major point of the
fundamental ontology that finds application in our proposed regional
ontology of ideology. This lostness is identified by Heidegger as an
acceptance by Dasein of the (categorically) consensus views of the
"they." He does not describe the "they" as an intentionally malicious
force, but rather as a quasi-conscious conglomerate of opinions, fads,
truisms, entertainments, and so on. The "they" is not a number of
individuals; the "they" is perhaps best imagined as something like the
difference between a finite number of individuals and the being of the
group. That there already exists such a recognized sub-discipline as
group psychology shall be testimony enough that the group is somehow
more than simply a collection of individuals. The "they" is a property of
Dasein as Mitsein.

Heidegger observes that fallen Dasein is dominated by the way
things are publicly interpreted by the "they." This domination generally
takes the outward (ontical) form of unthought agreements with the flow
of meaning that is continually generated among the "they" as gossip,
idle talk, news, analysis, etc.[25] All of this tranquilizes Dasein, claims
Heidegger, and causes it to divert its attention from its own authentic
possibilities toward real or fictional possibilities of others which Dasein
falsely imagines to be its own. In *Being and Time*, death is the authentic
possibility that Dasein most determinedly avoids, but it is not just death
as one's ownmost possibility that provokes falling into the "they"; it is
more precisely the sheer uncanniness (*Unheimlichkeit*) of the specter of

one's own thrown being and the nothingness that lies behind and beyond existence.

> When Dasein "understands" uncanniness in the everyday manner, it does so by turning away from it in falling; in this turning away, the "not-at-home" gets 'dimmed down'.[26]

In the ontology of *Being and Time*, Dasein is not simply carried away by the autonomous energy of the group, it is driven toward it from within. As Mitsein, Dasein naturally gravitates toward others, especially others with the Being of Dasein; others work along to constitute the exclusively linguistic world Dasein inhabits. As Heidegger imagines it however, Dasein both uses others to obscure itself and is used by others to reinforce the consensus of the "they." Though Dasein flees itself and, embracing inauthenticity, takes refuge in business and public activity, including good works, this is not a simple fugitive "hiding out." We remember that Dasein must traffic in the phenomena of falling, at best resolutely and at worst falling into the "they," if any work in the world is to be accomplished. Heidegger explains, "The Self must forget itself if, lost in the world of equipment, it is to be able 'actually' to go to work and manipulate something."[27] Dasein not only needs to get away from its mental self and the threatening uncanniness that lies at the edges of existence, it also needs that quality of consciousness which alows it to sustain itself physically, and these two conditions call Dasein to fall. On the one hand, Dasein is unable to bear a continual revelation of its own unconcealed truth and on the other, Heidegger is convinced, it cannot do its daily work without falling into the world of work. Falling is thus overdetermined in *Being and Time*. Once fallen, the temptation arises to totalize one's conception of one's situation and in that move to incorporate unintentionally the concealed possibility of choosing oneself back into authenticity.

The choosing of oneself into authenticity is not a matter of subjective will for Heidegger and it appears further that the achievement of something like a state of sustained authenticity is likewise independent of will, even prior to will. The decision for authenticity is a function of anxiety, as Heidegger lays it out.

> On the other hand, as Dasein falls, anxiety brings it back from its absorption in the 'world'. Everyday familiarity collapses. Dasein has been individualized, but individual-ized *as* Being-in-the-world. Being-in enters into the existen-tial 'mode' of the "*not-at-home*". Nothing else is meant by our talk about 'uncanniness'.[28]

This is the existential movement of Dasein that makes the difference between inauthenticity and authenticity, between ideology and religion. Schleiermacher seems to have seen this dynamic in a similar way:

> The human soul, as shown both by its passing actions and its inward characteristics, has its existence chiefly in two opposing impulses. Following the one impulse, it strives to establish itself as an individual. For increase, no less than sustenance, it draws what surrounds it to itself, weaving it into its life, and absorbing it into its own being. The other impulse, again, is the dread fear to stand alone over against the Whole, the longing to surrender oneself and be absorbed in a greater, to be taken hold of and determined.[29]

In assigning this role to anxiety, we are not suggesting the timeworn hypothesis that the origin of religion is fear. As a claim about ontic reality, the notion is not implausible, but it never reaches to ontology of religion; while there may well be some empirical justification for making such an assertion as part of the psychology of religion, that line of reasoning misses the point by not penetrating deeply enough to explain why religion, and not something else, should eventuate from such fear. Religion, an ontical phenomenon, could not originate without some ontological basis. That basis is the fact of anxiety in the existential analytic that *Being and Time* proposes. Heidegger insists that anxiety and fear, though related, are two very different states of mind. The important distinction to be made between them is that fear has a definite object and anxiety does not. Fear is described as directed toward possibilities within existence and anxiety is focused beyond existence, on nothing. Fear rivets one in the condition of fallenness, while anxiety yanks one out.

These abstractions may be given some weight by looking briefly at an illustrative text. We read in Ecclesiastes a testimony of anxiety:

> Emptiness, emptiness, says the Speaker, all is empty. What does a man gain from all his labour and his toil here under the sun? [30]

What we find in this book is not the tension of fear, but something like resignation. Koheleth has been given the reputation of speaking a sour discouragement, but this is not deserved. We find him/her not only speaking of the vanity of existence, but also counseling an enjoyment of life. This balance is crucial to the understanding of the difference between anxiety and fear. No such balance is granted to one who fears, for the situation is "weighted" at the location of the object of fear. Anxiety, on the other hand, is evenly spread around. There is nothing to do about it, no way beyond it. Given this, Koheleth's counsel is supremely sensible. We find it not only in the Bible, but also echoing in the later Heidegger's advocacy of waiting, for example, and in the thought of Heidegger's contemporary, Ernst Bloch, who writes, "We do paint images of what lies ahead, and insinuate ourselves into what may come after us. But no upward glance can fail to brush against *death* which makes all things pale."[31]

The advice of Koheleth to make the most of life, coupled with Heidegger's claim that anxiety individualizes, could be interpreted to lead to something other than an attitude of waiting, namely, a modest individualism. We want to register a strong suspicion that individualized Dasein is not necessarily individualistic Dasein for two reasons. The first reason is that while the individualist is a law unto himself, Koheleth's human being is always under judgement of God. The enjoyment of life occurs in an existence already structured by law. The second reason is that individualism appears in the ontology of *Being and Time* to be simply a deficient mode of Mitsein, a denial of the true Being of the "they" and the truth of one's own untruth as they-self. If the individualization that results from the experience of anxiety does not ground individualism, then the question remains as to what ontic phenomena it does have to do with.

Heidegger suggests an answer which is central to placing the phenomena of religion and ideology when he writes:

> But in anxiety there lies the possibility of a disclosure which is quite distinctive; for anxiety individualizes. This individualization brings Dasein back from its falling, and makes manifest to it that authenticity and inauthenticity are possibilities of its Being. [32]

Anxiety has to do with the phenomena of authenticity through the bringing back of Dasein from falling. Of special note is Heidegger's assertion that in this being brought back, both authenticity and inauthenticity become known as possibilities of Dasein. This is in significant contrast to the "flat" structure of fallen Dasein's self-knowledge, a spurious knowledge that is given by the "they" and takes the form of knowing oneself in the mode of being put to use for some purpose, as worker, buyer, patron, teacher, official, etc. Authentic Dasein, which has in every case already chosen itself, sees in a larger context than fallen Dasein, and this is the sufficient ontological basis for religion's claim of superior vision, insofar as religious Dasein maintains itself in resoluteness. It has nothing to do with empirical, factual knowledge at all. Though the vision of religious Dasein can claim priority, Heidegger says that self and world as disclosed in falling constitute the factical norm for everyday consciousness and activity.

> It has been shown that proximally and for the most part Dasein is *not* itself but is lost in the they-self, which is an existentiell modification of the authentic self.[33]

No empirical observation suggests otherwise. Heidegger's assertion rings true. If it is indeed the case that being lost in the "they" is the usual state of Dasein, then the implications for the understanding of religion and ideology are enormous, as ideology is recognized as the voice of the they-self. As the voice of the they-self, ideology can never be authentically true, and any Dasein which attends to ideology as truth falls into untruth. Because such falling is an existentiale for Dasein, there is no way to avoid it; writes Heidegger, " . . . Dasein is equiprimordially both in the truth and in untruth."[34] If falling into untruth cannot be avoided, at least it behooves one to make every attempt to recognize the signs and the implications of the different ways of being in the world so as not to persist in mistaking the voice and the agenda of the "they" for one's authentic own and, what is vitally important for Dasein as Mitsein, so as not to fall long and hard into mistaking ideology for religion. At this point in our inquiry, however, there is still not sufficient information to begin discriminating between religion and ideology in the domain of ontic phenomena.

It was claimed above that authenticity is a state of having chosen. This conceptualization places priority with inauthenticity as the condition of existential choice. Heidegger seems to be seeing the dynamic this way when he states, "Authentic Being-one's-Self takes the definite form of an existentiell modification of the 'they' . . . ."[35] As long as one can take seriously the thesis that there is a correspondence between authenticity and religion on the one hand and inauthenticity and ideology on the other, the movement from ideology to religion will be of greatest interest because it alone requires choice, while falling into inauthenticity/ ideology apparently does not. The question has been posed in various forms throughout history of why anybody should choose authenticity/ religion when the tranquility of being-fallen is so easy to attain; we have seen that, for Heidegger, the choice is not made by a willed selection, but occurs as a consequence of anxiety. That part of the psychology of religion which studies rituals has an ontological reason to examine their role in the evocation and dispersion of anxious moods.

In Heidegger's ontology, we do find decisions, including those following upon the experience of anxiety, but nothing like a sense of conventional personal responsibility, at least responsibility as it is a function of will. Kantian morality is far out of sight. Individual beings emerge as such, but they do not appear either as free and autonomous agents with respect to their basic state of being or as dependents on a higher authority; it is as a being with a specific potentiality for being that Heidegger is concerned to describe Dasein. Thus, when he speaks of freedom, which he does on occasion, he is not using the term politically, but in a way that belongs outside the dynamics of ontical phenomena generally.[36] The absence of voluntaristically-defined autonomy of the individual in Heidegger's thinking is sufficient grounds for renouncing the transcendental attachment of virtue or blame to religious or ideological Dasein. Such terms plainly belong to different levels of discourse. In the discourse of Christian theology, this issue of personal autonomy arises as a combined moral and existential dilemma with the heavily ramified question of what choice Judas had.

In the realm of psychology, this feature of Heidegger's ontology apparently harmonizes in some ways with the language of behaviorism, even though the general theory of behaviorism itself, which at points bears a striking resemblance to Nietzsche's concept of will-to-power, is not equipped to recognize any ontology as binding upon it or normative for construing its language. Though blind to the role of ontology in shaping its possibilities of factical realization, behaviorism remains a versatile psychological thesis. With some imaginative interpretation of its categories, behaviorism is a rich field for future inquiry.

Behaviorism might find the language of this ontology problematical because it appears to assert so much that cannot be verified by usual techniques of observation or introspection. It will be encouraged to pursue Heidegger's ontology, though, because it will value the malleability of Dasein. Upon closer examination, moreover, the apparently metaphysical constructs of *Being and Time* show themselves to be attempts at systematic, introspective description, which behaviorism accepts in principle. The reason why we concern ourselves with the reception Heidegger's ontology might receive from behaviorism is that as a practical matter, this study has a great deal riding on the truth of Heidegger's description of Dasein.

The truth of Heidegger's ontology is decided by its capacity to evoke a sense of Being that renders its own discourse intelligible and provokes further discourse that recalls the Being of beings. If it succeeds in this, then even a "non-metaphysical" theory like behaviorism is bound to acknowledge it as a matter of course. It is a practical matter. Practical matters are in the domain of care in this ontology and falling is the component of care that governs the Present. Fallen Dasein will dispose of this study one way or another, so it is in terms accessible to fallen Dasein that the case must establish itself if it is to have any material effect in the ontic domain. It is in the interests of behaviorists as human beings to find themselves within a viable ontology, but they never will be able to accept a Heideggerian ontology, at least, insofar as they sustain the Being of goal-directed researchers, that is, insofar as constituted in the mode of entities which understand themselves explicitly or implicitly as being determined by the technological agenda.

Behaviorism, as a radicalization of the consensus, sees the individual as the result of biological and social causal chains. *Being and Time* finds Dasein as thrown, already there, essentially mentalistic-linguistic, and does not speculate about material causality; thus there is no conflict between Heidegger's existential analytic and the theory of behaviorism at that level. Where behaviorism begins to represent the extreme challenge to Heidegger's ontology is in the question of Dasein's "there." The challenge becomes irrelevant if the "there" is properly placed as an element in the phenomenology of consciousness, as contrasted with the psychology of human beings. On the basis of a common recognition of the concept of Dasein's "there," Heidegger's introspective description becomes a theoretical issue for behaviorism and a case-in-point for the existential analytic with behaviorism's principled collapsing of authentic and inauthentic Dasein into one (as fallen Dasein always does). The question at this point is whether behaviorists have to behave this way.

In our reading of the existential analytic of *Being and Time*, this is exactly how the ideal behaviorist, fallingly occupied with entities in the world and imperialistically totalizing behaviorism's outlook, must understand theory, self, and subject. Behaviorism immediately closes itself off from the existential reality of the Self because it takes not beings, but behavior, as its starting point. In so doing, behaviorism performs a compound reduction of the being of an entity to presence, presence to (behavioral-) theoretical signification, and theoretical signification to instrumental-ethical signification. The individual is thus construed essentially as complex of appropriately-valued distinctive features, like a phoneme. Heidegger claimed that the unity of the Self would remain invisible unless an existential analytic were carried out and the Being of care disclosed:

> Selfhood is to be discerned existentially only in one's authentic potentiality-for-Being-one's-Self — that is to say, in the authenticity of Dasein's Being *as care*. [37]

Even though care is analyzed to be the basis of many of Dasein's least attractive attributes and activities, it is obvious that Heidegger is not suggesting repressing or otherwise altering the truth of Dasein's Being as care. He does claim that care cannot be recognized from within, but must come to be known from without, that is, from the vantage point of an authentic existence which is capable of encompassing it. What authentic Dasein can see is the truth of its Being, of which Heidegger asserts repeatedly, "Dasein's Being is care. It comprises in itself facticity (thrownness), existence (projection), and falling."[38] Only from the kind of standpoint granted by the fact of having chosen can the unity intuited as self be realized. From any other standpoint, says Heidegger, the vocabulary of self is invalid.[39] The standpoint of authenticity entails Dasein's recognition of its own self as Being-in-existence. From this standpoint, Dasein does not posit a self and then elaborate its structure as care; it discovers the phenomena of care and temporality and comes to see the unity of itself as a factical self. Heidegger writes:

> Care does not need to be founded in a Self. But existentiality, as constitutive for care, provides the ontological constitution of Dasein's Self-constancy, to which there belongs, in accordance with the full structural content of care, its Being-fallen facti- cally into non-Self-constancy. [40]

It is Dasein's Being-fallen into non-Self-constancy that behaviorism fixes upon when it denies the self. It is fallen Dasein, whose behavior is regularly modified by stimuli in the arena of publicness, that behavior- ism sees as man, unobscured by metaphysics and undergoing perpetual behavior modification at the hands of society and nature. As a technique of dealing with fallen Dasein, behaviorism shows itself to have grasped its subject, but not its limitations.

In grasping fallen Dasein as its subject, behaviorism's beginning is in a sense not so far away from Heidegger's. Heidegger explains why it is legitimate for him to have chosen to structure his own ostensibly authen- tic account of a non-metaphysical conception of human beings as he did, that is, with reference to fallen Dasein:

> So in orienting our analysis by the phenomenon of falling, we are not in principle condemned to be without any pros- pect of learning something ontologically about the Dasein disclosed in that phenomenon. On the contrary, here, least of all, has our Interpretation been surrendered to an artificial way in which Dasein grasps itself; it merely carries out the explication of what Dasein itself ontically discloses.[41]

If this is the case, then behaviorism and any similarly constituted science must see the beginning of Heidegger's project, since there is in some sense a shared point of departure. Even though they see the beginning, they do not follow along as far as the project goes. Heidegger has his own explanation of why the logic of his exposition must trail off into unacceptability for such sciences. As the work of fallen Dasein, that is, the they-self, the sciences are inclined to maintain existential understanding at the given level in the name of objective research.

> Every understanding has its mood. Every state-of-mind is one in which one understands. The understanding which one has in such a state-of-mind has the character of falling. The understanding which has its mood attuned in falling, Articulates itself with relation to its   intelligibility in discourse.[42]

In short, when Dasein is doing science and expanding the frontiers of knowledge, it is in no mood to be interrupted, especially by the thought of the permanent cessation of its activity. The Being of science is of special significance for the understanding of what falling means. Heidegger writes, "As falling, everyday Being-towards-death is a constant *fleeing in the face of death.*"[43] In light of this insight, the historical conflict of science and religion is revealed as ontologically determined insofar as science belongs to falling and religion belongs to authenticity. The only possible resolution of the conflict hinges upon authentic resoluteness of those who engage in science and authentic concern of those who articulate the ways of religion. Authentic resoluteness is always a possibility for Dasein, but it is a consequence of anxiety. Dasein not open to anxiety is not capable of choosing itself into resoluteness either. The opposition of religion and ideology as well as the included opposition of religion and science, which occurs when science supports an ideology so that its work may continue in tranquility, would have to remain as an unbridgeable split unless anxiety had some way to echo beyond the instant of its occurrence. Resoluteness is the way anxiety continues in effect, even when not in fact. As Heidegger describes it,

> "Resoluteness" signifies letting oneself be summoned out of one's lostness in the "they". The irresoluteness of the "they" remains dominant notwithstanding, but it cannot impugn resolute existence.[44]

For Heidegger, resoluteness is authentic disclosedness and authentic Being-in-the-world. As such, it has a special place in his analysis as the state-of-being which allows Dasein its full range of self-understanding. This is why resoluteness is designated the "most primordial" truth of Dasein.[45] It is primordial in the sense that any step away from this state of Being is a diminution of the factical existence (though not the Being) of Dasein. Heidegger understands resoluteness as the single possibility of care's authenticity and proposes that the true object of authentic care is resoluteness itself. In this way, he delineates how authentic Dasein can function in the world without losing itself totally to the "they" or to the idle talk, curiosity, and ambiguity which characterize fallen Dasein.

The concept of falling, then, is a characteristic that shows up in Heidegger's ontological narrative as belonging constitutively to the Being of Dasein. Grammatically, "falling" is verbal, so it is justifibly interpreted in terms of movement, as something that Dasein can be expected to "do" constantly, which can be said for the components of care in general. As an entity with the Being of care, Dasein "does" everything that is done in the world, cares for the world, cares for itself in the world, cares about itself in the world, and comes to presence as such in states of authenticity and inauthenticity alike. Thus, Heidegger can say, "Being-in-the-world is always fallen."[46] Falling is being construed as the condition of the presence of entities to Dasein and also as the pre-condition of Dasein's grasp of the Being of beings.

Dasein's Being-in-the-world, through which it is placed in relation to other beings that come to presence, is not the same thing as bare physical subsistence in the natural environment of Earth. It is how entities with the Being of Dasein (i.e., a specific kind of consciousness) exist. It is this existence that Heidegger is trying to describe. He explains further:

> As long as Dasein factically exists, both the 'ends' and their 'between' *are*, and they *are* in the only way which is possible on the basis of Dasein's Being as *care*. Thrownness and that Being towards death in which one either flees it or anticipates it, form a unity; and in this unity birth and death are 'connected' in a manner characteristic of Dasein. As care, Dasein *is* the 'between'.[47]

Heidegger locates thrownness in Dasein's past as one of the "ends" of Dasein, but he does not mean to identify it with physical birth. As he ontologically constitutes Dasein, facticity is given. Dasein not only has no consciousness of a "before the beginning," it has no Being prior to its advent in facticity; it finds itself already there, thrown.

The same is not true about the other end of Dasein, death. Just as facticity is not the same as physical birth in the ontology Heidegger constructs, so death is not the same as demise. "Demise" denotes a physical phenomenon, while the term "death" is reserved for the event in which an entity with the Being of Dasein ceases to have that Being. Having the Being of Dasein is not necessarily congruent with being a human who walks the Earth, which is why Heidegger made the distinction. Heidegger conceived his ontology to be valid under any physical conditions, though he did not stress this point. While Dasein, in a sense, finds itself already dead in the future, death itself is always an uncertain future possibility. Fallen Dasein maintains this ambiguity diligently, disavowing the possibility of knowing anything definite about many things through the device of pretending that everything worth knowing is already somehow known in principle.

While Dasein does not generally concern itself with its Being-in-the-world before its birth, it does frequently concern itself with its Being-in-the-world after death, by which is meant after its demise. Dasein's concern for its Being-in-the-world after its own demise is a manifestation of its Being as care, especially of falling in its aspect of curiosity, the element of futurity (as temporalized projection) notwithstanding. Dasein's projecting itself upon possibilities of the world as it will be after its demise may be nothing more than a falling continuation of Dasein's surrender to the they or it may be an inauthentic projection of authentic concern or it may be something else. The issue has various factical possibilities and does not call for an ontological judgement in advance. It does, however, provide a case-in-point of the concept of concern in *Being and Time*. As Heidegger describes it, concern splits up Dasein's Being-in-the-world into various activities such as "having to do with something, producing something, attending to something and looking after it, making use of something, giving something up and letting it go, undertaking, evincing, interrogating, considering, discussing, determining."[48] He adds, characteristically, a brief mention of deficient modes of concern, including, for example, "leaving undone, neglecting, renouncing, taking a rest."[49]

The purpose of these observations is to show that in the light of Dasein's always-present facticity, which follows upon thrownness and precedes death as Dasein's ownmost possibility, Dasein emerges as a being that exists between a unilaterally given past, before which nothing of oneself is known, and an undeniably possible future extremity, after which nothing of oneself is known. Is it any wonder, then, that Heidegger's Dasein typically flees into the factical Present and tends to lay near-exclusive priority on falling existence, proximally grounded in that element of care which focuses Dasein on apparently meaningful, factical possibilities? From the standpoint of existence, there is nothing else to "do." Heidegger writes:

> The Being of Dasein is care. This entity exists fallingly as
> something that has been thrown. Abandoned to the 'world'
> which is discovered with its factical "there", and con-

> cernfully submitted to it, Dasein awaits its potentiality-for-
> Being-in-the-world; it awaits it in such a manner that it
> 'reckons' *on* and 'reckons' *with* whatever has an *involvement*
> for the sake of this potentiality-for-Being — an involve-
> ment which, in the end, is a distinctive one.[50]

Dasein's concern is with making use of things for its own authentic or inauthentic purposes. The word translated as "concern" by Macquarrie and Robinson is *besorgen*, a verb that is used with a wide range of meanings, including attending to, taking care of, and procuring. It is a verb which demands concrete objects. Resolute and irresolute Dasein both take note of things and concern themselves with them; such concern is always the province of fallen Dasein engaged in a making-present. Heidegger's exploration of Dasein's concern with things shows up as a theme in his later writings when he discusses technology. Though the later essays are couched in different language and do not explicitly build upon the existential analytic of *Being and Time*, reading them in light of the earlier work, which Heidegger discussed in the *Letter on Humanism*, suggests that care may be understood as the ontological basis of technology. Among other things, technology can be viewed as an attempt by Dasein to realize its own potentiality-for-Being-in-the-world.

Dasein constantly faces the problem of realizing its own potentiality-for-Being-in-the-world. It always pursues its own projects, but its way of going about its work in the world varies. The constant in Dasein's existence is care and care is always realized in the Present as falling. On occasion, Dasein does maintain itself in resoluteness, but more often it loses itself in the "they," claims Heidegger.

> It thus entangles itself in itself, so that the distracted not-
> tarrying becomes *never-dwelling-anywhere*. This latter
> mode of the Present is the counter-phenomenon at the
> opposite extreme from the *moment of vision*. In never dwell-
> ing anywhere, Being-there is everywhere and nowhere.[51]

The problematics of falling, presence, and dwelling are carried on by Heidegger as he takes up the problem of technology.

Notes

[1] SZ, p. 43; BT, p. 68.
[2] SZ, p. 167; BT, p. 211.
[3] SZ, pp. 168-169; BT, p. 212.
[4] SZ, p. 127; BT, p. 165.
[5] Ibid.

[6] SZ, p. 128; BT, p. 165.

[7] SZ, p. 128; BT, p. 166.

[8] Ibid.

[9] SZ, p. 252; BT, p. 296.

[10] SZ, p. 129; BT, p. 167.

[11] John Rawls, *A Theory of Justice*. Cambridge, MA: Harvard University Press, 1971.

[12] This internal dialectic of existence is not exclusively a fabrication of Heidegger's ontology. It finds an ontic correlate, for example, in psychoanalysis. Jacques Lacan was one who devoted attention to this problematic. Stuart Schneiderman, in his recent book *Jacques Lacan: The Death of an Intellectual Hero* (Cambridge, MA: Harvard University Press, 1983) recounts Lacan's interest in the concept of existence as "ex-sistence," which recalls Heidegger's "ek-sistence," found in "Vom Wesen der Wahrheit" (*Wegmarken*. Frankfurt/M.: Klostermann, 1978, p. 186 *et passim.*) as well as *Discourse on Thinking* (orig. *Gelassenheit*, trans. J. M. Anderson and E.H. Freund. New York: Harper & Row, 1966) and the "Brief über den Humanismus" (*Wegmarken*, pp. 311-360). Lacan contrasts ex-sistence with "living" (the biological function) and "death" and, like Heidegger, ties existence more closely to death than to life. Schneiderman's report of how this worked out in the analytic situation, which was encountered after the bulk of this project was completed, is noteworthy for both the thought and the terminology he employs. In words that anticipate our title (i.e. the title of the dissertation, *At Cross-Purposes: Religion and Ideology in Terms of Heidegger's Concept of Falling*), Schneiderman writes, "Lacan gave the impression that he was hearing something other than what you were saying. He never put himself on the same wavelength as his analysand, but remained always at cross purposes. He never tried to find areas of agreement and accord, but scrupulously maintained a fruitful, well-tuned discord." (p. 119)

[13] SZ, p. 251; BT, p. 295.

[14] SZ, p. 170; BT, p. 214.

[15] Quoted in SZ, p. 171; BT, p. 216. Augustine is quoting 1 John 2:16. "For all that is in the world, the lust of the flesh and the lust of the eyes and the pride of life, is not of the Father but is of the world." (RSV) Also worthy of note for our purposes is the opposition of "pride of life" and God. This is one of the few places in Heidegger's writings where his Christian background overtly informs, or at least corresponds with, the ontology he works out. Why that is so lies outside the scope of this paper. Still, the passage in context is relevant. From *The New English Bible*: "Do not set your hearts on the godless world or anything in it.

Anyone who loves the world is a stranger to the Father's love. Everything the world affords, all that panders to the appetites or entices the eyes, all the glamour of its life, springs not from the Father but from the godless world." (1 John 2:15-16, *The New English Bible*. New York: Cambridge University Press, 1961.) We note especially the recurrence of the phrase "godless world," which becomes significant in connection with the place of gods in religions. (See remarks on divinities below.)

[16] Despite Heidegger's disclaimers, there exist a number of interpretations of *Being and Time* as a theological work, most egregiously involving substitution of "God" for "Being." Whether or not the book is theological, there may be some justification for reading it as a document of a religious quest. Throughout *Being and Time*, as well as in later works, Heidegger appropriates religious terminology and, as in his use of Augustine, turns religious problems to the purposes of his ontology. That he does not overtly discuss religion is evidence of nothing, for as he himself has written, " . . . if anyone is genuinely 'on the scent' of anything, he does not speak about it . . . ." (SZ, p. 173; BT, p. 218.)

[17] SZ, p. 173; BT, p. 217.

[18] SZ, p. 243; BT, p. 199.

[19] SZ, p. 175; BT, p. 219 *et passim*.

[20] SZ, p. 182; BT, p. 227.

[21] SZ, p. 249-250; BT, p. 293.

[22] The capitalized word "Present" signifies the temporal category according to a convention adopted by Macquarrie and Robinson to distinguish *Gegenwart* from *vorliegend*.

[23] Heidegger writes, "Just as understanding is made possible primarily by the future, and moods are made possible by having been, the third constitutive item in the structure of care — namely, *falling* — has its existential meaning in the Present." SZ, p. 346; BT, p. 397.

[24] SZ, p. 222; BT, p. 264.

[25] We recall in this connection Nietzsche's comment in *The Will to Power*, 132: "We feel contemptuous of every kind of culture that is compatible with reading, not to mention writing for, newspapers."

[26] SZ, p. 189; BT, p. 234.

[27] SZ, p. 354; BT, p. 405.

[28] SZ, p. 189; BT, p. 233. The concept of the not-at-home, which is etymologically transparent in German, should not be too quickly reduced to a simple affect. Heidegger's own later thoughts of "home" are partially indicative of the wider significance of the root (heim-) of the term. The fact that the word ("uncanniness") occurs in ontological discourse is also important. What Heidegger is especially warning against here is thinking *Unheimlichkeit* as the kind of weirdness that

substitutes an unlikely or monstrous presence for an expected presence, a connotation that is more prominent in German than in English.

[29] Schleiermacher, *On Religion: Speeches to its Cultured Despisers*, p. 4.

[30] Ecclesiastes 1:2-3, *The New English Bible*.

[31] Ernst Bloch, *Man on His Own*, tr. E.B. Ashton. New York: Herder and Herder, 1971, p. 43.

[32] SZ, p. 190-191; BT, p. 235.

[33] SZ, p. 317; BT, p. 365.

[34] SZ, p. 223; BT, p. 265.

[35] SZ, p. 268; BT, p. 312.

[36] Heidegger's sense of freedom has to do with Dasein's being what it is. "In each case Dasein has already compared itself, in its Being, with a possibility of itself. Being-free *for* one's ownmost potentiality-for-Being, and therewith for the possibility of authenticity and inauthenticity, is shown, with a primordial, elemental concreteness, in anxiety." (SZ, p. 191; BT, p. 236.)

[37] SZ, p. 322; BT, p. 369.

[38] SZ, p. 284; BT, p. 329.

[39] Heidegger illustrates in his own vocabulary: "The they-self keeps on saying "I" most loudly and most frequently because at bottom it *is not authentically* itself, and evades its authentic potentiality-for-being." (SZ, p. 322; BT, p. 369.)

[40] SZ, p. 323; BT, p. 370. Behaviorism's location of the Being of its subject in what it does bears a resemblance to Heidegger's formulation that " . . . the substance of man is existence." (SZ, p. 314; BT, p. 362.) He had already made it clear existentiality was not an obscure, metaphysical concept of a sort unavailable for scientific interrogation when he wrote, " . . . existing is always factical. Existentiality is essentially determined by facticity." (SZ, p. 192; BT, p. 236.)

[41] SZ, p. 185; BT, p. 229-230.

[42] SZ, p. 335; BT, p. 385.

[43] SZ, p. 254; BT, p. 298.

[44] SZ, p. 299; BT, p. 345.

[45] SZ, p. 297; BT, p. 343.

[46] SZ, p. 181; BT, p. 225.

[47] SZ, p. 374; BT, p. 426-427.

[48] SZ, p. 56; BT, p. 83.

[49] SZ, p. 57; BT, p. 83.

[50] SZ, p. 412; BT, p. 465.

[51] SZ, p. 347; BT, p. 398.

Any story purporting to kill other stories and the story-telling
impulse will lead, sooner or later, to its own demise.
— *James B. Wiggins*

. . . to be restored, our sickness must grow worse.
— *T. S. Eliot*

Nothing can be of ultimate concern for us which does not have
the power of threatening and saving our being.
— *Paul Tillich*

V. Technology

In more ways than we can name, technology continues to represent the greatest cultural variable in determining the future development of human existence. It is not a simple, one-dimensional variable that will let itself be calculated and mastered, because technology is more than the visible progress of mechanization and electronification that surrounds us and can be documented, charted, and projected; it is a mental phenomenon as well, perhaps even primarily. The mentality of technology goes back beyond the plans and calculations that proximally precede the setting up of physical technological installations, and reaches to the preconditions of technological thinking. As a mental phenomenon, technology can easily remain very much hidden. For all that is public and dependable in the standardized apparatus and reproducible routines of the technological world, there remains a vast reservoir of pre-technological nostalgia, proto-technological reductions, bizarre conceptions and misconceptions of what is possible and practicable, and so on.

Because of the vast scale of its influence and because of its style, that is, the way it presents its demands and determinations, the technological phenomenon seems to call for awestruck acceptance, but that response has not been universal. More important for the future development of technology and those who are destined to live through it has been the work of critical commentators, which has revealed facets of the phenomenon far removed from the products of laboratories and factories. Through criticism, technological civilization has come into an inheritance of a catalogue of complications of technology that have been delineated by that small minority who have not taken it for granted. It would be an unwarranted simplification to equate uncritical participation in the world of technology with a positive attitude toward it and critical reflection with a negative attitude, but it has none the less been usual for the bulk of critical energy in the twentieth century to be devoted to the problems of technology rather than the benefits it bestows.

One of the most widely-read thinkers toiling in these fields has been Herbert Marcuse. Analyzing the dynamics of modern society has brought him into a region of thinking where technology appears to have the first and last word. In the world of technology, there prevails a kind of being that Marcuse named in the title of his *One-Dimensional Man*. In the introduction to that book, he describes tendencies of the modern technological situation with reference to the dialectics of material change, but his remarks connect with themes of interest outside the ontology of dialectical materialism also.

> In this society, the productive apparatus tends to become totalitarian to the extent to which it determines not only the socially needed occupations, skills, and attitudes, but also individual needs and aspirations. It thus obliterates the opposition between private and public existence, between individual and social needs. Technology serves to institute new, more effective, and more pleasant forms of social control and social cohesion. . . .
>
> In the face of the totalitarian features of this society, the traditional notion of the "neutrality" of technology can no longer be maintained. Technology as such cannot be isolated from the use to which it is put; the technological society is a system of domination which operates already in the concept and construction of techniques.[1]

Marcuse is not alone in refusing to accept the fantasy of the neutrality of technology. Likewise, in his assertion that the social context of technological civilization is a totalitarian structure of domination, Marcuse articulates a not uncommon perception. Because of his social focus, however, Marcuse does not take his analysis of technology much further than this. If we were to remain at this level, then technology would appear as an instrument of ideology, even as religion appeared to Marx as such an instrument. To see what technology means for the religion-ideology-falling problematic necessitates going beyond an instrumentalist view of technology, however sophisticated.

In Heidegger's thinking of the question of technology, further insight is afforded into his understanding of both the ontology of falling and the ontical meaning of falling, even though the term "falling" has ceased to appear on the surface of the texts. The insights to be gained from following the idea of falling through the later material which touches on themes related to technology have direct relevance to the problematic of religion and ideology. While Heidegger directed a number of trenchant remarks toward easily accessible social phenomena of technology, his interest in the topic was clearly not only broadly political, but ontological-philosophical throughout. There is little to be gained from calculated speculations about how much of Heidegger's thinking concerning technology was ideologically motivated, but we may observe that a tenor of ontological resoluteness dominates the discourse in the material that deals with questions of technology, most of which originated as public addresses, including "The Age of the World Picture," "The Question Concerning Technology," "Building Dwelling Thinking," and others.

In these essays, Heidegger is still overtly attempting to think Being, but his strategy has changed. Whereas in *Being and Time*, he was trying to find a comparatively direct way to think the question of Being by conducting a phenomenological investigation of Dasein, in his work on technology, as in his later work generally, he follows a more indirect line of thought, preferring to clear the air for the ringing of Being's call; this he seeks to do by opening up the possibility of events of appropriation through rhetorical deconstructions of common understandings of technology. These deconstructions come in a series of phenomenological accounts which become impassioned enough at points to sound almost like the political pamphleteering of an opposition party. He tries to call attention to the problem in as clear a way as he can in order keep open the possibility of the full range of the revelations of Being. Some of his most direct remarks are the substance of the commemorative address for Conradin Kreutzer, delivered in 1955, in which he is found urging his hearers to look beyond the surface phenomena of technology:

> What is the ground that enabled modern technology to discover and set free new energies in nature?

> This is due to a revolution in leading concepts (*aller mass-gebenden Vorstellungen*) which has been going on for the past several centuries, and by which man is placed in a different world (*Wirklichkeit*). This radical revolution in outlook has come about in modern philosophy. From this arises a completely new relation of man to the world (*Welt*)

> and his place in it. The world now appears as an object open
> to the attacks of calculative thought, attacks that nothing is
> believed able any longer to resist. Nature has become a
> giant gasoline station, an energy source for modern technol-
> ogy and industry.[2]

If parts of Heidegger's work on technology have a negative tone, it is of necessity because they belong to a negative work, a dismantling of structures that are not just trivially dangerous, insofar as Heidegger's insights are valid. Other parts of the address sound disarmingly hopeful as the speaker imagines *ontologically* positive effects of technology that can be ours in the future if we can but see deeply enough into the nature of the danger of technology.

The nature of the danger Heidegger wants us to see is not of the same order as the threat to physical well-being of a polluted environment or a nuclear catastrophe, he says. It is not, at bottom, a physical danger. It is a danger to the Being of entities, including especially human beings. There is an often-quoted line in "The Thing" that stands at the head of a passage which presents an important moment in the progress of Heidegger's thought concerning technology, even though the hint is just a beginning on the way to the thinking of the problem.

> Science's knowledge, which is compelling within its own
> sphere of objects, already had annihilated things as things
> long before the atom bomb exploded. The bomb's explo-
> sion is only the grossest of all gross confirmations of the
> long-since-accomplished annihilation of the thing: the con-
> firmation that the thing as a thing remains nil. The thing-
> ness of the thing remains concealed, forgotten. The nature
> of the thing never comes to light, that is, it never gets a
> hearing. This is the meaning of our talk about the annihila-
> tion of the thing. That annihilation is so weird because it
> carries before it a twofold delusion: first, the notion that
> science is superior to all other experience in reaching the real
> in its reality, and second, the illusion that . . . things could
> still be things . . . .[3]

Heidegger draws on common perceptions in "The Question Concerning Technology" when he points out that it is usual to connect
technology with science by means of the idea that technology is basically
applied science. Given the ubiquitous presence of technological
apparatus whose design and construction are dependent upon the discoveries of science and which put into practice other discoveries of
science, this interpretaion is ontically undeniable, but it is incomplete.
Heidegger explains that there is a mutual dependence of science and

technology in the modern world, and that the nature of science has changed; the scientific way of being in the world has shifted from its ancient character of observation of the given in the world to its modern realization as a directed intervention that seeks to measure how the given conforms to pre-conceived parameters. The interventionist experiments of modern science require technologically developed apparatus; thus modern science stands in need of technology at least as much as technology stands in need of it. This little-noticed change in the methodology of science reflects a major change in the sense of how the truth of things comes to be revealed through science; that is a change which has far-reaching consequences, claims Heidegger.

Heidegger claimed in his essay "Kant and the Problem of Metaphysics" that the structure of knowledge in Dasein makes it possible for any being to be encountered as an object. In such an encounter the finitude of Dasein's knowledge is not only absolutized, which is unavoidable because the limits of Dasein's knowledge are synchronically the definition of the factical absolute in every case, but totalized in an implicit declaration of the sufficiency of the synchronic absolute ("the way things are"). As a consequence of this totalization, the part is taken for the whole as whatever aspects of the thing that are revealed to Dasein at the moment are imagined to be the thing in itself. Dasein loses sight of that commonality (Being) which makes encounter possible in the first place, and with its consciousness dimmed by this forgetfulness, it becomes impossible to know the entities one encounters as other than objects.

Fallen Dasein must apprehend entities in its world as objects which are there in order to be put to use; this attitude originates in falling and does not in itself distinguish the technological age. The difference between existence governed by the technological framework and any other mode of existence of Dasein (such as the narrative-mythological mode or the existentialist mode, to cite two examples of interest in religion studies) is that under technological scrutiny, entities cease to be free to reveal themselves as themselves. Instead, they show themselves as comprehensible creatures of particular scientific theories, forcibly annexed into the domain of the "standing reserve"[4] by the apparatus of technology. Modern science makes this move possible. It originates in a different essence from ancient science, a fact most importantly attested by its distinguishing itself from ancient science through the implicit claim of modern science that it can decide in advance how things will reveal themselves.

Underlying such decisions-in-advance, argues Heidegger, is the essentially unthought presupposition (or, perhaps, presumption) that the ordering of reality in this way is not only acceptable, but adequate or even superior to other ways. He claims that the advance of science and technology takes as its purpose to put the earth at the disposal of the technological system, "driving on to the maximum yield at the minimum expense."[5] What worries him is that in this movement all beings may be lined up into the disposability of the standing reserve. Heidegger's reservations about the technological future reflect a shift in his thinking from the careful distinction in *Being and Time* between how Dasein could comport itself toward beings which did not have the character of Dasein and those which did. In *Being and Time*, entities which are not Dasein can be objects of concern (*Besorgen*) and can be ready-to-hand, while Dasein is imagined as an object of solicitude (*Fürsorge*).[6] Once the meditation on technology gets underway, however, he no longer insists on the necessity of the separation, but he still wants to maintain it if it can be done. He begins to think that for the first time, revealed in the way that technology reveals, humanity stands in danger of projecting itself as part of the standing reserve.

There is a definite impulse toward just this sort of inauthentic projection in the phenomenon of falling. The reason why is that fallen Dasein is always already disposed to accept things, including itself, in whatever way they happen to have been publicly revealed by the dominant ideology. Fallen Dasein is always ready to include itself in the kind of totalized world view that keeps itself from itself, that trivializes its authentic possibilities as it absolutizes the fads and fascinations that perpetuate the flow of meaning. What makes the revealing of technology different from the revealing of other kinds of public interpretation is that technology puts at its own disposal specialized apparatus that gives it the appearance of a privileged (neutral!) access to reality. The danger that technology brings with it is related to this appearance of privileged access. The fact of presumed privileged access is the decisive difference between the way technological knowledge comes to presence and the way other revelations do. Specifically, the revelation of beings that occurs in course of technology's interventionist research is not able to remain one revelation among many. In the absence of technology, all revelations of beings stand in principle on an equal footing, namely, the given. Technology does not even engage other revelations in substantive conversation; it rather begins its drive for hegemony with considerations of methodology. At the level of methodology, technology possesses something that no other species of interpretation can offer: the means to show entities behaving exactly as technological scientists say they will, and in public, repeatable, incontrovertible terms. The possibilities for "intersubjective" agreement among observers are greatly enhanced by this methodology, and since fallen Dasein likes nothing so much as an easy agreement, it is naturally attracted to the results of the latest experiments and surveys, especially as they can be popularized and included as the already obvious in the stream of public discourse.

One of the most prominent aspects of public discourse is its narrative quality. Public attention does not rivet itself on a reality that is a collection of facts so much as it does on a moving story. Especially favored are networks of related stories that all tie in with each other and extend comparatively far into the structure of reality. Thus, when the American economy came to presence as a problem, public attention was drawn to a raft of stories of success and failure, to both optimistic and pessimistic projections of future economic performance, to strategies for survival, and so on. Another time domestic abuse stories took center stage with an urgency that would lead one to believe the problem had been invented just recently. In yet another time, the media delivered multiple hospital mistake stories, stories which appeared *en masse*, as if that problem were necessarily the latest in crises that demanded the attention of the American people, and then it just disappeared as if the problem had been solved to everyone's satisfaction. There is a nearly insatiable appetite for sensational stories because they maintain the *existential* tranquility of fallen Dasein, along with a sense of meaningfulness that keeps the attention focused on others, not on what they are, but on what they do and what befalls them (and inauthentic projections of oneself).

A part of the public attention to narratives is devoted to a matrix narrative, the consensus view of reality, which is an entity of varying composition that exists only as an abstraction. Like a natural language, it is only partially instantiated in any given individual. The matrix narrative determines much about the themes and structures of the stories that come to be situated within it. When Vahanian speaks in *God and Utopia* about a shift from mythology to technology, about a move from the universe of myth to the universe of technique, he is not just chronicling a shift in matrix narratives, but a shift in the kind of matrix narrative that qualifies to be such in this time.

The widespread currency of Thomas Kuhn's notion of the process of paradigm shift in scientific revolutions has not provided us with a better-known or more usable language than Heidegger's for discussing this problem, for Kuhn does not try to see through science to technology.[7] There is a major difference between a transition from later Newtonian to quantum mechanics and a transition from a universe of myth to a universe of technique/technology. One scientific paradigm, in the modern age at least, is essentially the same as another, however differently their theories may construct the physical universe, if they have in common a necessity to develop and employ technological apparatus for experiments. It is a matter of attitude toward beings' revelations of themselves. The mythological consciousness (scientific or otherwise) waits and watches while the technological consciousness forces. We need not concern ourselves with which of the two is "better" or what the selection criteria would be; what is important is to note that mythological and technological matrix narratives are not just ontically different; they are *ontologically* different.

All matrix narratives are attempts at totalization in principle. As such, they all tend to cooperate in the effort of consciousness to repress other stories of how things are. In the technological matrix, not only are other narratives repressed, but they are repressed for reasons that easily enter the realm of public discourse, and do so for purposes that are amenable to the task of keeping the they-self entertained, occupied, and as secure as possible in the sufficiency of material reality. To accomplish its mission, the technological matrix narrative *effaces itself as story* and becomes disarmingly simple matter-of-factness, a reasonable state of affairs that can be demonstrated to be the case on demand. In effacing itself as story, the technological matrix narrative also seeks to obliterate the category of story altogether as the genre appropriate to primary structures of consciousness. Technology as matrix narrative is in fact the story that purports to kill all other stories and the story-telling impulse as well. If Wiggins is right that we can expect its demise, the next question is how this demise comes to pass. To see this, we take a slightly circuitous route through ideology back into Heidegger.

Ideology, especially as it is related to falling, and technology go hand-in-hand in post-Heideggerian thinking. It is not only that technology pushes back the limits of human achievement and renders the horizon of inadequacy (ultimately, read death) more distant. There is also the reassurance of a system that calls for a minimum of "wild card" factors, and thus fewer challenges to the flow of meaning generated in the public discourse of the "they." Ideology's projected sense of human adequacy to events and its elevation of rationality (see "Theologies in Relation") support the spirit of technological calculation, and the achievements of technology are marshalled to support the ideology that attends their genesis. The combined effect works out to be a totalization of a single, fundamental sense of reality that presences itself unassumingly as common sense. Further, the concernful reduction of all phenomena to the categories of ideological rationality makes the manipulation and utilization of everything, that is, everything that is a signifier, easier to conceive and sanction. These are some of the basic themes that surface out of Heidegger's deconstructive critique of technology. They do not exhaust his thinking by any means, but are best understood as a preface to his thinking the beginning of the reconstruction of technology.

Heidegger has stressed the danger as well as the promise that has come into being as new developments have occurred in technology on both material and intellectual planes, though it has been the negative component which received the most attention and which has found its way into the body of often-quoted material. Not surprisingly, the task of the reconstruction of technology proves more difficult after all the understandings that must go before in a deconstruction; some possibilities will have been closed off. Looking at the situation ideologically, it has been much more in vogue among Heidegger's readers to engage in technology-bashing rather than imagination of salvation through technology. Also, when he preserves the tension with positivity, Heidegger strikes some as mystical, and therefore to be avoided. Yet Heidegger is not offering pious obscurities when he faces technology positively; his language reflects the difficulty of the task; if there is a mystical element in Heidegger's writing, it is not to be located in extrapolations from the existential analytic of *Being and Time*. Moreover, the negative work on technology was far from finished at the time Heidegger wrote, and he successfully communicates this sense to readers. Recent articles touching on technology have been sprinkled with bits of Heidegger's negative critique, but rarely has the positive side of his thinking been put to use, perhaps out of reluctance to depart from Heidegger's own emphasis. At the risk of stating the obvious, we note that just as "negative" does not mean "derogatory" in this connection, so "positive" does not mean "laudatory"; it means something more like "constructive." The presence of constructive proposals in the literature is crucial to the appreciation of technology's own revealing of its essence.

As a counterpoint to Heidegger's generally negative attitude toward technology, we insert Gabriel Vahanian's more positive thesis of technology as technique of the human. As occurs in Heidegger's positive meditations, Vahanian's thinking stretches language beyond convention, but he is well aware of this, even apologetic for the constructions that were required to venture beyond the usual. In simplest outline, Vahanian's thesis proposes that technology presents humanity with the possibility of continual change, of continually becoming human. This innocuous formulation is not just a glorification of the present ceaseless production of novelties; it is, rather, a sense that Vahanian seems to share with Heidegger of an opportunity for the human as something new, unprecedented, and more radically alive than ever before. Vahanian knows the subtlety of his suggestion and the ease with which it could be mis-read into conservative domesticity. He offers a clarification:

> And by the human is of course meant no flight forward, no starry-eyed mysticism, but rather the confrontation with the daily realities through which man is reconciled with his own reality, where heaven and earth, instead of confusing or dissolving one another, are articulated on the seventh day, the day of rest, or in the Easter dawn of the third day, or in the morning of the fullness of time.[8]

It is no accident or lapse of style that explanations of the *novum* come in language no less challenging than the theses that announce it. Both the thesis of the *novum* and its elaboration propose a radical transvaluation of all values from the far side of the division between a virtual now and then. Is it a mere coincidence that both Heidegger and Vahanian use the language of religion?

The appropriateness of religious language in connection with a technological future can come into view if we return to the thinking of story through the thesis of the epigram above. Already it has become apparent that technology's story, which tends to place all beings in the standing reserve such that they are present-at-hand for employment, can be and in fact tends to be a story to end all stories. It becomes that kind of story, implies Heidegger, whenever human beings accept themselves at the face-value declared by the calculated revelation of beings that shows up in the light of technological thinking. The general acceptance of technology's determinations is encouraged by technology's capacity to demonstrate the correctness of its story, a story that is held to be so objectively correct that it apparently transcends the category of story altogether and nullifies it to the point that stories as such become mere entertainment.

When stories become mere entertainment, that is, when their purpose is to tranquilize Dasein into one inauthentic ecstatic fascination or another, they lose the power to make a decisive difference in existence. When stories become just fiction or non-fiction, the question of truth becomes entirely a matter of the kind of correspondence that can in principle be falsified by experiment or the testimony of reliable witnesses, i.e., witnesses whose understandings already accord with common sense and the locally prevailing public consensus. Thus conceived, stories are denied on principle the possibility of true surprise, that is, of mediating truth as revealing or unconcealing (*alētheia*), if for no other reason than that the revelations of technology exclude all other revelations from reality.

Heidegger, like Blake, could see that technology tended to try to enforce a single version of reality through construction of comprehensive schemes of cause-and-effect coherence. Further, technology could and did point to the material aspect of its own achievements for validation, claiming essentially that one cannot argue with success. Heidegger disagrees:

> ... the unconcealment in accordance with which nature presents itself as a calculable complex of the effects of forces can indeed permit correct determinations; but precisely through these successes the danger can remain that in the midst of all that is correct the true will withdraw. [9]

The withdrawal of the true would not even be noticed by fallen Dasein, since ideology always presents its own story as the sufficient truth, but for resolute or authentic Dasein, the absence would surely be felt, specifically as existential distance. Paradoxically, as technology brings things closer in its own way by setting them up for maximum accessibility and usefulness in the standing reserve, it also removes them from nearness by denying all belonging together of beings whose *logos* is other than the logic of technology. Through its unplanned distancing of beings in their Being from authentic or resolute Dasein, technology in some moments forces Dasein away from its (that is, technology's) matrix narrative and its one-dimensional world.

Granted that technology is capable of all this and is even now informing an unintentionally international program that is hard at work to establish a single, fundamentally technological culture and consolidate its holding sway in the Earth, regardless of the consequences; granted that it does its best to undercut the impulse to tell stories; granted that it has developed the physical means of its own virtual destruction; still we do not expect technology simply to wither and die. If so, we must wonder what it would mean to talk of the demise of technology's story as Wiggins's words at the beginning of this chapter encourage us to do.

The demise of technology's story need not be equated with the actual demise of technology and its eventual disappearance from the Earth. The demise of technology's story need not either be part of an apocalyptic fantasy of the end of industrial society. The moment of the demise of the story of technology can be interpreted not only within the surface dynamics of history-as-chronicle, but within the less visible dynamics of existence as well, which is to say within the dynamics of authenticity and inauthenticity. The existential demise of the story of technology occurs when the technological matrix narrative is experienced in the mode of being no longer adequate as a primary structure significance, when it is experienced as a hollow text whose most significant symbols are unmistakably smaller than what they symbolize instead of larger, that is, in the event of authentic Dasein. In baldest terms, people can outgrow the story of technology.

This outgrowing does not mean a forsaking of the world in which technological development has come to pass and it does not entail either neo-primitivism or a move "back to nature." It is not primarily a realization of a need for alternative technologies or the wiser use of resources, important as these might be at this juncture in history. As Heidegger remarks,

> It would be foolish to attack technology blindly. It would
> be shortsighted to condemn it as the work of the devil. We
> depend on technological devices; they even challenge us to
> ever greater advances.[10]

Outgrowing the story of technology clearly does not mean the dogmatic uttering of a blanket "No" to all phenomena of technology; in light of Heidegger's thinking, it means being capable of both "Yes" and "No." He explains:

> We can use technical devices, and yet with proper use also
> keep ourselves so free of them that we may let go of them at
> any time.[11]

Being capable of both "Yes" and "No" means being able to make use of the things of technology without giving oneself over to technology. Heidegger not only believes this is possible, he believes that developing this way of being in the world is the only realistic option in this age. The odd occurrence of the word "proper" in the passage above does not refer to an implied extant moral code, we should note, but to an implied technique of the technological whose essence must be a mode of the authenticity Heidegger attempted to describe in *Being and Time*.

Heidegger is aware that his proposal of using the things of technology and yet staying free of them sounds paradoxical to his audience of non-philosophers, so he poses a question in their behalf:

> But will not saying both yes and no this way to technical
> devices make our relation to technology ambivalent and
> insecure? On the contrary! Our relation to technology will
> become wonderfully simple and relaxed. We let technical
> devices enter our daily life, and at the same time leave them
> outside, that is, let them alone, as things which are nothing
> absolute but remain dependent upon something higher. I
> would call this comportment toward technology which

expresses "yes" and at the same time "no," by an old word, *releasement toward things* (*Gelassenheit*). [12]

The concept of *Gelassenheit* shows up late in Heidegger's career, but it is not without a precursor. As early as *Being and Time*, he was trying to articulate how Dasein could function in the world and still not lose itself in the commotion of the "they." At that stage, thinking out the existential analytic, he called it "resoluteness." Resoluteness named an attitude of Dasein in which the possibilities upon which authentic Dasein had projected itself were not abandoned once the anxiety that brings Dasein face-to-face with its own death has dissipated. It was never a voluntaristic category, but the connotations of the word focused attention on Dasein to the exclusion of other entities.

With the concept of *Gelassenheit*, Heidegger expands the frame of reference beyond resoluteness without altering or retracting any of that part of *Being and Time*. The full semantic range of the original German word is brought into play as Heidegger intends not only the composure and self-possession of resolute Dasein, but also an acceptance of the situation and a willingness to renounce willing. It is important to the concept of *Gelassenheit* that the term does not occur in semantic isolation, but belongs in the phrase "*Gelassenheit zu den Dingen*," "releasement toward things." As with the concept of resoluteness in *Being and Time*, *Gelassenheit* is not imagined in the later literature, where it appears, as a free-floating, intransitive affect. It is more of a disposition or, in terms of *Being and Time*, a mood. Moods, Heidegger observed in *Being and Time*, always determine in advance how things will be revealed; one implication is that *Gelassenheit* allows beings, including perhaps the things of technology, distinct possibilities of self-realization. While the semantics of resoluteness readily suggest something more like determination to make a way in the face of resistances, the important element of circumspection that attends *Gelassenheit* is not so evident until the integral presence of the concept of things is noticed.

Gelassenheit zu den Dingen is only possible in the world of things, which is always already the scene of falling, making present, ideology, and technology. It is thus an attitude which is appropriate to where the danger is and *only* where the danger is. *Gelassenheit* is no dreamy, aesthetic reverie; it is a definite attempt at an encounter of beings, all on their own ways. It is also the coming to fruition of Heidegger's answer to Husserl. Especially, *Gelassenheit zu den Dingen* is non-technological being in the world *par excellence* by virtue of a rigorous letting-be of things. As an attitude, *Gelassenheit* eschews both the projected omniscience of ideology and the technological interventionism of modern science. Further, it is the true alternative to sado-masochistic Being-in-the-world, which is the prolepsis of technology and the ultimate enactment of the myth, that is, the structure, of ideology.

The meaning of *Gelassenheit* is bound up with Heidegger's understanding that the essence of technology is revealing and the danger that technology brings into the world is essentially a danger to revealing. With this thought, there occurs in Heidegger's work an unmistakable advocacy of a thoughtful move beyond a relationship to technology that is decided merely on the basis of personal likes or dislikes of the various phenomena that have accompanied technological development and into relationships with things in general such that beings are first understood ontologically and then, subordinately, technologically. This is the radical denial/acceptance of technology that Heidegger proposes. It is a possibility that offers much, but between the current situation and the promise of wisely appropriated technological development there is a need for care; fulfillment of the promise of technology does not seem to be implicit in the simple fact of the development of technology for Heidegger. He writes:

> That which presences the essence of technology threatens
> revealing, threatens (it) with the possibility that all revealing
> unfolds in ordering and (that) everything presents itself
> exclusively in the unconcealedness of the supply. [13]

Heidegger perceives how the manifoldness of revealing, which is the basis of novelty, could be twisted by the technological mind into something that can be regularized and controlled. Jacques Ellul's claim about the autonomy of technique notwithstanding, regularization and control serve the purposes of ideology. When it is said that technology is not neutral, the truth of the matter is that technology is not neutral between ideology and religion; but it is essentially neutral in relation to ideologies. The caricature of the objective scientist has its basis in the claim that technology delivers the facts, and the interpretations come later. The minions of technology may have their ideological preferences, but that is essentially beside the point. Ideological Dasein, on the other hand, is determined to make maximum use of technology because, unlike multivalent myth, which can be intractable, the technological matrix narrative comes already focused on a world of public reality that can be reliably instantiated and demonstrated without reference to improbabilities and without the uncomfortable necessity to put one's own Being at stake for the truth. For ideological Dasein, needing to maintain its lostness in the commotion of public reality, this low-risk approach to validity is preferable; from the standpoint of fallenness, even a lie that simulates truth is far superior to uncertainty.

The lie ceases to satisfy, however, once it has been recognized as such. Catalyst for that recognition is the experience of one's own historical finitude, which *Being and Time* discusses under the rubric of anxiety. Ontically, Dasein's consequent existential dissatisfaction comes to presence in the question "Is that all there is?". With this question, the presence of the Present is already exceeded in principle. What must ensue is a search for the hidden excess. This search can occur in two modes: in one realization, the search involves the placing of oneself, voyeuristically or otherwise, at the scene of the bizarre or the shocking or the horrifying; in the other, it can occur as a meditative attentiveness that distances itself (oneself) from the ideologically revealed world without severing the connections. In both cases, the goal is the same: to open oneself up to a life that will exceed the flatness of the consensus and that will free one from the matter-of-factness of the publically-interpreted given. In the technological world, the search can get underway when "Yes" and "No" to the things of technology occur together; only then has the disengagement from ideological structures progressed meaningfully and only then can technology be encompassed by Dasein, which is the condition of being meaningful. As Heidegger describes the event, it is plain that fallen Dasein's ideological self-assuredness must have been left behind:

> *The meaning pervading technology hides itself.* But if we explicitly and continuously heed the fact that such hidden meaning touches us everywhere in the world of technology, we stand at once within the realm of that which hides itself from us, and hides itself just in approaching us. That which shows itself and at the same time withdraws is the essential trait of what we call the mystery. I call the comportment which enables us to keep open to the meaning hidden in technology, *openness to the mystery.*
>
> Releasement toward things and openness to the mystery belong together.[14]

Openness to the mystery is for Dasein the completion of the movement out of technological thralldom. It is the principle that moves letting-beings-be out of the realm of caprice and into the realm of necessity. Like releasement toward things, openness to the mystery is not imagined as a voluntaristic concept. It is not exactly a species of grace either. Heidegger writes:

> Yet releasement toward things and openness to the mystery
> never happen of themselves. They do not befall us
> accidentally. Both flourish only through persistent,
> courageous thinking.[15]

Whereas at the earlier stage of his thinking, represented in "Conversation on a Country Path," which is reported to have taken place during World War II, Heidegger stresses waiting, there is no real conflict between earlier and later thought. Thus, when he is heard to say, "In waiting we leave open what we are waiting for,"[16] the waiting is not an idle passing time. It is the kind of waiting that occurs when one thinks without conceptualizing a goal in advance, without coercing thinking into instrumentality or mere problem-solving. It is this non-coercion that allows thinking to find its way, that really is a part of the making of a way (*Be-wegung*), perhaps the only part over which the individual has any control. In this light, it appears that the major dispositional difference between authentic and inauthentic Dasein might be patience. In *Being and Time*, one of the distinguishing characteristics of fallen Dasein was restlessness; in Heidegger's thinking on technology, impatience occurs as the interventionist compulsion of the skewed self-revelation of beings.

The unplanned demise of the story of technology occurs when human beings become thoughtful enough to accept the risk of relationship with other beings without interposing metaphysical precedents for security. In other words, it occurs when technological utopianism comes into its own *as a consequence of* a thinking that stays with technology but does not succumb to the nihilistic danger inherent in technology. In both "The Question Concerning Technology" and "The Turning," Heidegger meditates two lines from a poem by Hölderlin:

> But where danger is, grows
> The saving power also.[17]

The demise of the story of technology entails the growth of the saving power.

In a technological society, the demise of the story of technology virtually entails the collapse of all ideologies that sustain themselves by it. It does not entail the collapse of technology itself, for only when people have transcended technology's story does technology become a possibility which can be chosen with the full awareness of what is happening. At that point, and no sooner, can technology be transformed by thinking to become technique of the human, to use Vahanian's phrase.

Because technology pushes fallen Dasein past itself, past its Present and into a future that must be thematically imagined (if only because technique itself demands it), the meaning of technology as technique of the human is that technology has become the concrete historical realization of religion's original condition in our time; that is, it has become the agent which compels Dasein to decide its own Being. Realizing, even pre-ontologically, that such a compulsion belongs to the Being of Dasein is one of the conditions of the origin of religion. Until the advent of technology, Dasein had the option of remaining shielded in and by nature, but that is gone now. Dasein which does not grasp its Being as an issue is not shielded by technology; it is transformed. We can watch it happening parabolically on film as technologically-equipped explorers, exploiters, and governors enter the pre-industrial domains of isolated jungle cultures. Unshielded, Dasein has no choice but to wrestle with technology until it wins a blessing. Even so, it is technology which will name the *novum*.

Technology provides humanity with a possibility for factical existence grounded in the authentic resoluteness that Dasein achieves with the grasp of death as its ownmost possibility. It provides the occasion for Dasein to see how it can lose itself and how it can choose itself.

Technology creates the world in which releasement toward things and openness to the mystery become possible in a way that is unprecedented; for the first time, the Being of the things themselves hangs in the balance, and not because of the physical destructiveness of nuclear weapons. Without thinking its way into this situation, Dasein and its world remain unredeemed within the ideologically circumscribed universe of the "they" as everything that is not just more of the same gets suppressed. The new age never comes.

Technology may tend always to produce more of the same, but it also (and more importantly) constructs the world that Dasein falls into and that it must physically and spiritually venture out from. Technology, claims Vahanian, has taken over from mythology the function of identifying and placing humanity in the world. Unlike the virtually timeless orderings of traditional mythology, technology's determinations are not made *in illo tempore*, but right now, on the spot. The concept of faith becomes generally opaque because in the age of technology; there seems to be no distance between determiner and determined, and thus no distance to traverse in a leap.

Technology takes us to the moon but keeps us earthbound more decisively than ever before if it has its own way. If we have our own way, however, the image of the historical flight to the moon can be dramatically and informatively juxtaposed with the haunting scenes of primitive tribal villagers to become a metaphor of spiritual departure and return that is first made possible by technology. The thinking has not yet been done fully. Heidegger wonders:

> Will insight into that which is bring itself disclosingly to pass? Will we correspond to to that insight, through a looking that looks into the essence of technology and becomes aware of Being itself within it? [18]

Notes

[1] Herbert Marcuse, *One-Dimensional Man*. Boston: Beacon Press, 1964, pp. xv-xv.

[2] *Discourse on Thinking*, p. 50. Cf. "Gelassenheit," pp. 19-20. Original German terms were not inserted in the published text of the quoted translation.

[3] Martin Heidegger, "The Thing," *Poetry, Language, Thought,* tr. Albert Hofstadter. New York: Harper and Row, 1971, p. 170. Cf. Martin Heidegger, "Das Ding," *Vorträge und Aufsätze*, II. Pfullingen: Neske, 1954, pp. 42-43.

[4] Translates *der Bestand*. See Martin Heidegger, "The Question Concerning Technology," *The Question Concerning Technology and Other Essays*, tr. W. Lovitt. New York: Harper and Row, 1977. (Henceforward QCT) Cf. "Die Frage nach der Technik," *Vorträge und Aufsätze*, I. (FT)

[5] Op. cit. p. 15; German, p. 15.

[6] SZ, p. 121; BT, p. 157.

[7] Thomas Kuhn, *The Structure of Scientific Revolutions*, 2nd ed. Chicago: University of Chicago Press, 1970.

[8] Gabriel Vahanian, *God and Utopia*, tr. P. Lachance, P. Schwartz, R.D. Kozak, and author. New York: Seabury, 1977, p. 47. Henceforward GU.

[9] QCT, p. 26; FT, p. 26.

[10] Heidegger, *Discourse on Thinking*, p. 53. Cf. *Gelassenheit*, p. 24.

[11] Op. cit., p. 54; *Gelassenheit*, p 24.

[12] Ibid.; *Gelassenheit*, p. 25.

[13] "Die Frage nach der Technik," p. 34; translation mine. The original reads, "Das Wesende der Technik bedroht das Entbergen, droht mit der Möglichkeit, dass alles Entbergen im Bestellen aufgeht und alles sich in der Unverborgenheit des Bestandes darstellt." For comparison, William Lovitt translates the sentence thusly: "The coming to presence of technology threatens revealing, threatens it with the possibility that all

revealing will be consumed in ordering and that everything will present itself only in the unconcealedness of the standing-reserve." ("The Question Concerning Technology," p. 33.) In this essay, forms of the verb *wesen* present significant problems of translation. Lovitt's translation of *"das Wesende"* as "the coming to presence," the same phrase he uses to render *"das Wesen"* at most points, seems to obscure Heidegger's intention to name not the phenomenon of technology itself, but phenomena whose mode of presence is determined *by* technology. Further, Lovitt's choice of "consume" to render *"aufgehen,"* while not inconceivable, seems to contradict Heidegger's repeated claims that revealing does not come to an end in the technological age, but becomes only the kind of revealing that serves the purposes of technology. That Lovitt needs to put Heidegger's active sentence into the passive to make "consume" work is further evidence against the appropriateness of the rendering.

[14] *Discourse on Thinking*, p. 55; *Gelassenheit*, p. 26.

[15] Op. cit., p. 56; p. 27.

[16] Martin Heidegger, "Conversation on a Country Path About Thinking," *Discourse on Thinking*, p.68; "Zur Erörterung der Gelassenheit," *Gelassenheit*, p. 45.

[17] QCT, p. 28; FT, p. 28.

[18] Martin Heidegger, "The Turning," *The Question Concerning Technology and Other Essays*, p. 49.

Get the nothingness back into words. The aim is words with nothing in them; words that point beyond themselves rather than to themselves; transparencies, empty words. Empty words, corresponding to the void in things.

— *Norman O. Brown*

VI. Divinities

Historically, religion has been associated with "belief in" a god or gods; such belief has tended to be expressed in terms of propositions representing ontical facts about the divinities who have been believed in. At times, pure credulousness has been taken to be the essence of faith, as one reading of the *credo quia absurdum* that is attributed to Tertullian would have it. Ontically descriptive (i.e. "realistic") propositions having to do with gods, which the faithful are enjoined to believe by their clergy and by each other, have certainly been characteristic of religion as a phenomenon, but they are not part of the ontological constitution of religion.

While ontically descriptive propositions having to do with factical gods are not properly part of the ontological constitution of religion, the ontology of gods in general is. Through the ontology of gods that our critical theory develops (and it would be unjustified to dismiss critical theory from performance of this service), the possibility of gods becomes essential to the possibility of religion. It is important to think these signifiers ontologically. The ontological role of gods in religion has essentially nothing to do with particular powers or acts in history that religions may publicize in their own ways and for their own purposes; it consists solely in the fact that gods have a necessary place in the world that is implied in the existential analytic begun in *Being and Time*. The necessity of a place for gods in the world is the key point that separates religion and ideology in the ontologically-based, critical interpretation of the difference between religion and ideology that is being proposed.

If the necessity of a place for gods is simply inferred from phenomena and argued in those terms, the kind of god that emerges can only be a contingent one that lets itself be determined by human explanations of ontical phenomena. Inference from ontical phenomena must lead to "god-of-the-gaps" religion and theology. In this mode of thinking, the ontological problematic remains untouched and is, in fact, concealed by a wall of excuses designed to satisfy curiosity, in the sense that curiosity has been associated with falling in *Being and Time*. This satisfaction of curiosity operates contrary to the interests of religion even when phenomena that are associated with religion, such as the institutional church, appear to be strengthened as people are impressed by stories of the gods. In fact, such stories are destined to be pretexts for iconoclasm.

To get at the ontological problematic, it is necessary to look away from the explanation of phenomena and toward the interpretation of the world. In doing this, the thought of both early and later Heidegger is involved. Incidentally, the importance of the existential analytic of *Being and Time* for Heidegger's later work shows up with particular clarity in taking up the ontology of divinities. This regional ontology ultimately presupposes the kind of preliminary understanding of Dasein developed in *Being and Time*. We do not begin with that analysis, however, since a different thematic focus promises a larger view of the Being of divinities.

In "The Thing," Heidegger avers that the thing is defined in four essential aspects: earth, sky, mortals, and divinities. For a while, says Heidegger (playing on the German words *Weile* and *weilen*), the Being of the thing is the gathering of these four in unconcealedness. In the lexicon Heidegger develops, unconcealedness is never total exposure, it should be recalled. The now-classic example of the thing Heidegger chooses is the jug. He observes that the jug may contain a drink for mortals to quench their thirst or for the gods, as a libation which is an "authentic gift"[1] that lifts a celebration or ceremony into the realm of the divine. In this essay, Heidegger not only raises the possibility of the divine, a comparatively rare occurrence in modern philosophical writing, he specifies what he is speaking about as "the immortal gods."[2] He gives no other, familiarizing indication of the identities of these beings he associates so integrally with things, and when he speaks of God, as in "The Onto-theo-logical Constitution of Metaphysics,"[3] it is not with regard to things.

It could be speculated that he does not know how to name the gods or speak of them in any more specific way, but that turns out not to be the case for reasons that are more ontological than mystical. In another age, it would have been a matter of course for Heidegger to name the gods of which he spoke. In this time, however, it not only passes without causing a sensation, it would appear inappropriate for him to involve himself with (or commit himself to) the content of specific mythologies in discourse focused at a more general, anthropological level. In any event, naming names would add nothing substantially useful to his account if his intention was formally ontological; as Heidegger conceives ontology, it can not be dependent upon the truth-value of non-universal arguments or ontical propositions of empirical import.

Heidegger's taciturnity concerning the divinities cannot be ascribed to his assuming that the gods are so familiar to his readers that they can pick up that thread of his discourse in ontical reality any time they like. At the beginning of "What Are Poets For?" he makes his sense of the absence of divinities plain as he takes up a phrase from Hölderlin and characterizes the present age as "a destitute time."[4] Heidegger sees the destitution of the time as consisting not only in the people's forgetting of the gods, but more profoundly, in the fact that people have forgotten that they have forgotten the gods. This profound, compound forgetting is the distinguishing feature of today (or, we may surmise, the techno-logical Present in general) as a time in which the gods have "long since" flown. It is a time in which people can say, "God is dead," and possess only a vaguely mythological idea of what it means to them that they have said it. The advent of technology has played a part in filling the void left by the flight of the gods, but that is only because Being has already withdrawn in the way that is required for the coming into being of the technological attitude.

Because Heidegger's terminology so frequently has an overt reli-gious/theological ring to it, and because his generally unconventional treatments of notions of God or the gods tend to show up at significant junctures in his writing, it would be hard not to notice that in "The Thing," an address delivered in 1950, Heidegger explicitly recalls the gods, at least formally, and constitutes them as one of the poles of what he calls "the fourfold" (*das Geviert*).[5] In doing so, he considers each pole. One element of the fourfold is the earth, of which Heidegger spoke thematically in "The Origin of the Work of Art" as the concealing, that whereunto beings retreat. "Earth is that whence the arising brings back and shelters everything that arises without violation. In the things that arise, earth is present as the sheltering agent."[6] In "The Thing," a much later piece, the earth is again spoken of, this time as "the building bearer, nourishing with its fruits,"[7] a description which essentially accords with the thoughts of arising and sheltering. In the description of the fourfold, the sky is spoken of as raining and giving water so that it and the earth are united in the pouring of the contents of the jug. The relation is conceptually simple and elegant between these two poles of the fourfold.

The elegance apparently vanishes, though, as Heidegger applies himself to the task of communicating with the reader concerning the other two poles of the fourfold gathered about the jug. Mortals, as those who have need of the contents of the jug in ways that divinities do not, quench their thirst in the world where the jug is as jug. As Heidegger lays it out, the jug cannot be itself until the pouring out of its gift (as a gift, in contrast to a commodity) takes place. It is not difficult to see the necessity of mortals in this arrangement, not difficult to imagine how mortals and jugs might belong together. There is an obvious pragmatic necessity here, though it turns out not to be the most fundamental. If mortals withdraw, the jug cannot be jug because it cannot pour out its gift as gift. Can the same be said of the beings at the other pole, the gods?

Remaining with the jug, the effect on it is far less clear if the gods withdraw. Note: "withdraw," not "are withdrawn." It is clear that Heidegger sees the gods as belonging with earth, sky, and mortals, for he says so, but in the example of the jug, he has not really explicitly shown them to be necessary, only told the story of the jug as thing such that divinities can be given a place. What is the nature of this place? *The question is actually whether gods are **ontologically** necessary.*

At this point, for reasons we care not to guess, the logic of the address will not let itself be followed step-by-step. Heidegger makes a quick move from the assertion that the jug can be used in the pouring out of a libation for the immortal gods to the thought that, "In the gift of the outpouring earth and sky, divinities and mortals dwell *together all at once*. These four, at one because of what they themselves are, belong together."[8] The problem here is not whether Heidegger is justified in making the jump from one possibility of the jug to the inclusion of that possibility in the essential structure of the jug. Though at no point in this essay does he argue explicitly for inclusion on these grounds, it is not necessary in his methodology; he had already enunciated elsewhere the notion of truth as *alētheia*, or "unconcealment," which would allow him to speak of the jug truthfully when he describes a vision of it which includes gods. Additionally, it could be argued that any imaginable possibility of a thing is always already somehow included in the Being of the thing. The problem is why, in this time, Heidegger is justified in being obscure about who the divinities are to the extent that with the information given, the reader honestly could not locate the gods Heidegger is talking about and, indeed, could scarcely be sure of what Heidegger thinks a god is.

Heidegger leaves his readers light-years away from the metaphysical speculation about the gods he so steadfastly tries to avoid, but in doing so, he creates other problems that may or may not be edifying. First, such obscurity seems to undercut the reality of his description of the thing, and second, there is something strange about this obscurity concerning the gods when it is juxtaposed with the evident certainty that the gods belong with earth, sky, and mortals. This strangeness is not gratuitous; it arises out of the thinking of Being as Nonbeing, a point in the ontology of religion which is important for distinguishing it from ideology. In its absoluteness, ideology not only has no appreciation for Nonbeing, it conceals it at every turn to repress the fact of its totalization of a finite field of consciousness. Religion properly so-called not only implicitly grants the possibility of Nonbeing, it cultivates it as the gate of mystery. Ontically, this makes a great difference between religion and ideology.

Heidegger calls divinities "the beckoning heralds of Divinity."[9] The focus of the phrase is "Divinity," for it is only in the service of Divinity that divinities as such have any meaning. Further, it is only in the service of Divinity that the beckoning of divinities has any meaning. For the moment, let us not speculate about how Heidegger knows this; he did not volunteer any ontical testimony. Let us make the epistemological assumption Heidegger asks his readers to make and suppose for the moment that Being (the Being of Dasein? the Being of the gods? Being in general?) is responsible for this thought.

Of course, it says everything and nothing to name Being in this way, but it has the desired effect of placing attention at a level where the questions raised concerning divinities and Divinity can be pursued ontologically, with the least danger of falling unawares into easy or exciting metaphysical presentations. Attention to the Being of the Divine is germane to the understanding of religion and, beyond that, to the understanding of the factical means and purposes of intentionally religious communities of faith.

Returning now to the point at which Heidegger fairly leapt from the possibility that the jug could be used in the pouring out of a libation for the immortal gods to the ontological integration of the gods in a fourfold onefold with earth, sky, and mortals, the question remains of why the move was made, though now it is possible to suggest that it had something to do with the Being of divinities. There is a bit of internal evidence bearing on the question which shows up later in the address to indicate that this conceptual jump was made because Being in the mode of Nonbeing intervened in his thinking at that point. We note parenthetically that this is the kind of thesis that Werner Marx, who succeeded Heidegger at Freiburg, might encourage.

Just after he has concluded his last thematic phrases on the divinities, Heidegger begins a short disquisition on mortals. He says, "Death is the shrine of Nothing, that is, of that which in every respect is never something that merely exists, but which nevertheless presences, even as the mystery of Being itself."[10] As he wrote these words, he was meditating mortals and divinities together and in this meditation, his thoughts turned to Nonbeing at some point. From the placement of words in the text, it is uncertain whether that point belongs more to his thinking of mortals, or more to his (mortal) thought of the divinities, those nonmortals who also are not dead. The ambiguity is not uncalled-for.

By the time "Das Ding" is delivered, Heidegger is already on record in "What Are Poets For?" concerning the absence of the gods. Their absence, as he characterizes it there, is not the kind of absence that simultaneously eventuates in presence, as in the case of the past as outlined in *Being and Time*, which is also futural in its recollecting anticipation. It is an absence which must be brought to presence. The absence Heidegger was speaking of in "What Are Poets For?" is the kind of near-total darkness in which Being (i.e. the Being of beings) is for the most part ignored and only poets see at all out of their own Being. In this condition, where the light of Being does not shine forth in beings, except in the song of the poet, there is next to Nothing. That is what has happened to the world in the case of the gods who have flown. Heidegger credits Nietzsche with having had the experience of the world in which the gods have flown, which Nietzsche called the death of God, even though Heidegger himself did not agree with Nietzsche's interpretation of the experience; thus we hear him taking Nietzsche's words seriously without ever actually speaking Nietzsche's language as he considers the gods' having flown in the essay "Nietzsches Wort 'Gott ist tot.' "

The gods are not dead for Heidegger and they do not stand ready to die, so all speaking of the death of gods must be heard metaphorically. While divinities cannot die, they can, however, be concealed by Being. But, Heidegger claims, the compound forgetfulness that characterizes the destitute time is an oblivion even beyond the usual variety of concealment, for it is an absolute concealment, devoid of the positivity of revealing that is integral to Being's mode of concealing. Being as beings, which for Heidegger come to presence in Being by the light of Being, counts as concealed when beings do not shine presencingly (*anwesend*) to other beings; if there is absolute concealment, it can only mean that the light of Being has ceased to shine forth among beings, meaning local darkness, meaning Nonbeing, meaning Nothing. Nietzsche was the one who said for the record that God means nothing anymore. Heidegger, writing in a poetically-proclaimed destitute time in which the gods not only "no longer" come to presence as themselves but even cease to be-themselves (*wesen*), seems to reflect the temper of the time and the concealment of the gods when he speaks obscurely of the divinities, but there is reason to believe that it is not only in a destitute time that such obscurity is appropriate.

So far, the point here is mainly that Nonbeing/Nothing occurred to Heidegger in connection with the divinities, though we recall that it is in a hard-working speaking of mortals that the theme actually shows up. The discussions of mortals and divinities are very closely related. It is still not very clear, though, how Heidegger could speak of divinities if they have been so profoundly forgotten in this time. It has something to do with poetry. Language, as dead metaphor, could transmit to him or us the names of unfamiliar gods and senseless stories about them, but dead language is insufficient to explain all the thinking that is happening in the essays. Language as poetry in a broad sense has different properties, however. Poetry, when it works, brings Being to presence. And Being, coming to presence, brings Nonbeing/Nothing to presence in the same movement.

The reason why Heidegger can speak as he does of divinities is his experience of Nothing, which he describes as " . . . that which in every respect is never something that merely exists, but which nevertheless presences, even as the mystery of Being itself."[11] That the discussion of the experience of Nothing as the mystery of Being occurs in the course of an address on "The Thing" is not insignificant; it is highly probable that an experience of the thing in a way made possible by the thinking of *Being and Time* and his Kant studies allowed Heidegger the insight which informs this late essay. This comes out when Heidegger writes, "Only what conjoins itself out of world becomes a thing."[12] We know that Being is the principle of joining beings for Heidegger from his early writings. In this address, he is still meditating the uncanniness of the fact that there is something and not nothing, a thought which is brought back to him in the conjoining of the thing as thing with him as human being, a vital conjoining in which he mysteriously distinguishes the thing as thing from among "the countless objects everywhere of equal value . . . ."[13] When he wonders why this is so, then he arrives at the mystery of Being, for no existing agent of conjoining makes itself present-at-hand; as Heidegger thinks Being, he peers into Nothing and sees only the mystery of Being. "Man alone of all beings, when addressed by the voice of Being, experiences the marvel of all marvels: that what-is *is*."[14]

An additional aspect of what appears to be Heidegger's experience of the thing needs to be noted before further work can be done with the theme of divinities. This is the category of distance, with special reference to the idea of nearness. In his treatment of the thing, Heidegger has recourse to a conception of distance which is different from normal measurement in three dimensions, perhaps even essentially opposed to it. Here he is dealing with what might be called "existential distance" or "ontological distance," a kind of relationship that obtains among beings in their Being, something that is prior to the technology of measuring. He discusses his idea of distance in "The Thing," and relates it to contemporary events in some detail in another essay, "The Nature of Language," where he writes, "Nearness . . . is by its nature outside and independent of space and time."[15] In thinking the nature of distance in this way, Heidegger discovers that in his experience, farness is not simply the span of nearness multiplied. Nearness and farness are of the Being of the thing and are not mutually exclusive categories such that one is required to choose between them. In Heidegger's words, "Nearness brings near — draws nigh to one another — the far and indeed *as* the far. Nearness preserves farness. Preserving farness, nearness presences nearness in nearing that farness."[16] Still, says Heidegger, not everything that is (ontologically) near will necessarily be understood as near, or as far, for that matter; technology's distance-abolishing calculations have this effect on relationships, causing whole categories to disappear. The relationship of the thinking of distance to the thinking of divinities shows up more clearly when the connection of thinking with the phenomenon of technology is considered.

Heidegger is on record in several essays, including "The Thing," "The Question Concerning Technology," "Building Dwelling Thinking," and others as seeing several problems with technological thinking. One of most significant of these problems is that the Being of things is effectively ignored in favor of a thoroughgoing calculation of the uses to which a thing can be put. This problem, he feels, is closely related to the abolition of distance, as comes out particularly clearly in "The Nature of Language." The abolition of distance is not a way of bringing things (beings) immediately near, Heidegger claims, but instead is a way of excluding things from appearing as themselves, since nearness and farness are aspects of any thing *as* thing. Let us note parenthetically that for Heidegger, things are always beings while beings may only be things if they are somehow distinguished from the mass of objects. It is Being which grants things-as-beings/beings-as-things their possibilities of nearness and farness. In the same moment, however, Being, as the basis of the presencing of beings/things, has the possibility of being attended to or ignored.

Technological calculation's abolition of distance can be seen as a function of ideology; it proximately arises out of a refusal to see things as being anything other than immediately available for its purposes. This becomes a habitual attitude, a "dis-position," a re-placement of one's own being, as Hwa Yol Jung interprets it in one of his essays, "The Orphic Voice and Ecology."[17] When this dis-position is generalized from beings that are present-at-hand to the possibility of divinities, it automatically puts divinities into the same category technology uses to contain all other objects, namely, the potentially ready-to-hand. Phenomenally, this disposition shows up as cults of magic and petitions for boons, which leads us to the thought that the technological mind is not so recent a phenomenon as the rise of industrial culture might suggest; the existence of an essentially technological dis-position can be demonstrated in humanity's long history of casting divinities in the supporting roles of its perennial magical fantasies. Where the technological mind is in possession of magical technologies, the associated divinities remain present and ready-to-hand as just so much wonderful, if only dimly understood, equipment. Dasein's own Being, at stake in magical transactions, is equally obscure. The technological disposition working itself out in the absence of magical technology is not simply repressed; it gathers itself up and comes to expression in machine technology. Greatly extending the manipulative powers of humanity, machine technology promotes through its own logic the thesis that divinities are powerless because they share the uselessness of that which recalcitrantly resists readiness-to-hand. In the light of technological calculation, divinities apparently are superfluous. Just as the technological disposition represents the outer limit of ignorance of the Being of things generally, so it also represents the extreme of ignorance of divinities. As an extreme, it formally allows only one direction of change, and that is where the saving power of technology first comes to presence.

Heidegger himself does not write as if in ignorance of divinities, but he does not write as if they are steadily near either. The divinities he places in the fourfold come to presence for him somehow, but they are far away in a destitute time; if they are to come near, they must be brought near, as in the thinking of the thing or the work of art. They apparently are near in the thinking of Being (Heidegger's writing may be evidence of that, not to imply that he holds any privileged status that would not devolve upon or be granted to any thinker) but it seems that even then they maintain their distance. If this were not so, Heidegger would not have had to leap so precipitously from a description (or projection) of the occasional necessary presence of divinities (in the pouring of the libation to the immortal gods) to the assertion of their essential belonging with earth, sky, and mortals; even the quenching of the thirst of mortals would be imbued with an overt sacrality if the fourfold were actually, to use Heidegger's own terminology, perpetually presencing as a fouring in nearness in a onefold. It seems that Heidegger senses the asymmetry of the fourfold that he seeks to describe in "The Thing" and he moves to keep the fourfold as a onefold, even in the event that mortals happen to neglect the gods and thus unwittingly (or intentionally) place themselves in a virtual threefold.

Heidegger writes that in the saying of the name of one element of the fourfold, " . . . we are already thinking of the other three along with it by way of the simple oneness of the four."[18] It appears he is intending with the word "saying" that appropriating saying in which speaking both appropriates Being and is appropriated by Being (in dis-closure). Heidegger does not make it necessary for one element to be thought *as* an element of the fourfold in order to evoke the other three; he asserts that it happens as a matter of course, a point which is also made in a similar context in "The Nature of Language," where language as "world-enrouting Saying"[19] is characterized as "the relation of all relations."[20] The fourfold can be thought as being evoked in the thinking of any one of the elements only if this evocation is understood as an ontological evocation (i.e. Saying) and not as an ontical evocation (i.e. rendering present-at-hand). The reason for this condition lies in the nature of divinities.

If the elements of the fourfold were all present-at-hand as objects whose use entailed one another, the point of their necessary belonging together would be made at the ontical level. Even then, however, it would still be ontologically unsatisfactory. Perhaps if the elements of the fourfold were conjoined in a onefold as things, the point of belonging would also be made well enough, as might be demonstrated using the example of subsystems within a system, in which the subsystem cannot be itself except that it be constitutively included in a larger system. This possibility is also denied by Heidegger in the event of the fourfold because of one element: divinities are not present as themselves in the way that things are. This thought was an important part of his contention that divinities are not to be compared with any other beings that come to presence.

The fourfold itself cannot be analyzed as a thing. It does not behave as things do. That the fourfold should appear as a threefold is then exactly correct, if the Being of divinities is such that it is their nature to be in the fourfold in the mode of being-themselves (*Wesen*) instead of coming to presence (*Anwesen*). But, if it is of the nature of divinities not to come to presence as themselves, that is, as divinities, then the only way they could become known as such would be through a default of the sort that allowed them to come to presence as themselves. This sort of default seems to be just the opposite of what Heidegger is experiencing.

He writes portentously in the powerful opening pages of "What Are Poets For?" of the default of God: "The world's night is spreading its darkness. The era is defined by the god's failure to arrive, by the 'default of God.' . . . The default of God means that no god any longer gathers men and things unto himself, visibly and unquestionably, and by such gathering disposes the world's history and man's sojourn in it . . . .Not only have the gods and the god fled, but the divine radiance has been extinguished in the world's history."[21] Heidegger continues on to say that the time is so destitute is that " . . . it can no longer discern the default of God as default."[22] In Heidegger's own terms, there arise two separate questions which seem to be raised about divinities if this text is correlated with "The Thing." Specifically, is it of the nature of divinities to be seen as such or is it not to be seen as such? Further, does the default of a god sufficiently consist in not being visible or does it more essentially have to do with the extinguishing of the divine radiance from the world's history?

Granted that the compound forgetfulness Heidegger asserts of this age would remove divinities from presence, the question remains whether forgetfulness tells the whole story, even for Heidegger. There remains the problem of deciding whether the gods Heidegger speaks of in connection with the jug are only difficult for mortals to discern or are ontologically optional. Further, are the divinities associated with the jug the same ones who have fled? What does it mean to say a god has fled? One way of thinking the divinities as other than occasional guests turns on how the flight of divinities is understood.

Divinities, in Heidegger's words, have been described as messengers of Divinity. We can connect "Divinity" with "the Holy," another term Heidegger uses, and understand them both as aspects of Being. The Holy for Heidegger is (though not exhaustively) what the poet utters (as in the Hölderlin interpretations). The Holy, as Being itself, is the source of Divinity and thus the essence of divinities. The divinities, speaking for Divinity, which is divine by dint of its bringing the Holy (i.e. Being as the Holy) as such to presence, seem to have little autonomy, little say in the matter of their own presence or absence. It is Being which makes the decision and grants poets the say.

When we hear of divinities which have fled and a default of God, then, we should not understand thereby an autonomously willed leaving-of-the-scene or a heavenly miscalculation. True, in one way of imagining it, the divinities who have fled could indeed have fled the scene intentionally, but whose intention would be responsible? Divinities do not, at least within Heidegger's framework, appear to make autonomous decisions of that type; they only obey the law of the Holy. This is perhaps easier to grasp if Heidegger's original German is borne in mind. In the German of daily commerce, the word that corresponds to the English "decision" is *Entscheidung*, and that is the word Heidegger feels called to work with in "Introduction to Metaphysics." He marks the word as extraordinary by the addition of a hyphen between the prefix and the root in order to bring out both the fact of the *Scheidung* (split) in the structure of the situation and the stripping away of the appearance of the *Scheidung* (as an absolute) from the situation. *Ent-scheidung* names the gathering appropriation of the difference between Being (*Sein*) and what is rendered here as *"apparence"* (*Schein*).[23]

In Heidegger's "Introduction to Metaphysics," the thought of *Ent-scheidung* is associated with *logos*. For Heidegger, *logos* is the principle by which is accomplished the gathering together of what-is as it lies; *Entscheidung*, on the other hand, speaks less of discovery of the "logic" of the situation as it is essentially, and more of active structuring of the understanding of being in a situation. Heidegger provocatively characterizes *Ent-scheidung* as " . . . a separation in the . . . complex of Being, unconcealment, apparence, and Nonbeing . . . ."[24] It is crucial to see that the essence of the separation, which is a stripping-away of another kind of separation, is understanding the difference between *Sein* and *Schein*; maintaining that understanding is its authentication.

The decision according to which the divinities flee must be (at least in this ontology) a decision whose source is Being, a decision which is grounded in Being, which means, a decision determined by how Being is factically revealing itself in the situation. In this time, the revealing and concealing occurs according to the protocols of technology. It would be futile to try to assign any more precise local responsibility for such a decision as eventuated in the withdrawal of the gods, and it would be wrong to imagine it as an arbitrary, unilateral, strategic action of the gods. It is an event which is called for by the Being of beings.

In *Ent-scheidung*, there occurs also an awareness of the separation between Being and Nonbeing. In another, pre-technological, age, this quality of awareness might give one to appreciate the "suchness" of things; for those who live in a technological age, it makes the sanctity of the Being of things a pressing issue, for with technology, humanity has both the intellectual and physical means to introduce calculated, but unthought, possibilities into Being in the enduring project of fallen Dasein to fill every void. With the coming of technological calculation, however, there arises the possibility of calculating the existence of infinite new voids. The technological mind is undaunted by the challenge; with dramatically expanding manipulative power, there appears as an ontic ideal the imperative that everything which can be done, *should* be done, philosophical miscegenation as conservative values are grafted onto an ethics of the will to power, open contempt for the inexhaustibility of Nonbeing. The Being of beings is threatened and eclipsed with blinding speed unless the *Ent-scheidung* occurs which reveals the Being of beings and the emptiness of infinite calculation.

The absence of the gods as such is not the result of their willfully leaving the scene; it only looks that way from a "pre-Copernican" ontological standpoint. From that kind of standpoint, for as long as it is maintained, the absence of the gods becomes the condition of a metaphysical frustration which comes to presence as a vengeful atheism. With a moment's reflection, evidence piles up that it is we who have left the garden, we who have made progress. It does not seem that the withdrawal of divinities occurs as the kind of movement in which things which were present-at-hand simply vacate a space. This withdrawal of divinities into concealment, which is a withdrawal of the messengers of Divinity whose message is Being, does happen at the scene of things, viz. beings, but it is not a unilateral action of beings which simply "get away" and is not a reduction in the number of beings factically present.

If divinities had truly been present-at-hand as such in the historical past and were not forgotten, they would be available for recollection and would be in advent from the future. If they were doubly forgotten, as Heidegger writes in his telling of the story of the way things are in a destitute time, things would be as they are when technology determines Being. On the other hand, an alternative story waits to be told, for at the scene of things, in the region of beings, double concealment is indistinguishable from Nonbeing. By contrast, things which at a former time were present-at-hand and then later become simply factically absent but not forgotten, are only simply, not doubly, concealed. Does it happen that we sometimes try to fill a space with technology that already belongs to the divine?

In the story Heidegger tells, when divinities withdraw into concealment, they take the message of Divinity, which is Being, with them. In that case, even a remembering of names or stories would not be a true recollection of the absent divinities in their Being, but only the *apparent* recollection of divinities. In apparent recollection, apparent divinities which came to presence as such would be indistinguishable from true divinities. It is the case that beings which at a former time truly came to presence and are authentically recollected in their absence come to presence in their Being in the Present from the future; this is how they are remembered in their Being. For this kind of authentic recollection of beings to occur, at least according to the Heideggerian epistemology, the light of Being must continue to shine and illuminate their Being. In the instance of divinities, though, there is a major complication. When divinities withdraw as divinities, they must withdraw in the mode of the withdrawal of the light of Being; for this reason, they cannot ever be authentically recollected, since the necessary illumination is missing and beings do not come to presence as themselves. It seems that divinities do not behave as beings.

The question arises of whether divinities are beings. Up to now, the talk of divinities has been of divinities as a group, as if they somehow did everything together. The generality of Heidegger's language has favored this way of speaking. The problem, as it stands now, is that while authentic recollection of beings is possible as long as the light of Being illuminates them in some modality (even in absence), the authentic recollection of divinities is impossible in the destitute time that Heidegger describes, when the divinities — all the divinities — have fled, taking the message — the light — of Being with them. In that case, not only divinities, but all things, would withdraw into apparence or the actuality of Nonbeing. This brings us again to the edge of Heidegger's thinking of technology.

The way further into the situation of the allegedly defaulting divinities comes with questioning the assumption that the divinities as such drift together in and out of Being, as Heidegger seems to be implying. It is a question of whether the time must indeed be as destitute as he and Hölderlin say it is. The divinities in Heidegger's essays are grammatically plural, with reason, one assumes. They are, of course, ontologically united in their relation to Divinity. Beyond this, other questions about the ontology of the divinities Heidegger speaks of may still be asked. Are they dependent upon human recognition in any way? Can human ignorance really cast divinities into Nonbeing? Is it possible to think about divinities in their Being if they are logically unable to come to presence as such?

To continue with these questions we recall that, at least for Heidegger, divinities are constituted as such by their being messengers of the divine, of the Holy, of Being. If it should happen that they cease to bring Being to presence, then they would cease Being in the mode of divinities. To cease Being in the mode of a divinity does not entail absolute cessation of the factical being of an entity in this ontology; beings which are in the mode of divinities may conceivably be in other modes also, either simultaneously or consecutively, within the scope of the ontology's logic (which is not to be construed as the set of explicit propositions that constitute the ontology at any given time). It seems that beings which are in the mode of divinities are not absolutely dependent upon human recognition for their entire being, only for their Being as divinities. They are not "actually" cast into Nonbeing as demise if no one pays attention.

It is in light of this construction of divinities that we can understand Heidegger's characterization of the poet in *Erläuterungen zu*

Hölderlins Dichtung as a "half-god" who is essentially "between." In looking at the poet as half-god and half-mortal, the nature of divinities comes yet clearer at the ontical as well as at the ontological level. This half-and-half being, we propose in an extension of Heidegger, hears the hail of Being as mortal but speaks it as divinity, as one who brings Being to presence in beings. The poet must attend to Being in its finitude, in events of a world alternately exalted and fallen, and must speak in a language that carries in itself possibilities of both the luminous and the untoward. The poet is not, therefore, simply a divinity. Heidegger himself does not proceed much further along the line of thought distinguishing poets from "full" divinities but there is an important clue to his understanding of the question in a thread that runs through his later writing especially.

In the later writings, Being's revealing-concealing disclosure has been shown to be central, though it shows up as early as the opening pages of *Being and Time*. The importance of the play of revealing-concealing is extended beyond Dasein's relationships with things as Heidegger finds it essential to the Being of the poet. In these terms, the poet may be distinguished from the divinity in that Being itself is concealed from the poet even as the poet harks to Being's call to bring Being to presence in the poem. The poet has no call to think Being directly as such, for that (in Heidegger's estimation) is the work of the thinker. Not every attention to Being need be in the mode of thinking, it seems for Heidegger.

There arises at this point the question of what the difference is between a thinker and a divinity. It appears to be that the thinker resolves to attend to Being while no such resolve is demanded of the divinity.[25] The reason for the difference lies in the dissimilar relationships of these entities to Being: the thinker seeks a constantly self-concealing Being while the divinity is a channel for a Being that is constantly in advent. A thinker seems to be perpetually underway while a divinity reposes in its Being as long as the light of Being shines. A thinker does not cease to be a thinker if others pay no attention to what is conceived, said, or done, but, under arguably analogous circumstances, if Being is not attended to, then divinities (*as* divinities) cease to be and "flee" into Nonbeing (into the double concealment of compound forgetfulness). At first glance, the logic of the movement of divinities into double concealment appears to be acausal or co-dependent, but there is a decision of sorts that brings about the withdrawal of the gods, even if it does not address them explicitly at first, and it is a human one.

It is fallen Dasein which first ignores the gods and avoids occasions of authentic relationship with beings in its becoming preoccupied with what is assigned importance by the "they." This is the first forgetfulness, and it is not primarily a forgetting of the gods, since even when concealed for the most part, they may remain present-at-hand; it is really a forgetfulness of self, of authentic self, which knows what gods are for. To forget the essence of the gods, namely, Being, is essentially to forget the gods. So, in the first instance, forgetfulness of the gods is not a failure to recreate the experience of the presence of a divine entity, it is a failure to remember the kind of experience which is possible only if a divine entity is somehow present in the ensemble.

To fallen Dasein, even the most radiant advent of Being is invisible, factically and as a possibility, and this radical restriction of truth is the origin of the second aspect of forgetfulness. A traceless, unobserved movement of Dasein's understanding of the advent of Being from "something invisible" to "something impossible" constitutes the second forgetting. For the individual, the basic state-of-mind that typifies Dasein in a destitute time can thus be created instantaneously and without effort or awareness. An isolated, forgetful individual does not constitute a destitute time, though; that is a condition of culture. When the life of a culture is monolithically conditioned by compound forgetfulness, when no art and no community of faith are there to help restore authenticity, then we can speak of destitution. For Heidegger, the domination of life by technological thinking is exactly the way our particular realization of the destitute time has come into being, but it is premature to speak as if all is lost to destitution already; Heisdegger could not think his own thoughts in final destitution.

At this point, the gods of traditional religion seem far away. In a destitute time, Heidegger seems to turn to the poet as half-god, as psychopomp, as the only hope for the light of Being that is the necessary beginning and end, the alpha and omega, for the work of thinking. Is poetry, which perpetually recreates language and reasserts the metaphysics of uncertainty, the true counter-movement to ideology's self-satisfied certitude in a destitute time? Heidegger himself maintained that the Christian revelation was still viable (while keeping silent about others), but he did not explicitly relate his own thinking of divinities to the theology of the God of Abraham, Isaac, and Jacob, much less to the theologies of Thoth or Vishnu. We recall at this juncture that Heidegger also spoke of the saving power of technology.

It is in connection with the plurality of revelations that this thinking begins to bear on readily observable phenomena of religion and tie in with the religion-ideology problematic. We recall two points: first, that divinities are heralds of the Divine, the Holy, Being; second, that by implication, in the absence of all gods, none can be remembered in its

Being, while in the presence of one, any may be known and an authentic possibility of Dasein be repeated. Thinking this way, it appears to be essentially incidental which god is the herald of the Divine as long as the message gets through. Yet how does one attend to the message?

Heidegger chooses not to say what he believes authentic attention to a divinity is, but the literature of mysticism gives ample testimony of how others represent it. From autobiographical testimony in these writings, the structure of authentic attention to a divinity appears to have two aspects: a primary aspect and a reflective aspect. William James's descriptions of mystical experience in *Varieties of Religious Experience* present these two aspects repeatedly as narratives are divided into two segments, the first presenting an ineffable event and the second, a (pale) reflection. It is the reflection aspect, repressively limited as it is, which constitutes the remembering of the god and also *the first attention to a god as god*. This is because in the primary aspect of mystical experience, there is no "as."

If one's object of recollection is a divinity which has withdrawn as such, that means even the reflection has gone cold, though the god can still be inauthentically known and ideologically manipulated as a place-holder through the presence of a signifier. At any time, however, inauthentic recollection may be re-authenticated by the same or another divinity, presumably even a half-divinity, if Heidegger's essays that speak of divinities and poets have any basis. Authentication here means not an institutional official certification of objectively verifiable results, of course, but rather a rendering-authentic through the shining of the light of Being; only a god can bring, or reveal, the light of Being. In primary experience, absent of metaphor, all gods "say" essentially the same thing, and religions are ways of listening.

We return to the jug. As it stands now, the jug can not be known as a thing, viz. as a being, unless it is illuminated by the light of Being. Without that elusive element of the fourfold, a divinity, the jug can never be more than an apparent thing, remaining, in fact, an object actually concealed in its (Non-) Being. Apart from its thingness, the jug always remains an object available for technological manipulation and thoughtless use; apart from its thingness, however, it also remains unavailable as itself. It is only in the event of the completeness of the fourfold that the jug, or any other object, can become a thing itself. At this point, whatever is left of the original issue of whether divinities were occasional to the Being of the jug dissolves in a field-ground switch. It now appears that it is the jug that fades in and out as a thing; always there as an object, it is only occasionally known as a being, and indeed on those occasions when a divinity is being-itself (*wesen*) in the fourfold.

The divinity's being-itself happens in language, recollection. This recollection presences a possibility which surpasses apparence, giving a hint of the fact of difference and the incompleteness of presence through the acknowledgement of an absence. Thus, *Ent-scheidung* includes both separation and connection.

The notion that the jug, or any other object, is truly a being (or thing) only in the presence of a divinity has powerful implications for the structure of the religion-ideology problematic, since it undercuts all ideological ontology. Technology's determinations come to presence as errors and support none of ideology's claims. Still to be worked out, however, is what the presence-in-absence of a god means. It does not mean that all understanding must be explicitly theistically-oriented in the sense that thinking ought always to refer back to a god as an absolute standard of value; in its renunciation of classical metaphysics, Heidegger's projection of the way of thinking supports that particular fashion of religiosity as little as it creates ideological legitimacy. To see how this is so, we consider the presence of divinities further.

There is a principle in some philosophies of stage lighting that good lighting does not call attention to itself. If the lighting is very dim, actors on stage come to presence as distantly unreal, being half-hidden, and their movements are uselessly obscure. If, on the other hand, spotlights are directed for maximum brightness right at the audience, then everything washes out in a blindness that is its own kind of darkness. Heidegger sees in a light so dim, it is near to being extinguished (the danger of technology). The light so bright that it obliterates all else, and itself becomes darkness, is the immediate experience of Divinity.

Recall that a divinity realizes the Being of divinity by virtue of bringing Being to presence. It follows from this that for Heidegger, the divinity does not itself come to presence as a divinity; in other words, it does not come to presence as itself insofar as it is a divinity. The god withdraws as a phenomenon (not to mention as an object available for technological manipulation) so that Being may shine forth; the god, then, as divinity, does not come to presence as a being, but as Being.

Being, says Heidegger repeatedly, comes to presence only in beings, and gods are beings for which this is true in a special way. Whereas the Being of the jug comes to presence in the suchness of the jug, the Being of the god *as god* comes to presence as holiness, as the call of Being from itself to itself. Anticipating one of the key issues of future essays, Heidegger writes in *Being and Time*, "The call discourses in the uncanny mode of *keeping silent.*"[26] The caller, says Heidegger, is Dasein in its uncanniness, for Dasein is not addressed in its Being from without, but rather from within. It is in the silence of the wordless word that the call of Being rings. We do not locate it as emanating from any particular source except, perhaps, after the fact.

To carry this line of reasoning a step further, it can only be that the god who comes to presence as such either comes to presence as a recollection or comes to presence as a finite being. Heidegger himself takes cognizance of the possibility of confusing a god with the Holy, which is to say of confusing a being with Being. As Tillich pointed out in explaining ultimate concern, the confusion of the finite with the infinite is the essence of idolatry. The god which comes to presence primarily as a god present in the Present — wonderful, but not ineffable — can be signified and represented and is liable to be an idol or be idolized, it would seem. The god which comes to presence in absence, or which comes to presence in the Present as not-god, allows the light of Being to illuminate beings in their Being, rather than arrogating all radiance to itself. In Heidegger's thought, it is not the role of a god to call attention to itself *as* god, only to Being; for divinities who come to presence as themselves, this can only be done in the mode of not-god or not-present.

Is there a relationship between not-gods and gods who have defaulted? Clearly, the god who is spoken of by Heidegger as having defaulted is an absent god, but we are pushed to ask whether absence alone would constitute a default, especially considering that a case has already been made for thinking the presence of a god *qua* god as a kind of default. Heidegger's thinking about the default of a god is best reconnected with its context of a discussion of the double concealment of compound forgetfulness.

In forgetfulness, the default of the god occurs, but there is no blame to be assigned because the origin of forgetfulness is falling, an existentiale of Dasein which is never absolutely overcome. In falling, the light of being ceases to illuminate beings, which is much the same thing as a withdrawal of a divinity, only seen from a different perspective. That which withdraws is eventually forgotten and then the forgetfulness is itself forgotten. Heidegger gives enough information to come this far with the notion of forgetting, but remembering is yet another matter. Remembering Being from within this forgetfulness may not be possible; Being may perhaps only be grasped again in our time through the understanding of technology, of the infinity of Nonbeing and the opening up to Being that can occur when the possibilities of ignorance of Being have been played out to the end in fact or in thinking. At the limits of the finite is the opening for the infinite. Until it happens, however, the radically new truth that is promised by this thought remains veiled as impossibility.

If a god cannot come to presence as a god without calling attention to itself at the expense of the Being of beings in the world, and thus failing its commisssion as a herald of Divinity, there must be some other way the god can be discerned by beings who are in the mode of Dasein and still fulfill itself in its Being as god. Robert P. Scharlemann suggests a way of thinking this question in his essay "The Being of God When God Is Not Being God."

> The thesis I should like to propound here is that, in the theological tradition, the otherness of God (the being of God when God is not being God, or the freedom of God both to be and not to be) has remained unthought and conceptually forgotten in exactly the same manner as has the question of the meaning of being . . . . Hence, just as the symptom of the forgottenness of the meaning of being lies in our regarding the question "What does it mean for X to be what it is?" as nonsensical, so the symptom of the forgottenness of the otherness of God lies in our regarding as unintelligible the symbol of God (existent deity) which is the being of God when God is not being God.[27]

There remains for a god the kind of presence that a symbol has, which is the presencing of a different kind of Being from what comes to presence when a divinity appears as such. The god which presences as a symbol presences in the mode of absence.

If our brief account of the dynamics of hierophany holds, then it seems that gods can have the Being of gods only in epiphany or the event of withdrawal. In epiphany, the light of Being is pure and infinite. Following upon an epiphany, the light perceptibly fades, but the memory and the glow may remain. From the phenomenological analysis of *Being and Time*, it is clear that Heidegger's fallen Dasein would never miss the gods who withdrew as it turned to its various entertainments and preoccupations, but then it is not fallen Dasein which discerns the withdrawal of gods. Only those who watch and attend to Being would sense the change marked by the advent of absence and give a name to that which remains in the ensemble by dropping out of the ensemble. Authentic Dasein in general may possess the requisite sensitivity, but in this sphere, it is uniquely the poet who gives the names.

The names of the gods are only the names of the absence of Divinity. They are the stage-names of Nonbeing, of the *Scheidung* that separates *Schein* from *Sein*. This is how the infinite is named without thereby becoming finite. A god which is not forgotten, whose absence is remembered as absence and not counterfeited into sham presence, still beckons to mortals and thus gathers them as they attend to the Being of beings; such a god still gathers mortals who follow the way revealed by the withdrawing god, the god who disappears into Nonbeing as the Nothing beyond the Not-yet. Following the trail of the beckoning, withdrawing god into the Not-yet and attending to the light of Being, beings are free to disclose their own possibilities and realize their own potentiality-for-Being. The disclosure of Dasein's authentic possibilities is concomitantly a disclosure of authenticity itself and falling as well; it is a disclosure of Dasein's attainment of itself in its Being. The god, who by its own withdrawal and absence gathers beings unto itself by drawing them after it into the region revealed in *Ent-scheidung*, does Being's bidding by bringing beings to belong authentically in the Open, in their Being.

With the naming of the Open, the issue of nearness and farness returns in a new way. In the remembered absence of the god, the god is near in the sense of a recollected past and an adventing future. Still, the god is also far, because absent and withdrawing. Ontically, this nearness-in-farness is manifest in two ways: as the transitoriness of mystical experience that James and others report, and as the experience of a pivotal event which seems to change one's life, introducing a definite "before" and "after."

Religions tend to heighten the nearness of their gods while ideologies tend either implicitly or explicitly to emphasize the farness of all gods. Neither emphasis can be denied and both seem better thought in terms of absence than of presence. The absence of a god may eventuate in a feeling of being let down, but it is no cause for nostalgia or dismay about a "lost" god, since this absence is the condition of the adventure and discovery that lift human existence beyond mere biology.

In thinking the absence of divinities, another kind of nostalgia shows up as possible, even though it is never appropriate or authentic for Dasein. The thinking of the absence of gods may evoke myths of a "lost golden age," which is always fabled to have been strikingly different from whatever happens to be the case in the current epoch. Since the presence of the god maintains in those days an age of innocence, there is no motivation for a race into Nonbeing, which is the condition of the bringing up of its "there" to Dasein.[28] In *Being and Time*, the bringing up of its "there" to Dasein is a function of anxiety (*Angst*), which is experienced in the encounter with Nothing in one's grasping the possibility of death. Dasein's dash into Nonbeing is fraught with anxiety for its "there," which is disclosed as "being at stake." It is in this state of mind that the true import of decisions regarding gods becomes clear. Anxiety is the "push" that moves Dasein beyond presence into Nonbeing; and there is a "pull" also: "This projection into Nothing on the basis of hidden dread (*Angst*) is the overcoming of what-is in totality: Transcendence."[29] The beckoning heralds of Divinity are finally shown to be necessary to the Being of the jug *as thing* in that it is their absence which indirectly puts mortals in possession of the "there," without which they would necessarily relate to the jug as to any other object.

The absence of the god and the call to follow into the uncharted territory of Nonbeing grant the possibility of faith. Faith emerges here as a living according to a decision which unifies Dasein with the withdrawing god and preserves the light of Being. Thus, faith is shown to be the essence of religion.

Notes

[1] "Das Ding," p. 45; "The Thing," p. 173.

[2] "Das Ding," p. 45; "The Thing," p. 172.

[3] Martin Heidegger, "Die onto-theo-logische Verfassung der Metaphysik," and "The Onto-theo-logical Constitution of Metaphysics," *Identity and Difference*, tr. Joan Stambaugh. New York, Harper and Row, 1969.

[4] Martin Heidegger,"Wozu Dichter?" *Holzwege*. Frankfurt/M: Klostermann, 1972, p. 248; "What Are Poets For?" *Poetry, Language, Thought*, tr. Albert Hofstadter. New York: Harper and Row, 1975, p. 91.

[5] "Das Ding," p. 45; "The Thing," p. 173.

[6] UK, p. 31; OWA, p. 42.

[7] "Das Ding," p. 50; "The Thing," p. 178.

[8] "Das Ding," p. 45; "The Thing," p. 173. The translation would be clearer with a comma after "outpouring."

[9] "Das Ding," p. 51, translation mine. A. Hofstadter's English takes some liberties which radically affect the sense of the passage. Since the passage is not long but is important, we give the original German and a new translation to compare: "Die Göttlichen sind die winkenden Boten der Gottheit. Aus dem verborgenen Walten dieser erscheint der Gott in sein Wesen, das ihn jedem Vergleich mit dem Anwesenden entzieht." (Heidegger) "The divinities are the beckoning messengers of the godhead. Out of the hidden sway of the divinities the god emerges as what he is, which removes him from any comparison with beings that are present." (Hofstadter, p. 178) "The divinities are the beckoning heralds of Divinity. Out of its (Divinity's) hidden sway, the god appears in its being-itself (*Wesen*), which removes it from any comparison with that which comes to presence (*dem Anwesenden*)." (the translation used

here) The point we are concerned with is that the god's being-itself makes it ontologically impossible for the god to come to presence *as* itself.

[10] "Das Ding," p. 50; "The Thing," p. 178.

[11] "Das Ding," p. 51; "The Thing," p. 178.

[12] "Das Ding," p. 55; "The Thing," p. 182.

[13] "Das Ding," p. 55; "The Thing," p. 182.

[14] Martin Heidegger, "Nachwort zu: Was ist Metaphysik?" *Wegmarken*. Frankfurt/M: Klostermann, 1978, p.305; "What Is Metaphysics?" *Existence and Being*, tr. R.F.C. Hull and Alan Crick. South Bend, IN: Gateway, 1949, p. 355.

[15] Martin Heidegger, "Das Wesen der Sprache," *Unterwegs zur Sprache*. Pfullingen: Neske, 1975, p. 210; "The Nature of Language," *On the Way to Language,* tr. Peter Hertz and Joan Stambaugh. New York: Harper and Row, 1971, p. 103.

[16] "Das Ding," p. 50; "The Thing," pp. 177-178.

[17] Hwa Yol Jung, "The Orphic Voice and Ecology," MS.

[18] "Das Ding," p. 50; "The Thing," p. 178.

[19] "Das Wesen der Sprache," p. 215, translation mine. Original: "Welt-bewëgende Sage"; the usual translation of words related to the German *Bewegung* is some variant of the verb "to move," as in the rendering by Peter Hertz, "world-moving Saying." ("The Nature of Language," p. 107) The usual translation is justified on grounds that the German *bewegen* usually does mean "to move." On the other hand, Heidegger goes to great lengths, even so far as to include the introduction of a weird variant spelling, in order to distinguish his use of the word from the usual use. Given this, it seems appropriate to call attention to Heidegger's innovative departure from standard practice somehow. The neologism "enrouting" was chosen because its stem, "route," corresponds semantically to the German *Weg* and because it carries simultaneously the senses of moving and providing a way. There is an added "bonus" back in the etymology of the word, as it comes from the Latin *rumpere*, meaning "to break," which was used in the phrase *rupta via*, a broken road (of which there were many in the later days of the Roman Empire), thence *rupta* and the route. Further back, in reconstructed Indo-European, the word's original stem signified not only breaking, but also tearing out and tearing apart. This we connect up with Heidegger's concept of *Ent-scheidung*, usually translated as "decision." Being *en route* joins the breaks in the road just as de-cision conjoins beings in their Being.

[20] "Das Wesen der Sprache," p. 215; "The Nature of Language," p. 107.

[21] "Wozu Dichter?" p. 248; "What Are Poets For?" p. 91.

[22] Ibid.

[23] William Richardson suggests a translation of "*Schein*" as "seeming-to-be," which removes the ambiguity Heidegger built into his exposition with the choice of "*Schein*." The neologism "apparence" retains the ambiguity of the Latin *parere* and, in effect, goes Heidegger one better with the incorporation of the preposition *ad* into the word, which captures the directionality inherent in coming to presence. All is not gain, however, since the play in German between senses of "seeming" and "shining" in *Schein* are lost. Heidegger himself does not settle on a single sense of *Schein*. Cf. William Richardson, S.J., *Heidegger: Through Phenomenology to Thought*. The Hague: Martinus Nijhoff, 1974, pp. 263, 284-286.

[24] *Einführung in die Metaphysik*. p. 84; translation mine. Original: " . . . eine Scheidung im . . . Zusammen von Sein, Unverborgenheit, Schein und Nichtsein . . . ."

[25] This is a variant of the "resoluteness" of *Being and Time*, Section One. The category does not apply to gods.

[26] SZ, p. 277; BT, p. 322.

[27] Robert P. Scharlemann, "The Being of God When God Is Not Being God," *Deconstruction and Theology*, ed. Carl A. Raschke. New York: The Crossroad Publishing Co., 1982, p. 88.

[28] The doctrine of *creatio ex nihilo* appears in a new light with this thought.

[29] *Was ist Metaphysik?*, p.117; "What is Metaphysics?" p.344.

SECTION TWO

Ontologically, language and Dasein are mirrors for each other: we can see what our acts of thinking-being are by their expression in language, and we can understand language by an awareness of our acts of thinking-being. Dasein is a thinking that is a being, as language is a thing that is a thought.

— *Robert P. Scharlemann*

VII. Note on the Definition of "Theology"

The difference between religion and ideology is seen not only at the ontological level, in the structures that prefigure and determine existence prior to all factical symbol systems, but also in the theological language that takes up and elaborates the existential polemic. In order to present this difference as a tension which can seek faithful expression in theology, however, a sufficiently comprehensive definition of "theology" is necessary. While there may well be as many understandings of theology as there are theologians, it is still possible to evolve a sense of the term which does justice to common usage and yet grants the latitude for theology to bring both religion and ideology to language. If "theology" is to receive authentically inquisitive thematic attention, however, it is methodologically necessary to disrupt the tranquilized understanding of the they-self, which either does not care what theology is or is already satisfied that it knows what theology is. The they-self is disrupted by calling its ideology's "theology" into question in the course of a hermeneutic investigation.

Despite differences in definition, all understandings of theology belong to the *tradition* of theology. One of the traditional formulations of the definition of theology is "faith seeking understanding," a translation of the Latin *fides quaerens intellectum.* This phrase has been chosen because of its prominent place in the tradition and, by implication, in our ontology of theology. It has already determined understandings of theology for generations by giving the words; what these words say in the present situation, however, is a matter of interpretation. For clarity, a general interpretation of "theology" is called for prior to the rudimentary ontological analysis of the four situations of theology suggested below.

In the opening pages of a discussion of Anselm's proof of the existence of God, Karl Barth finds it apposite to discuss Anselm's understanding of the phrase *fides quaerens intellectum*. Barth's treatment is especially useful as a reference point which gives a traditional conception of the formula that spearheaded scholasticism. Anselm clearly thought that the rational path of theological thinking had two purposes, to prove theological propositions by reason and to make people happy that reason was able to do these things. This, says Barth, is what faith wants. Barth argues in Anselm's name against the idea that rational proof was a substitute for faith or that faith could be created by such exhibitions. Reason is no more a matter of necessity for faith than God is governed by necessity, Barth's Anselm says.

Barth's position is set forth when he writes, "It is my very faith that summons me to knowledge."[1] The knowledge that Barth is speaking of is knowledge of God, which is problematical but possible wherever traditional metaphysics reigns. Within that framework, there can be posited a correspondence between the thinking of one who is led by grace faithfully to seek God and the Being of God, which is held to be both knowable and incomprehensible. Theological knowledge is true because it is an expansion of the creeds; if it questions them or denies them, then it ceases to be faithful and loses its claim to truth, reports Barth. Even though theological statements may be true, they are not final truth for Anselm, if for no other reason than the incommmensurability of imperfect human knowledge and the perfect God. In Anselm's view, God decides what shall be revealed and what shall stay concealed at any given time.

Like the Heideggerian divinities, Anselm's God is not to be found initially present-at-hand. Writes Barth with a sympathetic assurance whose ontic basis is not readily apparent to the reader, "This remoteness is clearly an objective remoteness of God himself — God is absent, he dwells in light inapproachable."[2] What Anselm wants is for this absent God to show himself to thought and guide it to truth.

We see in this attitude something different from the worn caricature of the confident, calculating, Scholastic system-builder, but when all is said and done, correction of the old stereotype turns out to be mostly a matter of incidental interest. The belief in divinely guided reason as the way to truth determines that the results of an Anselmian meditation will look very nearly the same as if autonomous reason alone had built the metaphysical system; reason will have performed about the same operations on the same creeds and the joy at glimpsing the truth of the faith, even if it be recognized as a partial truth, will also probably be about the same. Even more radically than Aquinas, Anselm's faith in the God who reveals gives him faith in an *adaequatio intellectus et rei*. This *adaequatio* operates as the basis of systematic theology from Origen onward. As Heidegger summarizes it, preserving much of Anselm's basic outlook, in his early essay, "Phenomenology and Theology,"

> . . . theology is not systematic because it breaks up the totality of the content of faith into a row of loci, in order then to compartmentalize them anew within the boundaries of a system and from that to prove the validity of this system. It is not systematic through the production of a system, but the other way around, through an *avoidance* of that in the sense that it simply exposes to the light the inner *systema* of the Christ event as such, that is, it seeks to bring the believer as one who understands conceptually into the history of revelation. [3]

Resonances with Anselm's sense of reason notwithstanding, Heidegger's thinking of theology shows the effects of the centuries between him and the Scholastics as he refines his definition to exclude the possibilities that God can be the theme or object of theology, that the actual relationship of God and human beings can be explicated by theology, that theology is the study of religion, that theology is a study of the religious conditions and experiences of humanity, that theology is a kind of analysis that discovers God in man. Theology appears to Heidegger in this essay as a science whose knowledge begins in faith and returns to faith; he supplements this position in a later (1964) statement, saying that theology also has to decide out of its primary revelation how to define its own discourse, that it cannot let philosophy or natural science make those kinds of decisions for it. This is Heidegger's way of explaining how faith is primary for theology. It does not seem to support the idea that faith itself is a proper theme of theology, except insofar as one concretely attends to the faith of the faithful in a given religion.

"*Fides*," the word usually translated as "faith," is closely related to the Latin verb *fidere*. This verb does not mean simply "to believe"; that semantic task in Latin is handled for the most part by *credere*. *Fidere* has more to do with trust or remaining true (and the relationship of the Germanic "trust" and "true" is as close as the spelling suggests). The trusting and remaining true of *fidere* are not oriented toward propositions, especially not ontico-empirical propositions; they have much more to do with dispositions. *Credere*, which has to do with propositions that are either believed or not believed, is a moment of thinking. *Fidere*, on the other hand, is not a moment of thinking, but an attitude of being. *Fidere* speaks of having a feeling of confidence. Both *fidere* and *credere* are used in connection with religion, but, despite the semantic closeness of "faith" and "belief" in contemporary English parlance, these Latin antecedents of the modern English words are not interchangeable. Our interest in theology here leads to a thinking of *fides* with frequent reference to religion, though these religious overtones do not seem to be essential to the word etymologically.

With reference to religion, faith can be thought of in two aspects: a self-oriented aspect, which originates in visionary experience of authentically enrouting oneself, and an other-oriented apect, which originates in relation to a divinity. These two primary aspects of faith are not recently assigned, nor are they idiosyncratic segmentations peculiar to this project; they derive from the structure of existence as thought in the German tradition at least a century before Heidegger. As Friedrich Schleiermacher wrote, around the turn of the nineteenth century, "In self-consciousness, there are only two elements: the one expresses the existence of the subject for itself, the other its co-existence with an other."[4] Faith is a mode of self-consciousness. Recalling Nietzsche's genealogical thoughts about the origin of religion, we imagine the self-oriented aspect of faith manifesting itself ontically as a feeling of confidence, while the other-oriented aspect of faith would coordinately be imagined manifesting itself as a feeling of uncertainty. Since it contains these two aspects, faith is categorically a structurally complex phenomenon, irreducible to either of its components. When the feeling of confidence comes to the fore and dominates existence, its absoluteness is always conditioned by the contingency and insufficiency that are entailed in the relation of a mortal to a divinity. When relation to a divinity comes to the fore, on the other hand, Dasein's ontologically-mandated "there" still maintains itself as guarantor of difference and preserver of finitude. While in the discussion that follows, the feeling of confidence (not always called precisely that) is more in evidence, the feeling of uncertainty is never far off, since attention to one aspect of faith always evokes the other, even if not explicitly.

In the factical practice of religion, *fidere*'s feeling of confidence can be imagined as being identical with what Schleiermacher called a "feeling of absolute dependence."[5] This apparently oxymoronic juxtaposition of confidence and dependence approaches the idea that Schleiermacher himself seems to have had when he suggested that his readers " . . . now think of the feeling of dependence and the feeling of freedom as *one*."[6] Bringing the two apparently opposed notions of confidence and absolute dependence together (in a structure other than one of transference) sheds light on the preliminary understanding of faith in this discussion. The key word in (the English version of) Schleiermacher's formula, according to Richard R. Niebuhr, is "absolute," which he describes as a problematical rendering of the German *schlechthinnig*. The sense of this word in certain contexts is not far from the German cognate *absolut*, but the connotations of *absolut* are different, especially after Hegel. *Schlechthinnig* suggests that region of the English lexicon where we find "total," "utter," and especially "just plain . . . ," as in "just plain hooked." Qualifications and equivocations do not enter the semantic picture with *schlechthinnig* but the word must be understood to include the existential-structural complexity that Schleiermacher imagines in his proto-psychology. Within the implicitly or explicitly agreed horizons, in any event, there is no limitation on the quality that is named following the adjective. As Niebuhr interprets the term with reference to Schleiermacher's formula,

> Thus, in the phrase *absolute dependence* the substantive word conveys the sense of relation that Schleiermacher believed to stand at the center of self-consciousness, and the adjective *absolute* expresses the fact that this relation determines personal historical existence not in this or that particular capacity alone but in its entirety.[7]

Still, there are horizons, and the implication is that absolute dependence is still finite in the sense that Heidegger uses the term. As Schleiermacher puts it, " . . . our whole self consciousness in relation to the world or to its individual parts remains enclosed within these limits."[8] It is thus a dependence of the sort that obtains when a particular general understanding holds sway over consciousness so exclusively that no other possibility of understanding can suggest itself on the same (fundamental) level without necessitating a change in the existential paradigm. Within the horizon of understanding, all that is understood is grasped in a unified way, on the same basis. Beyond the horizon of understanding, there is nothing, for it is only as nothing that whatever may be beyond the horizon of understanding is grasped.

That Schleiermacher chose to speak of "feeling" and not "knowledge" places the kind of religion he imagines on a plane where strategies of empirical verification are not appropriate, but not beyond ontological investigation. For Schleiermacher, feeling was prior to knowing, though the two were related in the "abiding-in-self" (*Insichbleiben*)[9] of the subject. Because he assigned priority to feeling " . . . as the inner expression of the underivability of the self . . . "[10] in religion, Schleiermacher was not obliged to enter the religion/science debate and the philosophical theology he developed continues to place religion outside the pale of the empiricist challenge. For Schleiermacher, feeling is essentially autonomous, a primary experience, an experience of being in a particular way. In locating both feeling and knowledge in faith's aspect of "abiding-in-self," Schleiermacher implies that his words are not to be construed as setting up a dichotomy between feeling and thinking, as though it were a matter of choice whether one made decisions on one basis or the other. Feeling and thinking have their own domains such that feeling is both before and after thinking. In this sense of feeling, for example, one would not "feel" that a proposition is valid, since there is no content in feeling that would allow it to be confused with a hunch or hypothesis of validity. One might feel, however, that a proposition is (existentially) true.

The feeling of absolute dependence carries with it a sense of coherence, a sense that one's way of being in the world, as given in one's religion, is at one with the world. To step outside this horizon of understanding would be to step outside all that truly is and is possible. The feeling of absolute dependence thus proximally originates in a recognition that *who* one is and *how* one is in Being can only come to pass if one *is* in existence according to one's religion. Religion should not be conceived in this connection as a set of propositions to be believed, as Schleiermacher also warned against in his separation of religion from objective and conceptual knowledge; it wants to be understood essentially as a **way of being**. The way of religion is sometimes spoken of as a path, conveying the experience through shared linguistic competence with an ontical metaphor that is not only concrete, but also, consonant with the discourse of this project, recognizable as related to Heidegger's thought of *Be-wegung*, enrouting. Ontologically, the way of religion is not a way that "goes anywhere"; it is a way of being underway, *en route*. This being *en route*, it was observed above, binds that which is broken into a unity. This unity is exactly the spatio-temporal unity described in Section II of *Being and Time*. It is by virtue of this unity that all within the horizon of temporality belongs together.[11]

The feeling of absolute dependence, then, is not just a sense of impotence which causes one to look to a more powerful being to do what what one wants to do and somehow cannot. Harvey Cox, interpreting Dietrich Bonhoeffer, disagrees and, in considering an idea of Bonhoeffer's that is reminiscent of Kant's opening in the essay "What is Enlightenment?" offered the thesis that a mature humanity would be beyond religion. Cox wrote:

> But need this man be "nonreligious"? Since for Bonhoeffer
> religion implied an element of dependency, a weakness that
> must be matched by a strength from elsewhere, a need for

answers not to be found by man himself, on his terms, the "man come of age" would *not* be religious. There will be those today, of course, contending with some justification that religion need not mean all of these things and that therefore Bonhoeffer's nonreligious interpretation would not be as radical as it first sounds. Perhaps they are right. Perhaps the meaning of the word "religion" can be so radically redefined that Bonhoeffer's challenge will evaporate. But I doubt it. For the vast majority of people today, especially in America, "religion" still means very much what he had in mind. [12]

Cox is speaking here of an ontical experience of religion which happens to be shared by a large number of people. This ontical experience cannot be surveyed in order to determine anything about the ontology of religion, only to provide exemplary phenomena for the ontology to explain. So, what most Americans happen to think about religion at a given time is essentially irrelevant to the thinking of the ontological problematic of religion itself. In arguing for a religionless humanity, Cox was making a proposal with ontological implications, but his discourse, at least in this brief essay, is all focused at the ontical level. At the ontical level, the feeling of absolute dependence may manifest itself in the way Cox and Bonhoeffer observed, but it may also show up as a sense that all which lies within one's horizon of understanding, including oneself, is truly *as* it is. For as long as the feeling remains, the seamless coherence of this experience logically, radically excludes all other interpretations.

While the world-picture that emerges to the faithful appears ontically unified and exclusive, it does not entail a world always already reduced to the clarity of a single dimension or a single interpretation. What-is may well be as it is in modes of plurality, ambiguity, paradoxicality, or strangeness. In part, this arises from the shifting perceptions that occur in the course of the *Weltspiel*, that is, the polemical play of the fourfold, and in part from the intrusion of anxiety into the closed-off complacency of falling. What lies within one's horizon of understanding is thus not expected to be thoroughly known or revealed, but insofar as it is revealed, it is interpretable in ways that either coerce it to fit in fallen Dasein's closed reality or let it be in the Open. Ontical interpretations are, for Heidegger, basically pre-given by mood in the sense that their epistemological basis is located in mood. "The mood has already disclosed, in every case, Being-in-the-world as a whole, and makes it possible first of all to direct oneself towards something."[13] Explains Heidegger, "Indeed *from the ontological point of view* we must as a general principle leave the primary discovery of the world to 'bare mood'.''[14] Schleiermacher's notion of "feeling of absolute dependence" implies, then, that ultimately there is a resolution which essentially unifies all phenomena within the horizon of understanding; there is no telling, however, what the specific nature of the resolution will be or whether there will ever be an ontical experience of the resolution as such. Authentically, the resolution is the experience of the Open; in falling, it is manifested as the matter-of-factness of taking things for granted.

Ontically, taking things for granted is a trust that what is within the horizon of understanding is factically as it is and belongs where it is in both physical and existential space. One has confidence in the world as it is. Taking-for-granted is not essentially a confidence in the reliability or usefulness of objects present-at-hand in the world, but confidence on principle in the world as it is in its totality, which is the logical basis of all other varieties of confidence. This basic attitude of confidence in the world as it is can be analyzed as an equiprimordial correlate of confidence in oneself as oneself is in the world, thus being inseparable from self-confidence. Such a self-confidence is very different from the mood in which an individual feels self-sufficient and in control of events. The self-confidence that correlates with confidence in the world as it is can be understood as a trusting of the self that is true to its way, a self which is always an already and a not-yet by virtue of one's enrouting historically in the world. A self-confidence of this description can arise only in the experience of being-in-a-way and is absolutely (categorically) dependent upon being-in-a-way. Absolute dependence equals absolute confidence for one who keeps faith. . . .

We understand *fides* existentially, then, as a remaining true to oneself as being-in-a-way. This is not to be construed as inflexible "fidelity to one's convictions," which Schleiermacher warned against.[15] The phenomenon of convictions arises out of being-in-a-way but there is an important distinction to be made between being-in-a-way and convictions in terms of Heidegger's framework. The sense of being-in-a-way is ontological and comes to presence in the phenomenon of mood " . . . in which Dasein is disclosed to itself *prior* to all cognition and volition, and *beyond* their range of disclosure."[16] It appears that convictions, which in this framework are products of the they-self's falling concern, are cognized rationalistically out of one's ideology and volitionally employed as equipment which brings self and world "into line" and which always effects a subsequent modification of authentic being-in-a-way. Convictions, if observed as the non-uniform sedimentations of moods, reveal what Heidegger claimed to be a disclosure of Dasein's thrownness, namely, " . . . an evasive turning away."[17] Convictions, in deriving from the they-self, belong to a metaphysics of presence and the history of the oblivion of Being. This is not to say that convictions in themselves have no legitimate place in human existence, only that their place is essentially derivative.

For epistemological reasons, *fides* cannot be an intentional remaining true to the way *as* way since the way can be known only insofar as one is in it and realizes it. As Heidegger recognized when he said that one who was on the scent of something did not speak about it, one who is on the way has no ontical experience of an independently subsisting way which is present-at-hand and available to be spoken about. Except as projection of convictions, an inauthentic possibility in the present framework, a way cannot come to presence and still be a true way. Thus, faith is ontologically prohibited from owing anything of its Being to ontical phenomena which have been brought to presence in empirically intended propositions or specific expectations of the behavior of other beings. *Fides* indeed has more to do with dispositions than propositions, since religion as being-in-a-way grants the position that is prior to all dispositions, and faith grants the continuity which maintains enrouting.

At the opposite end of the phrase *fides quaerens intellectum* is the word that is usually translated as "understanding." In making this translation, a danger arises in the possibility of identifying the Latin word too closely with its English relatives. In that misreading, *intellectus* is perceived through one's semantic competence as the virtual equivalent of "intellect," with overtones of the contemporary sense of "intellectuality." "Intellect," in the semantics of modern English, conveys much heavier connotations of rationality and detachment than *intellectus* does in Latin. As in the case of *fides*, a look at verb forms is again revealing of the sense and resonances of the noun.

Intellectus is related to the verb *intellegere* (also spelled *intelligere*; the slight variation does not seem to be semantically significant). This verb basically means "to perceive" or "to understand." It does not mean "to think rationally about something." The verbs *cogitare* and *reri* mostly cover that semantic ground. It is only recently that *intellectus* has seemed like a word closely connected with figuring out. Heidegger's analysis of technology can be read to suggest that the technological world view has determined the word's present semantic situation to be such, since for technique, there is a categorical refusal to recognize any mode of understanding other than one based on calculation, so what *intellectus* does would only be conceivable as calculation. Jacques Ellul expresses this same thought in *The Technological Society*:

> Technique has become autonomous: it has fashioned an omnivorous world which obeys its own laws and which has

> renounced all traditon. Technique no longer rests on tradi-
> tion, but rather on previous technical procedures; and its
> evolution is too rapid, too upsetting, to integrate the older
> traditions.[18]

At an earlier time, the semantic field of *"intellectus"* covered understanding at all levels; the sense was one of integrated understanding, a
cooperation of rational and non-rational. The tendency to reduce understanding to a single dimension, which simplifies Being and facilitates the
operations of technique, now works against any broader conception of
intellectus.

Close to the origin of *intellectus* is the verb *legere*, which means "to
choose," then "to survey" and "to read." This root shows up in English
words such as "select" and "elect." There are endless "etymological"
interpretations that can be developed from the reconstructed Indo-
European **leg-* root, which similarly has to do with choosing. This
thought of choosing is further articulated in the Latin *legere*, which has
the additional sense of "gathering." This sense shows up in the German
lesen, which means not only "to read," but also "to harvest." *Intellectus*
takes *legere* and couples it with *inter*, a word used for relations expressed
in English by both "between" and "among." This yields a combination
which speaks of "choosing among" or, more properly, "among-choos-
ing." It is legitimate, even by conservative standards, to follow this kind
of etymological possibility in Latin since *fides quaerens intellectum* was
originally thought in Latin and the phrase's etymological relationships
are very close to the surface there.

The conventions of preposition complementation in English grammar favor a reading of "choosing among" that places a direct object after
the verb to form a complete verb phrase. By this reading, *intellectus*
would become a choosing among things which separates things such that
some are chosen (and thus set apart) and some are not. This is not the
most plausible reading in the present case, though, partly because it
makes *intellegere* indistinguishable from *selegere*, the verb that directly
gives us "select." It also fails to think the verb *intellegere* in its own
terms, with deleterious effects on the thinking of *intellectus*; specifically,
construing *intellegere* as a selection among things in which an action is
directed at an object, departs from a thinking of the verb and leaps to a
presumption of its meaning, which is subsequently analyzed for its effect
on a posited object. If *intellectus* is to be thought at all, then thinking
must remain with the verb of which it appears as a participle, in which it
participates, as Heidegger would suggest. Resembling a participial form
of the verb *intellegere*, *intellectus* is able to retain a heavily verbal

character. The noun is the name of the action of this verb, a point which favors its rendering as "understanding" on the condition that the verbal character of "understanding" is kept in mind; its occurrence in a direct object situation tends to nominalize it strongly, but this is to be resisted.

The preposition "*inter*," which relies on context for the distinction that shows up in the English pair "between" and "among," places the action of choosing in a semantic space defined by "among" or "between." The action of the verb is governed by its prepositional component. While it was not legitimate to think the verb by going outside it to focus on an affected direct object because there would be a presumption of precisely what was not known, viz. the meaning of the verb, it is legitimate to think the verb by going more deeply into its action on its own terms. One way into this depth is by way of a consideration of any entailments of the governing prepositional component of the verb. The "*inter*" places the action of the verb between or among some things, but what these "somethings" are remains unspecified for the most part. All that can be assumed is that the "somethings" must be possible elements of the world. For this reason, the action of *intellegere* is placed between or among possibilities. This strategy of interpretation also works to recommend the translation of *intellectus* by "understanding," since the "under" has, in its comparatively recent Germanic past, the meaning of "among" as well as the sense of "below," and thus plausibly yields an interpretation of "understanding" as "a standing among." When one stands among (possibilities), that is when one can have experience; our language encourages us to see experience as bound up with understanding. Heidegger observes the connection as he writes in *Being and Time*, "Understanding signifies one's projecting oneself upon one's current possibility of Being-in-the-world; that is to say, it signifies existing as this possibility."[19] This element of experience in the structure of understanding further links "understanding" with *intellectus* by way of the alternative translation of *intellectus* as "perception." This aspect of the word does not come to the fore just now, but it is not totally concealed either.

In light of these attributes of *intellectus*, there is not much reason to sustain the reading of "intellectual analysis" which is superficially suggested to speakers of English by the appearance of this word. *Intellectus*, then, is understood to mean "choosing among possibilities." In this interpretation, the ambiguity of the "among" cannot be lost, so it is necessary to remember both senses, namely, that the choosing takes place in the midst of possibilities and that possibilities are themselves chosen. *Intellectus* is located in the world as given and never leaves it; it is definitely not the kind of flight from concreteness that has become known as "intellectualizing." It is, rather, a de-cisive (*ent-scheidend*) choosing, in that what is chosen is joined in the choosing and understood ontologically as joined, even though ontic experience may not deliver this information explicitly. As far as the usual sense of "understanding" is concerned, it is not hard to reconcile the thought of "a grasp of the meaning of . . . " with the fact that the meaning which is grasped in understanding is necessarily one of an inventory of possibilities, at least one of which must be chosen according to the logic of the field within the horizon of understanding. This choosing, which is a grasping of possibility, does not entirely eliminate the possibilities not chosen, or grasped, from understanding, for all that lies within the horizon is always already grasped in a preliminary way on the basis of the spatio-temporal horizon itself. Unlike the choosing of *selegere*, which is a kind of selection that divides and extracts, the choosing of *intellectus* joins and remains among. It is not purely positive, but preserves both positivity and negativity, understands both positively and negatively. This will be a significant point in connection with the warrant of theology and our construction of the relationship of theology to religion and ideology.

Lying between *fides* and *intellectus* is *quaerens*, a present participle which is traditionally rendered into English with the Germanic "seeking." Seeking can happen in two modes. In one mode, the seeking is an attempt to find something that is needed. In the phrase "faith seeking understanding," this reading of the word "seeking" posits a deficiency in faith that stands to be remedied by the finding of "understanding." The second mode of seeking has the sense of looking for something from a position of superiority, as in the situation of authorities seeking a fugitive from the law. In the first case, the issue that calls for a seeking is one of completeness/incompleteness, while in the second it is a question of absoluteness, as interpreted above in connection with "a feeling of absolute dependence." There are reasons to lean toward emphasizing the second mode in this interpretation of "faith seeking understanding." From this construction of "seeking," any reading of the traditional guiding definition of theology which casts faith in a position of insufficiency that somehow requires it to seek help from "understanding" or which presumes that faith does not understand is excluded. Faith seeks understanding in some other way. A closer inspection of *quaerere* suggests how.

The primary meaning of *quaerere* is more connected with asking and interrogation than with what is conventionally understood as seeking. *Quaerere* is the root of words like "question," "inquire," and, tellingly, "require." *Quaerere* is not associated with naive ignorance or "being in the dark"; this word in Latin has undertones of doubt and connotations of directed action. It does not suggest a general skepticism either, though, and it does not name the kind of asking that is associated with the catholicity of "an inquiring mind." *Quaerere* also does not have to do with free-form curiosity. It is questioning with an agenda which seeks "the facts" and aims toward establishing a basis for judgement. It is not an opportunistic or playful kind of questioning, not roguery (in the old sense of the word that had to do with a vagabond's kind of mischief, trickery, and play). One must therefore be careful with the translation of *quaerens* as "seeking"; the word's own associations bring it much closer to "questioning." It is, moreover, apparently a kind of questioning that will not relent until satisfactory answers are forthcoming, and it is a questioning that doubts in advance every answer that is proposed. *Quaerere* in Latin names a questioning that arises not out of inquisitiveness for its own sake, but in order to monitor a situation for some specific purpose. It signifies a responsible action of seeking out what is to be monitored.

The traditional definition of theology which has been proposed to guide this section's discussion of the four major types of theology can now be restated in a way that brings out a preliminary sense of "theology" that will be adequate to serve as a proximate point of departure. This preliminary sense of "theology" is already more than an ideologically-given definition because it has evolved from a hermeneutic inquiry into the tradition of "theology." On this basis, we read *fides quaerens intellectum* to say "remaining-true-to-oneself-as-being-in-a-way monitoring and questioning one's own choosing-among-possibilities." Thus focused, theology appears as the coming to language of this monitoring questioning through which the absolute sway of the decisions of religions and ideologies is faithfully maintained in the choices and joinings that are made in the midst of beings in the world. These choices must always answer to faith. And faith answers to Nothing.

There is one further implication that is contained in *fides quaerens intellectum* which bears note. It has to do with the answers to faith's questions. The formula does not specify what kind of question faith poses. It seems, though, that the questions of faith must be yes-or-no questions; a choice as possibility either accords or does not accord with the pre-given totality of the world. The nature of a possiblity's accord or discord only comes to language in interpretation, and interpretation is always a projection of one's Being-in-the-world. Theology is this projective interpretation in which religion or ideology and possibility are reconciled in one or the other of Dasein's modes of Being-in-the-world.

Notes

¹ Karl Barth, *Anselm: Fides Quaerens Intellectum*, tr. I.W. Robinson. Richmond, VA: John Knox Press, 1960, p. 18.

² Op. cit., p. 38.

³ Martin Heidegger, "Phänomenologie und Theologie," *Wegmarken*, translation mine. Frankfurt/M: Klostermann, 1978, pp. 57-58. Original: " . . . die Theologie ist nicht dadurch systematisch, dass sie das Ganze des Glaubensgehaltes in eine Reihe von Loci zerstückelt, um diese dann wieder in den Rahmen eines Systems einzufächern und hernach die Gültigkeit dieses Systems zu beweisen. Sie ist nicht systematisch durch Herstellung eines Systems, sondern umgekehrt durch eine *Vermeidung* desselben in dem Sinne, dass sie einzig das innere *systema* des christlichen Geschehens als solchen unverdeckt ans Licht, d.h. den Gläubigen als begrifflich Verstehenden in die Offenbarungsgeschichte zu bringen sucht."

⁴ Schleiermacher, *The Christian Faith*, p. 13.

⁵ Op. cit., p. 16.

⁶ Schleiermacher, op. cit., p. 14.

⁷ Richard R. Niebuhr, op. cit., p. 183.

⁸ Schleiermacher, op. cit., p. 15.

⁹ Op. cit., p. 5ff.

¹⁰ Niebuhr, op. cit., p. 181.

¹¹ We recall that Heidegger eventually repudiated the logic by which spatiality was derived from temporality in paragraph 70 of *Being and Time*. In admitting into the discussion a spatio-temporal unity of uncertain ontological character, we leave aside the question of deriving space from time or vice-versa. In the question of why there is something and not nothing, there echoes a kind of surprise at the negation of nothing that has come about. Unspoken is the knowledge that with the negation of nothing, which is the condition of spatiality, has come the negation of eternity, which is the condition of temporality. All that is demanded to fulfill the formal requirements of the kind of existential analytic we have been using is recognition of the fact of a spatio-temporal unity as an existentiale of Dasein. We should note that recent discoveries in the physical sciences, which challenge usual perceptions of space and time, have no bearing on the analysis of the structure of Dasein. If certain tentative findings are extrapolated, there are apparent radical implications for the thinking the Being of human beings, but not as Dasein.

¹² Harvey Cox, "Beyond Bonhoeffer? The Future of Religionless Christianity," *The Secular City Debate*, ed. Daniel Callahan. New York:

Macmillan, 1966, p. 213. We restrict ourselves to what is written in the essay quoted above as an example of one point of view. We are not concerned here to relate it to subsequent publications by Cox in which either refinements or modifications occur.

[13] SZ, p. 136; BT, p. 176.
[14] SZ, p. 138; BT, p. 177.
[15] Schleiermacher, op. cit., pp. 8-12.
[16] SZ, p. 136; BT, p. 175.
[17] SZ, p. 136; BT, p. 175.
[18] Ellul, op. cit., p. 14.
[19] SZ, p. 387; BT, p. 439.

An atheist for atheism's sake knows no God as the wholly Other — or as that which makes man quite another — because he views himself as God. An atheist for God's sake on the other hand, destroys all images, traditions, and religious feelings of his own that unite him with God in an illusive fashion; and he does so for the sake of the inexpressibly living, wholly different God. His atheism is negative theology.

— Jurgen Moltmann

VIII. Concerning the Warrant of Theology

Concern for the warrant of an utterance arises with the perception that there is something at stake which will be decided or disposed in the utterance. This is the general way in which utterances emerge out of the matter-of-fact to become present-at-hand and is an instance of the general fact of care as an existentiale of Dasein. The way Heidegger explains it, "Care, as a primordial structural totality, lies 'before' every factical 'attitude' and 'situation' of Dasein, and it does so existentially *a priori*; this means that it always lies *in* them."[1] There is no question of warrants until one is confronted with an utterance that stands out *as decisive* for the world that comes to presence through the primordially-given structural totality of care, and becomes questionable by virtue of its presence-at-hand. In that case, all interested parties seek to satisfy themselves that the utterance in question is both possible and meaningful. An inquiry into warrants formally clarifies the basis of an utterance and makes way for further questioning or elaboration. Every decisive utterance must be ready to answer a warrant call, Anthony Flew suggests in "Theology and Falsification," even though there are certain to be differences of opinion on what constitutes philosophical defensibility.[2] It is perhaps an indication of the inherent decisiveness of theology that theological discourse has frequently been presented with warrant calls. It is also an indication of the nature of religion's presence-at-hand that Flew can conflate the truth criteria of philosophy and religion.

In asserting that all decisive utterances must be ready to answer a warrant call, only one claim is being made here concerning the standpoint from which the call may issue or the standards by which the reply will be judged: formally, all warrant calls originate in questions of truth as *adaequatio intellectus et rei*. While not occupying himself much with the term *intellectus*, Heidegger makes use of this formula in *Being and Time* in a way that dovetails with the reading of the term proposed in Chapter VII above; for his own purposes, he suggests an unconventional interpretation of *adaequatio* that leads him to abandon the reading of the word as "agreement in particulars" and instead think of it primarily as naming a kind of relation of entities grounded in Being, the knowledge of which " . . . demonstrates itself *as true*."[3] Further, says Heidegger,

> What gets demonstrated is the Being-uncovering of the assertion . . . .What is to be demonstrated is not an agreement of knowing with its object, still less of the psychical with the physical; but neither is it an agreement between 'contents of consciousness' among themselves. What is to be demonstrated is solely the Being-uncovered of the entity itself — *that entity* in the "how" of its uncoveredness. This uncoveredness is confirmed when that which is put forward in the assertion (namely the entity itself) shows itself *as that very same thing. "Confirmation"* signifies *the entity's showing itself in its selfsameness.*[4]

Warrants are determinations that what-is will be confirmed as it is, not necessarily that knowledge will match up with prior convictions. A warrant is an explication of the basis of that discourse in which the basis of the discourse shows itself to be viable. Today, perhaps the most common type of warrant call in thoughtful conversation originates in analytic philosophy; while this type of warrant call is neither the only possible way to question the foundations of an utterance nor the only appropriate one, it is one that is often heard and one that could conceivably be directed at the present project. Though warrants have been most prominently discussed in the conversations of analytic philosophy, warrant calls are by no means restricted to that specialty. The warrant calls of analytic philosophy appear to have their primary use in matters of logical consequence and empirical falsifiability, that is, whenever the notion of truth-as-agreement operates. In the limited sphere of these types of questions, a warrant call is the beginning of establishing to which domains a present-at-hand statement belongs or can belong, an operation which conseqently determines meaningfulness, truth, or falsity of the statement virtually in advance, viz. according to the positivistic assumptions that apparently operate throughout analytic philosophy.

We do not have to accept all of analytic philosophy's assumptions here to make use of some of its procedures regarding warrants.

Even though analytic philosophy's warrant calls seem to have their greatest utility in science and law, one of analytic philosophy's classic cases involves theological metaphysics. It deals with theology's presumed warrant to speak of God and it illustrates both the strength and weakness of conceiving warrants in terms of agreement as the refinement of powers of discrimination goes hand-in-hand with a dramatic narrowing of the field of vision. In considering the example at hand, allowance for the somewhat dated character of the argument should be made in view of the fact that about a half century of theological ferment has taken place since the critique was made and also that the term "theology" is taken there more or less at face value within the philosopher's own framework. Still, the general outlook of A.J. Ayer represents a necessary step on the way to understanding the nature of religion that must be made by anyone who tries to think the problem through. Ayer's analysis of some surface features of myths and creeds is significant not only historically but also in the dynamics of the present as the voice of common sense.

In the essay *Language, Truth and Logic* Ayer is found defending empiricism against the claim that judgements of value constitute a kind of knowledge. The positivist sense of "knowledge" (i.e. of the things themselves) operates throughout the discussion. In the course of his analysis, Ayer performs his own philosophical house-cleaning; he rules out normative ethics on grounds of their not having any empirical basis, allows a discipline of descriptive ethics because it logically must have an empirical basis, distinguishes expressions of feeling from assertions of feeling, and also argues " . . . that the phenomena of moral experience cannot fairly be used to support any rationalist or metaphysical doctrine whatsoever. In particular, they cannot . . . be used to establish the existence of a transcendent god."[5] At this point, Ayer is not only pursuing Kant, he is also articulating mainstream analytic philosophy's position on religious knowledge, or at least a position that can be taken as typical of that way of thinking. Ayer's logic is essentially duplicated in Flew's article, "Theology and Falsification," and even in Sidney Hook's "Modern Knowledge and the Concept of God."[6] While Ayer's account of theology is largely beside the point as far as the main work of the present project is concerned, it bears inclusion at this juncture because it relates to a warrant that has historically been claimed by some traditional theologians, is still claimed by some today, and is often associated with theology in one of the popular conceptions of the field. By recapitulating Ayer's argument, we gain access at a key point to the thinking of warrants and at the same time take the opportunity to put further distance between "theology" as it comes to presence in this project and the type of theology Ayer criticizes.

The critique begins on what Ayer explicitly sees as a point of commonality between himself and the theologians he is addressing. He proposes conversation with the initial thesis " . . . that the existence of a being having the attributes which define the god of any non-animistic religion cannot be demonstratively proved."[7] Ayer quickly moves to enlist all reasonable persons to his position with the observation that there can only be proof with certainty and that such certainty requires that the premises from which the existence of the god is deduced have to be certain. Empirical propositions, he continues, are only probable at best, and since the existence of a god is an empirical question, it must be uncertain because of the categorical uncertainty of the premises (which are themselves empirical propositions) from which it must be deduced. The only alternative that would provide the kind of certainty that is recognized by analytic philosophy would involve *a priori* propositions. From the closed circle of tautologies that ensues from such propositions, however, only the logical, not the empirical, existence of a god can be deduced. While it is not part of this project to take issue with Ayer point-for-point, we note that elements of unclarity exist in the argument where the notion "god of any non-animistic religion" is introduced as speaking of "a being"; there is a hint of compatibility with the understanding of gods developed above in the discussion of divinities, but there is no basis for adducing any common ground or even any real possibility of fruitful comparative analysis, especially given the remainder of Ayer's chapter on this topic.

The critique in *Language, Truth and Logic* does not stop with the exclusion of certainty of the existence of the gods of non-animistic religions. Once the empirical certainty of these gods has been ruled out, Ayer shifts register and sets out to exclude the empirical probability as well. Ayer's strategy is slightly different when he deals with this question. The empirical probability of a god is analyzed as resting on some manner of perceptible manifestation. Any empirical account must restrict itself narrowly to description of this manifestation alone. Ayer sees that it is unacceptable to define a god exclusively in terms of empirical manifestations, that is, from presence.

If one attempts to go beyond the empirically verifiable data of presence in the quest for a more satisfactory formulation describing a more sufficient god, Ayer reasons, the statements become "metaphysical" and leave the arena of truth, falsehood, and probability altogether. Statements which depart the field in this way cannot logically be taken as literally significant within the framework of analytic philosophy, and within this framework, literal significance is the only significance that is recognized. Thus, it is not possible to arrive at either the empirical certainty or the empirical probability of any being like the traditional Christian God.

Since such a god in the full sense of being God is not an empirically discoverable or knowable entity, utterances which presuppose or logically depend upon the certain or probable existence of that god are, in the terminology of analytic philosophy, "nonsense." Further, this evaluation of language bearing on the problem of gods extends to two other positions on the question, namely, denials of the existence of a god (common atheism) and suspended judgement concerning the factical existence of a god (empiricist agnosticism). In the first of these two additional cases, the thrust of Ayer's critique is that the negation of a nonsense statement is itself nonsense for being bound by nonsensical terms. In the second case, the point is that agnosticism posits a false presumption of verifiability, since Ayer has already shown that the problem is not just a temporary hiatus in epiphanies which causes uncertainty about the existence of a god, but the specifications of an eternal principle.

In view of these findings, Ayer holds that the word "God," when used to refer to an empirical entity of the sort he has described, is not a genuine name. In this, he follows the early Wittgenstein, whose position on this subject is typified in his *Tractatus Logico-Philosophicus* with the sentences:

> In a proposition a name is a representative of an object. Objects can only be named. Signs are their representatives. I can only speak about them: I cannot
> p u t   t h e m   i n t o
> w o r d s .[8]

Since "God" does not refer to an object that can be spoken about sensibly, it is not a name in the ordinary sense for Ayer. On this point, the observable consequences of taking Ayer's position to heart are remarkably close to those of ancient Hebrew piety. Continuing on the tack of the God-as-object critique, he observes that purported descriptions of such a god by mystics are also strictly nonsense, even though they are allegedly based upon mystical experience as a type of empirical encounter. The mystic, according to Ayer, is only reporting a nonverifiable, subjective state. He cites no examples of the kind of description he is criticizing. This completes the picture of Ayer's position in its major points.

Whatever the adequacy of Ayer's analysis, it is at least true that he believes himself to be dealing with issues of religion and theology in a rigorously meaningful and forthright manner. His own claims to meaningfulness are strengthened in the arena of public discourse by the supporting apparatus of a quasi-explicit conception of meaning which allows the logic of his argument to come to the surface insofar as he is aware of it. Though Ayer seems to think that he has formulated a critique that is both relevant and valid for all theology (his chapter title is "Critique of Ethics and Theology"), he has missed this particular objective by a wide margin. Still, he has performed a valid critique of a part of theology, namely that genre of theology which takes itself to be truly as he describes it. In his analysis, then, he can be heard as cautioning against a particular conception of theology which happens to be his own, by all appearances and as Quine has led us to expect; that Ayer intended all theology and mistook the part for the whole is an incidental matter of indifference to the ontological problematic of religion and ideology. What is important for this discussion is that Ayer has apparently found a way to deny theology a warrant to engage in discussion of empirical questions; the condition of resting with Ayer is that thinking be limited to the metaphysics of presence.

Although Ayer's critical undertaking now has the look of a rearguard action, his own suggestion that he is thinking out Kant's problematic more radically than Kant (since no god is posited in *Language, Truth and Logic*) gives his work a possibility of importance it could never have solely on the basis of the depth of its philosophical or theological insight. Even given the early Wittgenstein's contention that philosophy is both before and after science,[9] Ayer does not appear to have considered such a possibility for the *Wissenschaft* of theology. This datum suggests that his intentionality limited understanding of theology such that it was always and only an ostensibly empirical discipline (god science) which would be found to be either warranted or unwarranted by the rules that applied to all empirical disciplines. For Ayer, that condition on knowledge amounts to a dismissal of theological discourse. At this point in the history of theology, given the radical challenges of contemporary critical theory, Ayer's conclusions are not especially provocative in themselves, though other aspects of his position remain contested. These conclusions are no longer important for their novelty, but rather as the basis for constraints on theology.

Constraints on theology condition the ways in which both religions and ideologies can come to language. Because they are systematic, philosophical correctives, they are specific in the way that positive warrants are, but instead of establishing what is possible to say, they establish which possibilities of language will not be realized for as long as they remain in force. There is reason to avoid conceptions of constraints as simple limitations, bounds, restrictions, or statements of arbitrary preference. As the term is being used here, it does not, moreover, signify a type of proposition that could be taken as absolutely true or as absolutely necessary.

Constraints on theology belong to the class of synthetic propositions, statements whose substance is not necessarily contained in their subjects so, for example, one could never arrive at the set of constraints for theology simply by thinking "theology" phenomenologically or, for that matter, by investigating the traditional definition of theology, *fides quaerens intellectum*. Constraints are system-specific; in the case of theology, the constraints in effect are contingent upon understandings prevailing in a community of faith at a given moment in its history. In Heideggerian terms, they belong to the worldhood of the world.

A constraint is not a simple conservative restriction because the possibility that it closes off must already have been explicitly posed *as* a possibility. It is not like a sign that simply says, "Do not go beyond this point," but rather more like one that says, "Do not go to the corner of Lin Sen North Road and Nanking East Road in Taipei when you feel lonely," or, more formally, "Avoid X under conditions Y." Further, the possibility that is closed off by a constraint must have been thought at least far enough along for its undesirable characteristics and/or ramifications to have emerged somehow into presence-at-hand. These characteristics or ramifications become the basis in presence for the constraint. That a possibility has been found undesirable is evidence that it has been thought and understood up to a point; the implication is that what is proscribed in a constraint is therefore not the absolutely unthinkable, but simply the not-to-be-thought, or more precisely, the not-to-be-thought-*as*. The not-to-be-thought differs from the absolutely unthinkable in that it always remains a possibility for thought (even as imagination or as nonsense), while the unthinkable is by definition a null set about which all speaking is highly restricted, since the unthinkable comes to presence as nothing. The not-to-be-thought also differs ontologically from the unthinkable; whereas the unthinkable is for the most part excluded from thought by definition, the not-to-be-thought is excluded by principled decision. Let this be an indication of the role of decision in theology, though by no means a full description. It should be clear that the decisions which are represented in constraints do not restrict subjects of propositions *to* certain possibilities; instead, they restrict subjects *from* certain possibilities, and that entails a prior grasp, however incomplete and problematical, of the possibilities under consideration.

The purpose of constraints is to guard against error. For the moment, let us leave aside the most prominent Heideggerian sense of error as the untruth of concealedness so that error can be imagined as a projection of a decision which does not accord with prior decisions that somehow still hold sway. There is no assumption in this context of agreement with some objective truth, only narrow reference to specifications of existence that arise from factical religions and ideologies. Constraints on theology are negatively decisional, and what they are concerned with, namely, error as violation of a paradigm, is negatively decisional also. In this connection, it is necessary to bear in mind that error is not simply the result of a unilateral determination of Dasein to realize a particular possibility, but a phenomenon that occurs within pregiven horizons and the world that is constituted by the unified structure (the worldhood of the world) that obtains in that particular case. As Heidegger explains the situation in *Being and Time*, "Thus the significance-relationships which determine the structure of the world are not a network of forms which a worldless subject has laid over some kind of material. What is rather the case is that factical Dasein, understanding itself and its world ecstatically in the unity of the 'there', comes back from these horizons to the entities encountered within them."[10] Dasein's world of significance-relationships is experienced ontically as "the way it is" in a unified structure; whether in the mode of religion or the mode of ideology, Dasein for the most part maintains itself as a structure that functions locally with a measure of situational coherence that it may or may not appropriate. Observes Heidegger, " . . . existing is always factical. Existentiality is essentially determined by facticity."[11] Instances of incoherence, which occur as disruptions of the totality of significance-relationships of the world, impinge on those entities within the world which have the Being of Dasein and come to presence as error, that is, as proposals whose claims are contrary to fact. If there were no existing structure of significance-relationships, then errors would never present themselves as such because the required antecedent conditions for the possibility of error would not obtain. "Significance is that on the basis of which the world is disclosed as such," Heidegger writes.[12] The phenomenon of warrants, including constraints, presupposes a grasp of the world.

From their limiting function and constant reference to an existing structure of significance-relationships, it is clear that constraints are functionally conservative, even though their exposition may appear iconoclastic, as Ayer's treatment of theology does. Constraints are conservative because they define certain sets of decisions as error from the standpoint of an existing structure of significance-relationships. The historical circumstances in which a given structure of significance-relationships occurs are beside the point and dominance in the sociological sense is not essentially an issue in the emergence of a structure of significance-relationships as a reference for a constraint. Any existing structure, regardless of its antiquity or novelty or the extent of its acceptance among members of a group, can be taken as *the* existing structure of significance-relationships for purposes of the thinking of a problematic or in political exchange.

While existing structures of significance-relationships have a certain priority in setting terms, the limits of that priority are discoverable, and an existing structure can be overcome, or replaced, by a change of mind or mood. In Heidegger's framework, the concept of state-of-mind as an existentiale provides the ontological basis for this possibility. There is a justification of sorts for the possibility of discovering and overcoming prior structures of significance-relationships in that the order in which decisions occur is irrelevant to the logical status of the decisions; in a sense, all decisions are equal because all have the same formal ontological status. This equality is the basis of the critiques of the status quo as ideology, which Marx encouraged. A chronologically later decision, then, has several possibilities with respect to an existing structure of significance-relationships: it may be subsumed in a relation of inclusion under existing decisions, may integrate existing decisions as convictions into an updated structure of significance-relationships that is essentially not at variance with the earlier one, or it may supercede previous decisions. Heidegger's thought on state-of-mind and mood clarifies a point in a possible mechanics of decision as a function of religions and ideologies.

The point in question has to do with avoidance of some possibility. Specifically, why is a possibility to be avoided, especially one that has previously been embraced? Why does what has been thought become not-to-be-thought?

First, from the fact of mood, what has been thought is analyzed as having been embraced on the basis of a mood of Dasein which first made attraction possible. Heidegger's interest in moods focuses on how moods reveal Dasein as it is in its inconstancy, but in his exposition other aspects of mood are brought up. The relationship which Heidegger proposes between mood and state-of-mind is such that the scope of mood determinations also includes understanding, which is significant, considering the decisive importance of *intellectus* in theology's representations of religions and ideologies. As Heidegger explains this complex of proto-psychological concepts, "State-of-mind is *one* of the existential structures in which the Being of the 'there' maintains itself. Equiprimordial with it in constituting this Being is *understanding*. A state-of-mind always has its understanding, even if it merely keeps it suppressed. Understanding always has its mood."[13] There is thus no separation of Dasein from its world in this view. As Heidegger's analysis construes it, "Existentially, a state-of-mind implies a disclosive submission to the world, out of which we can encounter something that matters to us."[14] The central concept informing the ontological construction of the relationship of decision to possibility is "that-which-matters." Ontologically, the basis of relationship to that-which-matters is grounded in falling. Heidegger claims, "The understanding which one has in such a state-of-mind has the character of falling."[15] **Theology is thus affirmed as ontologically connected with the problematic of religion and ideology, specifically through the concept of "falling."**

That-which-matters is not static; it varies with one's moods. Further, the way in which things matter varies with the mood. Following Heidegger's thinking, this implies variation in understanding as inevitable. These variations do not affect entities in isolation, but as part of the world. A shift in the understanding of that-which-matters is not simply a local revision, but a global one. In the event of such a change, previously grasped possibilities (now excluded) remain present-at-hand and demand attention. When these possibilities are thoughts that come to presence as the not-to-be-thought, they are handled by constraints.

While the not-to-be-thought is an error within its own structure of significance-relationships, there remains the possibility of worlds within which that idea is attractive and "valid," as Thomas Szasz is continually reminding us both generally and with reference to his own field. In the dynamics of religion and ideology, this point defines one of the key issues. Since Dasein is constituted in such a way that both ways of being in the world are necessary for it and at the same time both ways of being in the world are constantly being left behind, Dasein is faced with the fact of itself as "having-been" continually undercutting itself as "to-become" in a ceaseless progression through understandings, moods, and states-of-mind; its "there" can become problematical for that reason alone. Ontically, this shows up in the phrase, "I just don't know what to believe."

It is precisely at this moment, when the nullity of its existential basis so confronts it, that Dasein evades its truth, falls into the they-self, and lets itself be told what to believe; and it is in the arena of theology that this dynamic of conflict between authentic and inauthentic possibilities of Dasein works itself out publicly. It can happen on a large scale as well as privately, in the mind of the individual, with the founding of new religions and ideologies, as novel sorts of significance-relationships come to be and different ways of being in the world become possible. These new structures naturally decree errors and new constraints may appear. Gabriel Vahanian observes, " . . . all religion begins by desacralizing what it dissents from . . . ,"[16] by which he means not that religion originates in desacralization, but performs this act as its first order of business. It can just as well be said that all ideology begins by negating what it dissents from, by which is meant that ideology's first order of business is to plunge Dasein into the they-self. From either of the two possible general standpoints, errors will be visible.

Ontologically, then, there is no way for error of the general type specified in constraints, which has been shown as something other than a simple being-mistaken, to be eliminated entirely, even given a powerful apparatus for generating constraints. As soon as a factical decision comes to pass and negates some possibilities in favor of others, the "not" appears. When the decision happens to be a decision concerning think-ing, the "not" is realized as a not-to-be-thought, but only subsequent to Dasein's having entertained the possibility. This entertaining of the possibility itself could only occur in the event of a question. Even after a choice is made, its questionability does not entirely disappear; the basic questionability of all decisions presents itself to Dasein at every turn and Dasein always wants fallingly to turn away; this falling turning away from the questionability of all decisions manifests itself as convictions. In his own way, it seems, Schleiermacher recognized that faith construed as fidelity to convictions must mean the end of the possibility of religion.

Constraints logically ought not to exist because they are demon-strably superfluous. The "not" of the not-to-be-thought is always already sufficiently determined by the structure of significance-relation-ships, which says, in effect, "this and whatever accords and not-every-thing-else." By this wording, it is clear that what is excluded is infinite and is concealed for the most part besides. Constraints are specific, and this characteristic alone prohibits them from ever exhaustively listing all that is excluded by a structure of significance-relationships. The same rule that makes most objects trivial in existentiell experience also makes most exclusions trivial; the class of possibilities posed *as* possibilities is all that stands outside the infinite number of trivial exclusions.

Trivial exclusions are not to be thought as dismissals of the inher-ently insignificant. That which is trivially excluded by a structure of significance-relationships is only that which has never appeared as an issue. Ontically, Dasein is always being confronted by novel possibilities, so the question of exclusion is always coming up. If a novel possibility accords with the existing structure, a more complex structure encompas-sing a larger domain comes into being. If a possibility does not accord, however, it does not simply disappear, but becomes thematized in the formulation of a constraint. It cannot be known in advance which specific possibilities will need to be thematized in constraints, but the essential specifications are all pre-given along with the totality of the world. Because a constraint is specific, it carries in its text indications of the positive warrant which is the pre-condition of its existence but, under most conditions, no adequate sense of a concept can be constructed on the basis of a constraint alone. A constraint suppresses not only what it explicitly forbids, but the structures of significance-relationships in which the suppressed could operatively occur. In the narrow sense, constraints are like navigational aids; in a broader sense, they are instruments of totalization.

What a constraint can do is point to the existence of a warrant that may or may not be present-at-hand. Ayer has provided the case-in-point. Throughout his chapter on ethics and theology, he expounds on what theology can never be. He gives us the choice of interpreting his remarks as aimless shots-in-the-dark or as an instance of directed discourse guided by an ideology of theology, as we have noted that Quine, for example, would claim.[17] Ayer himself would most likely agree with Quine. In that case, the choice of interpreting Ayer's remarks as directed discourse raises the question of what, exactly, they are directed at. He named theology in his title and his language suggests that his attack was directed at all of theology. In spite of the negative language Ayer uses, a specific positive notion of theology can be discerned.

Existing, discovering a problem, and writing within his own structure of significance-relationships, Ayer set his sights on the phenomenon of theology as it came to presence for him. That he apparently believed a caricature of one current of another epoch's theology to be the totality of theology is of minor importance. The main point is that Ayer wrote as he did in order to circumscribe meaningful discourse in such a way that positive descriptive theology and anything close to it in certain particulars would be specifically relegated to the not-to-be-thought. He did not effect the exclusion by claiming a superior revelation (at least not in those words), as has often happened when traditional religions confronted each other head-to-head, and he did not do it by arguing about the deleterious social effects of theology and theologians in the course of history, as Hook and other liberal humanists did. Ayer attempted to achieve the categorical exclusion of theology from meaningful discourse by obliterating (in language) what he understood to be the basis of theology's warrant, the experience of God. Note: not an elimination of God as such, but the experience of God as an empirical event and also the God of language (not-God). In making the attempt, he appears to have made an honest effort to employ a number of premises that would be accepted as he presents them by those with whom he proposes to take issue; he was very selective. (Ayer's fidelity to all of the structures of significance-relationships he touches upon, of which he explicitly intends to exclude only a part, is not germane, but in a fuller discussion of this point it would be an issue.) In attacking the basis of the warrant of one variety of theology, Ayer claimed to have constructed a constraint that would invalidate the entire discipline.

As Ayer understood it, and as many still do, theology was essentially to be conceived as discourse about God. If that were the case, an important part of the warrant for this discourse would have to be that God can be experienced empirically. In that event, the basis for the warrant is experience, construed as empirical experience of God. Ayer grants that there may be extraordinary experiences, but he objects cogently to interpreting them using the category of "empirically knowable God" and then extrapolating all kinds of content. The focal point of his analysis is precisely this one category of interpretation, since when that category of knowledge is set into a proposition that asserts its viability, it yields a warrant for some sort of "theology." In light of the Heideggerian concept of gods articulated in the first section of this project, the kind of position Ayer takes has its validity, but it obscures more than it reveals about its theme.

There is a significant point about the relationship of the basis of the warrant for theology to the phenomenon of theology that is illustrated in the case at hand. The inference made from Ayer's critique was that the basis of theology's warrant was an experience, specifically the alleged experience of God as such. The subject matter of the theology that was warranted out of this experience was the content (subsequent to interpretation in problematical categories) of the experience itself. This content became thematic for theology, though it was already inseparable from the primary categories of interpretation. Further, to stay with the present example, this content's history also included its elaboration in the categories of classical Greek philosophy. These categories provided the faithful with concepts which allowed a different kind of discourse, a language that might once have seemed to allow a more precise articulation of the primary grounding experience of faith, religion, and theology. The Greek categories were employed by theologians as guides suggesting "where to look" and how to talk about the theme of theology; they became the *categories of intentionality* of that mode of theology.

Categories of intentionality are themselves thematized in philosophy, not in theology. In theology, it is the grounding experience of its warrant that is thematized and no other. For any theology, only one theme is appropriate, though a theme may be complex. In the chapter that follows, below, four genres of theology are described, each articulating a specific type of theme. In a way that is formally similar to medieval scholastic theology's appropriation of the categories of Greek philosophy in order to elaborate the basis of its warrant, viz. its theme, these four types of theology are constituted in ways that also make use of philosophy, only this time it is not the philosophy of the ancient Greeks in general and Aristotle in particular, but modern Western philosophy in general and Martin Heidegger in particular. The purpose of philosophical consideration of categories of intentionality, even if the discussion must be partial, is to bestow what is to be thematized in a particular genre of theology.

For any theology, the discovery of its theme is of paramount importance. It is the intentional act which must precede all theological discourse. Where themes come from is yet another question. An old bit of folk epistemology will do for now. People say, "You don't know what you've got till it's gone." In principle, this says everything that needs to be said about how theology gets its themes. On the way to an understanding of religion, it is necessary to consider the possibility of remaining the aesthetic observer of everything, including God, but once detachment is seen to be impossible, the next thing to do is let go of themes like Ayer's. Theology has no use for them when the work is really underway.

To the point, theology's themes have been analyzed here to originate not in presence, but in absence. Themes are not selected for theological reflection on a hunch that it might be possible to say something interesting about them; they are selected, rather, out of the necessity to address an absence — not an absolute absence, but a felt absence. Theology needs to speak about only what is actually felt to be needed to be the voice of religion as the search for what is missing.

Dasein in both authentic and inauthentic modes has needs which are addressed by different genres of theology. Up to this point, what has been sketched is a rationale for the existence of warrants for theology by inference from the existence of a specific constraint. The reason a warrant is important is that theology needs a position of its own from which to speak. In former times, this did not seem to be a problem; theology's right to speak was so totally unquestioned that no specific inquiry was made into theology's warrants and they remained obscure. Certain philosophical problems also remained obscure as a result. Now, technology's rise and unrelenting imperialism, along with the recently enhanced possibilities for ideological modes of being-in-the-world, have swept away much of what was once the supposed foundation of theology's legitimacy, and gaps in our discourse, both overtly theological and not, become evident. As Gabriel Vahanian describes the change, "The world has moved. And rightly or wrongly exposed the illusory character of the religious scaffolding which previously held it in place."[18] In the process, the possibility of theology has been called into question. How this question is answered determines whether theology speaks by right in its own domain or as an interloper condescendingly granted sufferance by technology for purely technologically-defined purposes. For theology to win its viability under these changed circumstances, it needs a viable warrant and, in fact, appears in our ontology to have at least four, granting the possibility of at least four distinct genres of theology.

Notes

[1] SZ, p. 193; BT, p. 238.

[2] Anthony Flew, "Theology and Falsification," *New Essays in Philosophical Theology*, ed. A. Flew and A. MacIntyre. New York: SCM Press, 1969. Flew believes that religious statements should be philosophically defensible.

[3] SZ, p. 217; BT, p. 260.

[4] SZ, p. 218; BT, p. 261.

[5] A.J. Ayer, *Language, Truth and Logic*. New York: Dover (n.d.), p. 114.

[6] Sidney Hook, "Modern Knowledge and the Concept of God," *The Quest for Being*. New York: Delta, 1956, 1960.

[7] Ayer, op. cit., p. 114.

[8] Ludwig Wittgenstein, *Tractatus Logico-Philosophicus*, trans. D.F. Pears and B.F. McGuiness. London: Routledge and Kegan Paul, 1961, #3.22-3.221, p. 23.

[9] Wittgenstein, op. cit., 4.111.

[10] SZ, p. 366; BT, p. 417.

[11] SZ, p. 192; BT, p. 236.

[12] SZ, p. 143; BT, p. 182.

[13] SZ, pp. 142-143; BT, p. 182.

[14] SZ, p. 137; BT, p. 177.

[15] SZ, p. 335; BT, p. 385.

[16] Vahanian, GU, p. 37.

[17] See Willard Quine, "The Scope and Language of Science," *Ways of Paradox*. New York: Random House, 1966, and "Ontology and Ideology Revisited," op. cit.

[18] Vahanian, GU, p. xi.

I will ask questions, and you shall answer.

— *God (Job 38:3)*

IX. Theologies in Relation

With a sense of the meanings of religion and ideology, with a provisional working definition of theology in place, and with reasonable grounds for believing that theology in general is an activity which proceeds on the basis of a warrant, the nature of the specific warrants for theology and the different genres of theology that are called into existence by them can come more clearly into view. The contemporary question, posed by liberalistic culture, of the viability of theology in pluralistic contexts invites (or perhaps demands) an interpretion of the phenomenon of theology which can recognize theology's warrants and its relationship to the two impulses of religion and ideology. This entails an interpretation of theology in which a typology is proposed to differentiate the abstract notion of theology in general into a feature-laden spectrum of actual theologies. These individual theologies can then be placed according to their warrants in generic relationship through an ontology which is regionally explicit and not entirely sunk in the obscurity of reified ideology.

Traditionally, theology has belonged in a setting that was structured according to the teaching of a living, organized religion. Phenomenally, these settings have been diverse, but in structural terms, all the settings of traditional theology are reducible to one, namely, the world as conceived in light of the teaching of a given religion. Granted that any religion participates in the falling of its followers and theology is easily implicated in this falling, it is still true that traditional theology developed into an important aspect of the religious way of being in the world and continues to be thought of as such.

The fact of the matter appears to be that theology belongs also to the non-religious, ideological way of being in the world, though not in the same way as it does to the religious. For those who live within the horizons of their world in a way structured by a living, organized religion, there is the absolute confidence of absolute dependence and the tacit matter-of-factness of the world that comes with falling into a situation of this type. There is also an institutionalized agreement (maintained by ideology) on some basic things, such as the legitimacy of the religion itself within the culture (or sub-culture) and one or more culturally acceptable representations of the religion's general structure of significance-relationships; these come to presence as categories of self-understanding given by the religion. Bearing in mind that reified categories of self-understanding, no matter what the source, are the substance of ideology (including "religious ideology"), and remembering that religion and ideology are ontologically unified, let us consider initially how a religion's logical categories of understanding in ensemble can be the basis of warrants for traditional kinds of theology, following the commonly accepted view that "(a) theology mediates between a religion and a culture."[1] When a sectarian agenda is set by a warrant for theology, what results can be either confessional theology or philosophical theology, depending upon how the categories of the discourse function. Because they are better established, we look at these two before analyzing how non-sectarian warrants function.

Confessional theology is charged by a standing mandate to preserve the religion's given complex of self/world in its absolute unity and to insure coherence in the futural projections of the community. Its functions are especially to illuminate and preserve the structure of significance-relationships against the ravages of absurdity and the experience of anxiety by claiming, or appropriating, the nothingness which continually draws beings into itself. This claim is made in the name of a divinity in recognition of that which proximally draws the religious person onward through existence in a way that is both meaningful and beyond meaning. As a way of being in the world, a religion logically entails the significance of the world as the condition of its own significance. But, as Heidegger notes, "Anxiety discloses an insignificance of the world; and this insignificance reveals the nullity of that with which one can concern oneself — or, in other words, the impossibility of projecting oneself upon a potentiality-for-being which belongs to existence and which is founded primarily upon one's objects of concern."[2] Religions, as present-at-hand, tread a fine line between necessity and irrelevance. For this reason, confessional theology takes its categories of understanding ultimately seriously.

By taking its pre-given categories of understanding ultimately seriously, confessional theology only appears to reify them to the ideological, or exoteric, consciousness. Confessional theology's warrant from religion essentially calls for a way of thinking which is vitally concerned with its original matrix in the mode of its absoluteness. As a way of thinking, confessional theology is virtually self-sufficient; in its own terms, it is not pressured to examine or relativize its own foundations because those foundations are as secure and as true as the absolutely accepted primary categorizations codified in the religion which grounds it. As long as the general structure of significance-relationships represented by the religion retains the integrity of its self-evidence, there is no challenge to coherence except that of anxiety itself (which the religion seeks to appropriate by interpretation) which would redirect the eyes of faith from the reality of its own religiously pre-given conceptions to an explicitly alternative structure of significance-relationships, to the ontological status of the world itself as function of Dasein's own spatio-temporal horizons. This is to say that for confessional theology, the (tautological) understanding of its own understanding will always take precedence over all other interpretations. This is what Heidegger was advocating when he placed upon theology the responsibility for the nature of its own discourse and what Ayer was arguing against. The tension between these two thinkers is indicative of the tension between religion and ideology.

Confessional theology, as it appears essentially in our extrapolation from the ontology of the previous chapters and the working definition proposed above, is the seeking of understanding which occurs when Dasein finds itself, groundless, in the condition of a lack of understanding in the confrontation with nothingness. Because understanding can never attain satisfying completeness in the face of nothingness, confessional theology is granted an internal, logical justification for perpetual activity. In earlier times, that justification was claimed on the grounds that God revealed different things at different times, not an unthinkable position for theology grounded in narrative. Though the canon of a religion may be (declared) closed, the possibilities of its community of faith can never be factically closed until it comes to an end. As long as a community of faith exists, confessional theology has a role to play in the elucidation of the religious doctrine that binds the community and defines its general way.

Since doctrine is a phenomenon of institutionalized religious practice, confessional theology, as the explicit elucidation of doctrine, has a place in any community of faith that is characterized by the presence of normative, institutionalized religion. This would include virtually all traditional societies, where the institutionalized religion so suffuses daily life that doctrine, as a kind of cultural metalanguage, is factically interwoven with every understanding, even though no explicit codification may have occurred. It would also include the obvious cases of organized, bureaucratic religions in both traditional and pluralistic contexts.

A more telling way of placing confessional theology might be to enumerate those contexts in which it may not occur. There is only one type. True confessional theology (in contrast to artfully constructed linguistic replicas placed in service to ideology) may not occur where the notion of doctrine itself (not just points of particular doctrines) is in question and thus where the presence of socially-given constraints on religious doctrine is an explicit and accepted possibility. This seems like a very strong exclusion, but it is justified. A given doctrine may be in question within a community of faith without making that community any less religious, but if the notion of doctrine itself comes into question and the resolve of the religious is effectively weakened, then not only does confessional theology become present-at-hand to the group as a problematical contrivance, but the religion itself comes to presence as insufficient. In the anxious turning away from the authentic grasp of its "there," which occurs when the sense of nothingness overwhelms and overflows religion's appropriating language, Dasein hopefully turns to the critique of religion proffered by ideology and falls into totalization of the presence of the Present. From that kind of fall, the only possibility for recovery of a theological voice lies with the faithful impulse to subvert the presence of the Present, which realizes itself in a mode which is not strictly theological because it in some sense anticipates the possibility of theology. Without digressing too far, we might note that such anticipation is existential rather than chronological.

Within a Heideggerian critical theory, confessional theology is thought as ontologically connected with the possibility of resolve and Dasein's contrary tendency to flight from anxiety. The connection can be observed in the ontical presence of confessional theology, in which its discourse provides a semblance of order, reflecting the existing structure of significance-relations. Ontically, confessional theology appears to be narrowly representing the interests of one particular interpretation of the world, but this appearance can be misleading if it is generalized to the ontological level; confessional theology is not essentially interpretation of things in the world. Ontologically, confessional theology functions to shield resolute Dasein from the inauthentic claims of the "they" by presenting an interpretation of religion which can be authentically grasped by Dasein. What this means comes out with a closer look at resoluteness.

"Resoluteness," writes Heidegger, "as *authentic Being-one's-Self*," not only " . . . does not detach Dasein from its world," but " . . . pushes it into solicitous Being with Others."[3] Further, he writes, "Dasein's resoluteness towards itself is what first makes it possible to let the Others who are with it 'be' in their ownmost potentiality-for-Being . . . . Only by authentically Being-their-Selves in resoluteness can people authentically be with one another . . . ."[4] In short, resolute Dasein *as* resolute does not seek to lose itself in the creation of an ever-new "they." In shielding resoluteness, confessional theology can be seen to have an important role in any community of faith, since resoluteness is of the essence to a community of faith. This also means that confessional theology can not be a public interpretation of things (for that is what the "they-Self" is continually generating); confessional theology, in remaining with the religion which warrants it, attempts to hold Dasein in authenticity, even at the cost of appearing as nonsense to the conventional wisdom.

In its attempt to sustain Dasein in authenticity, confessional theology comes up against the phenomenon of "idle talk." In the Heideggerian lexicon, "Idle talk is the possibility of understanding everything without previously making the thing one's own."[5] Idle talk, as has been noted, is a closing off of authentic possibilities and it is powerful indeed.

> The dominance of the public way in which things have been interpreted has already been decisive even for the possibilities of having a mood — that is, for the basic way in which Dasein lets the world 'matter' to it. The 'they' prescribes one's state-of-mind, and determines what and how one 'sees'.[6]

This domination of Dasein, which originates in falling and is therefore ideological, constitutes a constant temptation for Dasein which is given with Being-in-the-world.

Ontically, the temptation to relinquish authority to the "they" has to do with the contrasting ways in which idle talk and confessional theology come to presence. As a correlate of religious resoluteness, confessional theology comes to presence as ontically indefinite, useless, and vague. This is because of the ontical uncertainty which is decreed by every true religion. Ontologically speaking, Heidegger claims, "To resoluteness, the *indefiniteness* characteristic of every potentiality-for-being into which Dasein has factically been thrown, is something that necessarily *belongs*."[7] This is not gratuitous paradox; the deep existential definiteness of resoluteness translates into existentiell indefiniteness, Heidegger is saying. In accord with the logic of his existential analytic and in anticipation of the regional ontology of religion that would develop from it, he is explaining how Dasein always tends to turn away from existentiell indefiniteness since existentiell indefiniteness is associated with death, which is Dasein's ultimate possibility of indefiniteness. In the mode of resoluteness, Dasein affirms itself even while facing indefiniteness and thus death and nothingness. A few pages later Heidegger continues, "When Dasein is resolute, it takes over authentically in its existence the fact that it is the null basis of its own nullity."[8] It is from the specter of this nullity that Dasein is constantly tempted to flee by falling into concernful Being-alongside-things and so on. Confessional theology, in its steady affirmation of the way of its warranting religion, can play a part in maintaining Dasein's authentic appropriation of the structure of significance-relationships codified in the religion, but it can never make nothing into something with which Dasein can then concern itself.

Confessional theology mediates Dasein's relationship with the nothing into which it is inexorably drawn. It does so specifically by concerning itself with religion as the way into Nothing which Dasein takes in the course of relationship with a divinity as such. This concern of confessional theology gives it a certain appearance of groundlessness or arbitrariness, but that is because confessional theology refuses to concern itself with things in the relational terms characteristic of falling. The system of systematic theology, we recall, is not the kind of calculated structure that a naive science builds up from raw data, but a derived structure drawn from its warranting revelation. As Tillich describes it in words that express Heidegger's understanding of theology as well as his own, "The concrete *logos* which (the theologian) sees is received through believing commitment and not like the universal *logos* at which the philosopher looks, through rational detachment."[9]

In refusing to concern itself with things in the manner of falling evasion, confessional theology, as a phenomenon of resoluteness, leaves Dasein with its anxiety intact and in possession of the facts of its thrownness and its "there." "'Resoluteness,'" says Heidegger, "signifies letting oneself be summoned out of the lostness of the 'they'."[10] Essentially, though, confessional theology still leaves resolute Dasein with Nothing and its situation, of which Heidegger claims, "The irresoluteness of the 'they' remains dominant . . . ."[11]

In spite of this tendency to irresoluteness, Dasein also always ontologically retains the option, which is presented concretely in confessional theology, of a resoluteness which projects itself upon some factical possibility, in this case a specific religion as a mode of enrouting. Dasein's enrouting is existentially definite and it is precisely the definiteness of Dasein's factical enrouting which determines why confessional theology must always happen in the name of some particular divinity: it is a definite beckoning divinity which Dasein names and follows into Nothing. In this reading, the named god of a religion appears to be the existential counter-phenomenon to the "they," and the doctrines of religions appear as ways out of the lostness of the "they," in which Dasein maintains itself in the condition of a lack of understanding.

There exists an inverse, acausal relationship between the becoming problematical of the idea of doctrine and the ontical condition of a lack of understanding. In the condition of a lack of understanding, authentically grasped as such, there is a presumption that greater understanding is possible. Since Dasein always has an understanding, a lack of understanding is only an existentiell modification of Dasein's condition. The ontical condition of a lack of understanding, authentically grasped as such, is also the condition of openness to confessional theology and the religious way it represents; an authentically grasped lack of understanding is itself a way of being religious. By contrast, questioning the possibility of doctrine itself already represents a deviation from the way of religion in a turning away from the prospect of Nothing to look for some standard against which the essentially unprecedented appropriation of Nonbeing can be evaluated. A lack of understanding, then, which belongs to all religion, is not to be thought of as some kind of fault or blindness that religion foists upon humanity; it is both a name for the incompleteness of an understanding set to the task of grasping what lies beyond itself, and it is the state of Being of Dasein in which Dasein authentically grasps itself as inadequate to comprehend its "there." Dasein finds that ideology has and does not have something to offer.

This complex lack of understanding attracts attention to itself and is consequently addressed by confessional theology from its, viz. religion's, self-sufficiency. From the standpoint of self-sufficiency, confessional theology can unhesitatingly draw on its own resources, which are originally the resources of the religion which grounds it (by virtue of its absoluteness) and constitutes it (by providing all categories of understanding). This absolute self-sufficiency reveals itself to be both the strength and the weakness of confessional theology; **within** the horizon of understanding of the grounding religion, confessional theology participates in the absoluteness of the religion, while **outside**, its discourse just comes to presence as essentially meaningless. The important point is not that confessional theology is something of a hothouse flower because it withers just outside its community of faith, for all theology does that; it is to see that confessional theology is absolutely dependent upon the truth of its grounding religion for its warrant to speak. Confessional theology's warrant has two parts: one part which calls for interpretation of the way of the religion in its own terms as a way of resoluteness, and another part which calls for defining the way of the religion, which comes to presence as tradition and a factical community of faith, as an authentic alternative to the finalistic defining of things which occurs in the decisions of the "they" in ideological metaphysics. From this two-part warrant, the tasks and themes of confessional theology are determined.

The implications of the warranting relation between religion and its associated confessional theology are best illustrated by reference to concrete examples. In the following example of confessional theology, it can be seen how statements that would be analyzed philosophically as being unwarranted are more properly understood as being religiously warranted, and, insofar as the analysis of confessional theology presented in these pages is viable, confessional theological statements are not religiously warranted solely by appeal to privileged knowledge. Given a concrete example, it becomes possible to consider in greater detail both the general nature and the content, or instructions, of a warrant for confessional theology.

We take for our example of confessional theology Seyyed Hossein Nasr's *Ideals and Realities of Islam*, in particular an essay titled, "The Quran — the Word of God, the source of knowledge and action." This traditionalist essay is useful not only as confessional theology (its primary purpose) and as an example of confessional theology (our primary interest), but also as one of the necessary poles to highlight a distinction that will be made below between confessional theology and philosophical theology, a distinction which in this discussion does not appear to be as important as it actually is until the logic of warrants for theologies independent of specific religions arises as an issue. We select it also because the religion/ideology tension is very highly-charged for Islam at this juncture in its, and our, history.

Nasr's essay is an especially revealing example of confessional theology, since it appears at several points to go beyond its own context and into the spiritualities of other traditions. The promise of this piece is not more comparative religion material, but cases-in-point of one religious way's understanding of other religious ways *as such*. This essay, written with Western readers in mind, superficially appears to violate the description above in which it was claimed that confessional theology was only concerned with its warranting religion in the mode of its own absoluteness. Nasr frequently includes observations of non-Islamic religious phenomena which have the appearance of comparative exposition, so the question of the horizontal limits of confessional theology's concerns is sharply posed in this essay as an example of its genre. As it stands, the essay as a work of confessional theology counters any impression which might have been given that confessional theology is understood to be done in artificial isolation from the world. Confessional theology's exclusive concern with its warranting religion in its absoluteness means not the stereotype of parochial isolation, but that whatever presents itself as part of the world within the religion's horizons of understanding (which are always coextensive with religious Dasein's own horizons) will necessarily be integrated into religious Dasein's existing structure of significance-relationships before alien categorizations can affect the existing structure. This dynamic is responsible for the datum that one of the hallmarks of confessional theology is the steadfastness of its faith in the face of seemingly persuasive challenges from the world of consensus reality.

An important category in Islamic spirituality is that of the "sacred book." The central position of the Quran in Islam makes this category one of the most significant, so Islamic confessional theology will be mandated to devote considerable energy to illuminating this category. In this cross-cultural essay, one of the first tasks Nasr takes on is the authentic establishment of the category his title deals with. In a purely Islamic context, this step would scarcely be necesary, but in view of the wider audience the writer intends, he is called upon to reveal the foundation of his discourse as the Quran itself. From the text of his essay, it is clear that Nasr feels he has a sufficient basis and he calls no other support into authenticating service for what ensues. This apparent self-assurance is characteristic of confessional theology.

From an external perspective, Nasr's reasoning appears to be tightly circular: The Quran is a category of the religion because the Quran itself says it is. It is not especially interesting that the Quran gives all of the categories in Islam, for sacred texts (written, oral, or tacit) generally give the categories of any religion; what is interesting is that the Quran makes itself a category, and thus presents the classical intellectual problem of religious solipsism in clearest outline. The "illogical" terms of decision are not hidden from the believer; indeed the theme of the unconventionality of the sacred, which is so pronounced in Islam, begins with Quran's challenge to the faithful to remain true to the path even when it is bizarre or unreasonable. The cost in human suffering is reckoned to be cheap in the currency of eternity. On the basis of the account of confessional theology above, it appears that Islam not only challenges, but also safeguards the resoluteness of the faithful by calling them to attend to that which proximally provides a codification of the religion's general structure of significance-relationships. In so doing, the fact of Nothing remains before their eyes, just beyond the Quran. Ontically, the Quran is always there; ontologically, Nothing is always there.

Nasr knows, as should all theologians who write in a time of theology's presence-at-hand, that a set of ontical categories which are not one's own will appear arbitrary and probably unserviceable. Since it is the Quran which proposes the categories of Islam, it is the Quran itself which will ultimately appear arbitrary in this case. Nasr writes, "Many people, especially non-Muslims, who read the Quran for the first time are struck by what appears as a kind of incoherence from the human point of view."[12] Two points are worth noting. The first is Nasr's observation that the Quran will appear incoherent especially for non-Muslims. This is precisely what should happen according to a conception of religion which focuses on religion as a primary structure of existence. For those outside the Islamic structure of significance-relationships, and thus outside the Islamic structure of self-understanding, the Quran as founding document of an alien sensibility must appear insufferably wrong insofar as it differs from the founding text of the reader's own religion. Not only would the alien text see something where there was nothing and nothing where there was something, everything within the horizon of understanding would be strangely placed, viewed at an odd angle, differently related as Dasein came back to itself from different limits and encountered itself and others in a different way.

The second point worth noting is Nasr's phrase "from the human point of view." Were the Quran a purely human text, a philosophical text, let us say, then it would be subject to warrant calls for every decisive statement it made, and it would be required to meet prevailing standards of intelligibility if it were not to come to presence as nonsense. In its own terms, however, the Quran is not a purely human text, but a divine dictation, and therefore an account of structures and decisions beyond the reach of all human qualification. The practical consequences of this understanding of the text for studies such as the present one is that there is no philosophical questioning of its primary categorizations and no calling for their warrants, since a) outside the structures presented in the text there is nothing; b) all qualifying impulses originate outside the structure of the text; so, c) all such qualifying impulses are ontologically baseless. Through this logic, Islam is especially energetic in its exclusions.

Nasr's essay is an example of how the textual origins of all confessional theology warranted by specific religions come to presence — as fundamentally other to outsiders and not really amenable to translation or rationalization, only to direct exposition by either confessional theology or phenomenology of religion. The absoluteness of primary structures of decision and the interpretive categories that inhere in them is attested in Nasr's remarks concerning the relationship of the Quran and knowledge. Our expectation is that confessional theology will speak the unity of all that lies within its own given structure of significance-relationships. Nasr would certainly concur; he writes, "The Quran is then the source of knowledge in Islam not only metaphysically and

religiously but even in the domain of particular fields of knowledge."[13]
In its own terms, Nasr's statement is interpretable as a faithful assertion
that all understanding owes its existence to the categories of the founding
religion. In this focus, it looks like a straightforward description of life in
the Islamic world. Ontologically, the Quran, as that which brings to
presence the Islamic way of Being-in-the-world as such, must be the pre-
experiential source of all knowledge within its spatio-temporal horizons.
The basis of the Quran's being the source of all knowledge lies in its
articulating the *logos* of the Islamic world.

It is the function of confessional theology to concern itself with the
logos that happens (*sich ereignet*) in its religion. In *Being and Time*,
Heidegger interprets *logos* as " . . . a letting-something-be-seen."[14] This
is exactly what Nasr reports the Quran is doing as source of all knowledge. The Quran, as the articulation of the *logos* of its matrix, appears as
what Heidegger also calls *logos*, " . . . the Laying that gathers."[15] In its
broad scope, it appears to do this in an obvious and direct way; and by its
acknowledged strikingly poetic language (in Arabic), it accomplishes the
gathering Laying of beings logically in its normative, performative discourse. How that takes place, Heidegger ascribes to the apophantical
function of *logos*, as that which lets something be seen.

> And only *because* the function of *logos* as *apophansis* lies in
> letting something be seen by pointing it out, can the *logos*
> have the structural form of *synthesis*. Here "synthesis" does
> not mean a binding and linking together of representations,
> a manipulation of psychical occurrences where the 'prob-
> lem' arises of how these bindings, as something inside, agree
> with something physical outside. Here the *syn* has a purely
> apophantical signification and means letting something be
> seen in its *togetherness* with something — letting it be seen
> *as* something. [16]

That there is a connection between *logos* and knowledge is clear in
Heidegger's writing from *Being and Time* onward, but the role of
language, specifically poetic language, unfolds gradually in his thinking.
In his meditation on Stefan George's poem, "The Word," in the essay
"The Nature of Language," Heidegger is brought to one of his clearest
statements in this regard. Speaking there of the poetic experience with
language, an experience which we note has frequently been reported by
Muslims in connection with the Quran, Heidegger writes,

> It points to something thought-provoking and
> memorable . . . .It shows what is there and yet "is" not.
> The word, too, belongs to what is there — perhaps not

> merely "too" but first of all, and even in such a way that the
> word, the nature of the word, conceals within itself that
> which gives being. If our thinking does justice to the matter,
> then we may never say of the word that it is, but rather that
> it gives . . . .The word itself is the giver. What does it give?
> To go by the poetic experience and the most ancient tradi-
> tion of thinking, the word gives Being.[17]

In this focus, it is not gratuitous hyperbole for Nasr to speak of the
Quran as source of all knowledge. Moreover, since the Quran is not a *sui
generis* phenomenon, it is not responsible for being the ultimate source of
anything, but a source which points beyond itself.

As it stands in its two aspects, Nasr's statement on the Quran as
source of knowledge in Islam shows only half of the nature of understanding that obtains in confessional theology generally. Just a few pages
later in the same essay, Nasr reveals the other half, which is less obvious.
We find him there speaking of the experience of a world by a subject
which experiences itself as traveling through it. He speaks of a kind of
" . . . fundamental distinction between the traveller and the world
through which he passes . . . "[18] and describes that distinction as " . . .
the basis of every human experience, whether it be physical, psychological or religious."[19] The person-world split is a matter of fact for Nasr,
and not an optional interpretation. Surprisingly though, Nasr then
proceeds to expand upon his description by saying, "The Quran reflects
this reality."[20] There follows a discussion of the correlation between
reality and the Quran. Nasr speaks unreflectively, ontically, almost
ingenuously, in his theo-logical report that the Quran "reflects" reality.
True to his ontic experience, Nasr is prepared to acknowledge only one
reality, and that is the one he knows as a Muslim. In so doing, he
uncritically places the Quran as *both* the source of all knowledge *and* a
reflection (rather than, say, a presentation) of reality. Philosophically,
Nasr's position may not make much sense, but confessional theology is
not bound by most analytic philosophical considerations and it disre-
gards any that would condition it.

Confessional theology is always free to disregard philosophical
considerations because from the outset its warrant is perceived to come
from beyond philosophy. From the few ontological observations that
have been made up to this point concerning confessional theology and
Nasr's essay, which we have taken to be typical of its genre, several
additional points about confessional theology can now be made. First,
confessional theology's independence of philosophy is warranted entirely
from the internal logic of its religion, since the only purpose of confessional theology is to provide the interested faithful with an explicit

reconciliation of a religion as such and their own structure of significance-relationships, which has always already occurred. Confessional theology is, then, a report of what is revealed to be authentically significant in the way that it is revealed to be authentically significant. Confessional theology is done in the name of a specific god in order to unfold the structure of significance-relations in absolute purity and religiously coherent continuity. It is something like this that Carl Raschke seems to have had in mind when he described theology as a "supplement."

> The idea of supplement is bound up with the notions of
> both addition and substitution. The supplement "carries
> on" from where the primary text left off. [21]

When confessional theology "carries on," it is especially careful not to get carried away.

Second, confessional theology is not commissioned to bridge the gaps between its own religion and others by "meeting them half-way." As Nasr's example shows, a work of confessional theology can speak of other religions, can speak to other religions, and can even acknowledge their legitimacy, but this always occurs on the way to clarifying its own categories and confirming its own religion. This is why Nasr can write in the middle of his essay on the centrality of the Quran, " . . . we know that in Buddhism the very beauty of the Buddha images saves."[22] He is not talking about Buddhism, but Islam.

In summary, confessional theology is the conserving and consolidating moment of a religion's interpretation. This theology's warrant, which is absolutely contingent upon the religion it speaks of, allows it to be no more and no less. Ontically, the possibility of confessional theology remains open as long as its religion is sufficient unto human existence and as long as faith persists.

We recall that faith was characterized as having two aspects, a self-oriented aspect, which was associated with what was rendered "enrouting" oneself (*be-wëgen*), and an other-oriented aspect, which was associated with Dasein's relation to a divinity. The self-oriented aspect was also correlated with an ontical feeling of confidence, and this was claimed to be specifically a feeling of confidence in the truth of one's way. Truth counts for a great deal in confessional theology both ontically and ontologically.

Faith's other pole, however, decrees that confidence is always faced with doubt, for the way of religion is always absolutely (logically) contingent upon an incalculable other and because Dasein ontologically finds itself as thrown, it knows not whence. Dasein, as portrayed in the early Heidegger corpus, is doubly problematical as its own basis and it is this double difficulty that Dasein evades in falling. In falling into the world of daily affairs, the world as it is known in the way of religion does not disappear, but becomes questionably real, ontologically uncertain. The intrusion of the various other circulating interpretations of existence (which are actually the public obfuscations of existence put forward by the "they") makes other ways available and makes them attractive as well, immediately casting doubt upon the way of any factical religion as the true way. Such doubt naturally raises the possibility of untruth in both the conventional sense and in the sense that Heidegger gives the term in *Being and Time*.

Truth, as Heidegger speaks of it, is an uncovering of "the entity as it is in itself."[23] He emphasizes that it " . . . is not an agreement of knowing with its object, still less of the psychical with the physical; but neither is it an agreement between 'contents of consciousness' among themselves."[24] Upon introduction of the concept of truth as uncovering, the notion of a sacred text which determines the way of all uncovering within its domain makes Nasr's comments about the Quran that much more comprehensible as ontologically founded claims. Because ontological validity funds no claims about ontic facticity, Nasr's comments do not *prove* the exclusive truth of Islam, only claim its truth. The sufficient basis of the claim is existence in the Islamic world itself, where what-is comes to presence as it is. What-is in the Islamic world includes Nasr himself.

Truth is about uncovering, or disclosedness. The sacred text, which points Dasein to Being, and the religion it founds as the way of being are essentially inseparable. The sacred text and its religion, within which Dasein authentically grasps and appropriates its own possibilities of existence, even while understanding and relating to other beings in their Being, cooperatively orient Dasein to attend to its own disclosedness and thereby understandingly realize its own disclosedness. Confessional theology helps preserve the reality of the most easily lost of the four in the fourfold, namely, the divinities which come to presence in absence, through this orientation of religious Dasein to the truth of its own disclosedness. In his existential analytic, Heidegger can be heard explaining some of the implications: " . . . with Dasein's *disclosedness* is the *most primordial* phenomenon of truth attained."[25] This most primordial phenomenon of truth is Dasein's own being in the truth, which is realized as essentially non-relational certainty. "(C)ertainty is grounded in the truth, or belongs to it equiprimordially."[26] The Being of truth as uncovering is the origin of confidence.

The phenomenon of truth is related to care, and thus to falling, but in a negative way. Care imparts to Dasein the structure-of-Being which first becomes explicit through it, but furthermore, says Heidegger, in the structure of care, that is, in Dasein's manifold involvements, " . . . the disclosedness of Dasein lies hidden."[27] Care allows Dasein to be in truth while concealing Dasein from itself. Dasein may grasp other entities in the world but in this grasping, Dasein tends to lose itself in the world for the sake of effective participation in the world. This is the basic structure of falling. For Heidegger, falling determines a second mode of Being for Dasein, a mode that is no less essential to Dasein and disclosedness than authenticity. "Because Dasein is essentially falling, its state of Being is such that it is in 'untruth'."[28] He then adds, "The upshot . . . is . . . that Dasein is equiprimordially both in the truth and in untruth."[29] This equiprimordiality subverts the facile privileging of truth in the *ontology* of Dasein.

Heidegger's argument for this assertion, which focuses on the covering-up of death at the behest of the they-self, gives an analysis of Dasein's evasive being untrue to itself which superficially does not relate very closely to the problematic of theology warranted by religion. The connection exists at a fundamental level, however, and is made through the concept of resoluteness. Heidegger writes in a passage that is crucial to making use of his existential analytic in the religion-ideology problematic, "Resoluteness appropriates untruth authentically."[30] With this thought, we are able to understand how a theology for falling creatures can be possible: resoluteness is the ontological basis for the second genre of theology that is warranted by religion, **philosophical theology**, and falling is its condition.

Resoluteness comes into play whenever Dasein's "there" is disclosed. This "there" is always proximally located in a definite, factical world because Dasein must project itself upon factical possibilities, says Heidegger, and it is only in resoluteness that Dasein can project itself authentically. When Dasein thus projects itself, it always does so in a definite existentiell resolution, that is, it knows how to describe the appearance of what it is doing. "The resolution is precisely the disclosive projection and determination of what is factically possible at the time," explains Heidegger.[31] If religion is thought as a way of projection, let us follow this line of reasoning a little further and think resoluteness as a distinctive feature of religious Dasein; resoluteness allows religious Dasein, through its authentic grasp of what Heidegger calls its "Situation,"[32] to decide which particular possibilities to project itself upon and which to avoid. The interpretation of these factical possibilities within a religion's pre-given general structure of significance-relationships by resolute Dasein is philosophical theology.

Philosophical theology appears because it is called for in the event of a recognized possibility of a given religion's untruth. Ontologically, untruth is always a possibility for Dasein, but it is accepted in religion as the fact of human inadequacy; in falling, an existentiell reversal occurs as Dasein ontically experiences untruth as truth (the always-shifting "truth" of the "they") and truth as uncertainty. With that move, Dasein loses confidence in the way of its religion. The loss of confidence comes as the religion appears to be covering up entities (including oneself) instead of revealing them as they are, and closing off possibility (especially one's own) instead of opening it up in the way that a religion is supposed to. This is not a matter of having to choose some possibilities and leave others behind; it is about the disappearance of the prospect of the *novum*.

The possibility of the untruth of a religion does not mean that confessional theology disappears; it does mean that in certain lights confessional theology appears as inadequate. When Dasein is lost in the "they," then sacred text, religion, and their confessional theology do not ring true. Confessional theology seems unwarranted in this kind of situation because it is warranted by the truth of its religion; philosophical theology, on the other hand, is warranted by the possibility of the same religion's untruth, a possibility which ontically appears when Dasein falls into the "they." It is the function of resoluteness to keep Dasein out of the "they," but for that function to be realized in existence, Dasein's own Situation must first be authentically appropriated as an ensemble of factical possibilities upon which it is able to project itself. Philosophical theology tries to bring Dasein to do exactly this.

Just as the thinking of an ontology of confessional theology was taken a few steps further with the aid of a concrete example, so also may such an example help define the Being of philosophical theology. Gabriel Vahanian's *God and Utopia* can serve as a case-in-point of what has been claimed as true of philosophical theology and, at the same time, it can represent a few points which bear on theology in general; in that book, Vahanian is doing two things at once: he is thinking problems of theology and he is thinking theory of theology as a related problematic.

Vahanian begins thinking theology as a problematic in the preface of the book, where he right away takes issue with a conventional understanding of the task of theology. He introduces discord in a manner that bears directly upon the distinction being suggested here between the two genres of discourse that have been designated "confessional" and "philosophical" theologies. In constructing the categories of confessional and philosophical theology, the first priority is to preserve a sense of the relationship that originates in their complex, but still essentially unified, ontological basis and avoid a conception of these two types of theology that has them playing to different audiences.

In our keeping the moments of truth and untruth together (both ontically and ontologically, following Heidegger), the implication is that confessional and philosophical theologies are speaking to one and the same religious Dasein. The role of resoluteness in the conceptualization of philosophical theology also points in this direction. Thus, what are called "confessional" and "philosophical" theologies do not correspond to the traditional dogmatic and apologetic theologies Vahanian cites when he claims, "Indeed, nothing has been more harmful to the understanding of faith than the now 'classic' distinction between a theology for internal use and a theology for external use, between dogmatics and apologetics. Such a split has only succeeded in aggravating the cleavage between church and world. . . ."[33]

The point was made above that confessional theology comes to presence as nonsense outside its own religion; the fact is, philosophical theology does too and thus it has no business "outside," in the sense of selling or justifying the claims of a religion to those in a different community of faith. Even Anselm's proof of the existence of God was a proof that its author was perfectly content to admit was only convincing to the faithful. To expect more of any theology is effectively to presuppose the non-integrity of symbol systems; philosophical theology is always placed within its own symbol system and no other.

The ideal of philosophical theology is to avoid idle talk directed at the non-faithful. Except perhaps as part of the missionology of a religion which imagined its truth to be accessible through stimulus-response interaction, philosophical theology is an internal matter. It is made clear at the outset of his discussion that Vahanian wants nothing to do with the theory of theology which posits a dogmatics/apologetics (inside/outside) division. In the placing of his own work, he envisions the human race as his audience. It is also clear, however, that the book belongs somewhere in the field of Christian theology, even though Vahanian assiduously seeks to confront the reader with the magnitude of the distance he sees between himself and the bureaucratized, institutionalized religion of Christianity. Indications are that Vahanian's work is not only nominally located within the Christian symbol system, but also that there is a definite traditional-religious way in which Vahanian moves, which is appropriate for philosophical theology.

One wants to notice textual evidence that points to the writer's generic intentionality unless the surface of the text is so completely mistrusted that nothing the writer says makes any difference. For the present, let us not adopt that particular style of radical suspicion. The fact of the philosophical theologian's being located within a specific religious symbol system (in contrast to assuming a transcendentalistic perspective) shows up in Vahanian's writing in phrases like " . . . the biblical perspective of creation and redemption,"[34] in which the definite article is used comfortably, as if there were a single biblical perspective of creation and redemption, or phrases in which referents and propositions appear as if they were self-evident facts or universally agreed hypotheses; it is not part of the agenda for philosophical theology to make concessions to any context in which it expects to receive an equivocating response. Thus, even in the face of its religion's presence-at-hand, its language is unequivocal. Only when one speaks within a specific tradition, within a specific symbol system — as one who follows the path of a specific religion — is such language possible. Here is the pole of confidence.

Does not this imputed confidence alone place *God and Utopia* within the field of *confessional* theology? Not necessarily, since accompanying any apparent occurrences of the sense of truth (as unconcealment) that characterizes confidence, there are co-occurrences of untruth (as exposed deficiency). That duplexity is the structural description for philosophical theology, which is above all a discipline striving to articulate awareness of which possibilities lie within its field of appropriation and which do not. **The real question in this case is not whether a religious factor is present, but rather what sets the agenda for the discourse.**

It is already granted that a theology warranted by a specific religion will be essentially religious, even (and maybe even especially) when it is at odds with ontical realizations of the religion. While confessional theology elaborates the categories of its religion in an uncritical way, in their truth, philosophical theology attends to its religion's basis and takes note of the factical limits of its religion's coming to language. Philosophical theology thereby concerns itself with the possibility of untruth, not so much as prevarication or misrepresentation, but as concealment of Being. In the authentic appropriation of the possibility of untruth, philosophical theology may effect an apparent transvaluation of its own ontical basis, as in fact happens in *God and Utopia*, but ontologically, the essential enrouting of the religion remains unchanged.

The most important specific alteration of the categories of its proximate ontical basis (i.e. Christianity) that *God and Utopia* proposes is the addition of "technology" as a major interpretive element. To be sure, ideology possessed (indeed midwifed) the category of technology long ago, but it is only with Vahanian's work that technology actually moves from being something interpreted to a principle of interpretation and becomes a primary religious category. The important difference between Vahanian's sense of the word and other treatments of technology is that Vahanian is not proposing to interpret technological phenomena from a religious perspective as if they were external entities; he is rather proposing in effect to symbolize technology's modifications of human existence, including the devices that are its most visible manifestations and, much more important, the unprecedented people who populate the world of technological progress. Unlike Heidegger, who envisions for Dasein a kind of necessary snapping back to awareness of Being as the dynamics of technology bring Dasein into a confrontation with the impossible, Vahanian will make the very dynamics of technology from which Heidegger prescinds constitutive of the religious perspective; this is done by making technology's artifices the way of the authentically human. This is technological utopianism. While the shift that is embodied in the thought of technological utopianism is interesting in itself, its importance for this study is as an example of the impact philosophical theology must have on its tradition if it is to fulfill its mission. Since traditional Christian religiosity is familiar, it is not necessary for us to go into the origins of Vahanian's thinking to see something of the iconoclastic flexibility that philosophical theology requires if it is to be more than window-dressing.

With the thought of transposing religion from mythology to technology, Vahanian is attempting to make a critical consciousness integral to religion. This transposition of a currently developing (and thus incompletely understood) philosophical tool from the periphery of religious practice to the center is the only way for human utopianism to be free of ideological constraint as he pictures it. It is also a way for religion to have a hand in the appropriation of the epoch's most vital cultural energies. With the word "utopianism," Vahanian appears to be naming a variant of what our ontology has imagined as the appropriation of nothingness. With the concept of "technique of the human," he seems to be reworking a dominant theme of our time to suggest an element of a nonsectarian Christianity which is capable of a radically different, nonsubstantialistic, *non-essentialistic*, yet definitely religious understanding of the being which appropriates. It may not always be a change of this magnitude that the task of philosophical theology demands, but anything less extensive (i.e. which leaves some elements of the way of the religion untouched) is either confessional theology or metaphysics. The scope of philosophical theology's transformations is absolute. In Vahanian's novel treatment of technology's Christian possibilities, philosophical theology can be seen working both sides of the culture to discover (that is, uncover) the human as the technological and humanity's opportunities in technology. This is what philosophical theology must do to maintain resolute Dasein's integrity. It can also be seen frequently straining the language of the past to the limits of intelligibility as it tries to construct the religion of the future.

The authentic appropriation of the possibility of untruth requires of philosophical theology that it possess a wider inventory of categories than confessional theology. Since it is enrouting movement that is the essence of a religion, and not its inventory of interpretive categories, this revision does not destroy a religion, but continually reconstructs it to broaden its ontical scope. To some, such reconstruction is tantamount to heresy, but for true religion, the real heresy is to be found in the covering-up of possibilities of the uncanny and unprecedented. In the process of reconstruction, religion's categories themselves become present-at-hand and available for deconstruction; the result is that relationships among existing categories must change, not only because of the addition of a new category, but also because of radically new perceptions of the efficacies of the old ones. Since it is philosophy, and especially metaphysics (including its *post mortem Dei* variant realization, criticism), which is most concerned with categories of interpretation, philosophical theology is always tempted to fall into philosophy; ideology, through language, paves the way. Philosophical theology, as authentic appropriation of the possibility of untruth, never intends to align itself with untruth as truth, though it may fall into just that possibility if resoluteness is lost; as long as resoluteness remains, however, it is the unspoken aim of philosophical theology to disappear into confessional theology, even though it never can, at least within a Heideggerian ontological-critical framework. On the contrary, philosophical theology is always springing out anew from the polemics of truth and untruth.

If philosophical theology is defined in this way, *God and Utopia* may serve as a good example of the genre in spite of its non-Heideggerian orientation. The point, of course, can never be to force philosophical theology into working with "orthodox" Heideggerian themes and vocabulary; it is rather to see from the perspective afforded by the Heideggerian ontology developed here just how unorthodox the discourse of philosophical theology can, and perhaps should be. Vahanian alludes to this point when he writes, "I hope the reader will indulge the author's habit . . . of defining some categories en route, while their meaning is unfolding or as the argument is drawing to a close. The reason for this is simple enough: it has been difficult to denounce antiquated notions and at the same time marshal these reflections under the aegis of traditional thought."[35] Even though a work of philosophical theology is warranted by a specific tradition, it can never be entirely "traditional" in the conservative sense frequently attached to the term; it is traditional insofar as it intends to remain true to the tradition (community of faith) within which it occurs by the resolute, authentic appropriation of the possibility of untruth and enabling of Dasein's consequent projection of itself upon factical possibilities that can be given for the first time by the structure of significance-relations and mediated by the religious symbol system.

God and Utopia shows how theological discourse can remain true to the religious origin of its warrant even while departing from it by taking it in unaccustomed ways. Ontically, this is the philosophical theologian's task, since philosophical theology is charged by its warrant to enable the religion to do what it ontologically must as it has ontically never done before. As Vahanian explains, speaking perhaps for all philosophical theologians, "What is important is to be in this world in such a way that everything has its place and that there is a time for everything . . . ."[36] More than anyone else, the philosophical theologian resolutely endeavors to make this happen.

It would be convenient to let our ontological sketch of philosophical theology conclude on this note, but the problematic does not allow religion and philosophy to be reconciled yet. When a religion warrants philosophical theology, it is because there is trouble in the air. The trouble has already been formally identified above as the perception of the possibility of untruth, a possibility which is radically disequilibrating for religious Dasein; as soon as the factical possibility of untruth exists, even a Dasein called back from its lostness in the "they" to some authentic way may not find the way of a given religion adequate to its needs and Being-in-the-world. Projecting itself resolutely upon a given religion's world as factical possibility, Dasein may find that "it (the religion) does not relate" when (according to Heidegger's analysis in division 44 of *Being and Time*), in fact, it is Dasein itself that is not relating, or, to put it more accurately, when its own religion does not relate to life, Dasein is finding itself being called away from an authentic grasp of its Situation and into an inadequate general structure of significance-relationships and way of being in the world given by a religion.

By this analysis, a part of one's disaffection with religion in general must be traceable to a disaffection with some specific religion, or even several. Disaffection with religion formally arises out of an original projection onto a factical religion as an authentic possibility which could not be sustained; that kind of disaffection must be **essentially religious**. Philosophical theology watches this happen and moves "Darwinistically" to try to find a new equilibrium. Vahanian expresses this dynamic in ontic language: "Challenging every absolutism used to dress up gods (or, for that matter, men), theology unmasks the tyranny of false assurances and deceptive hopes nourished by religion."[37] These words should not be interpreted to mean that all theology has an adversarial relationship to the warranting religion at all times — because confessional theology obviously does not — but rather that at the level of philosophy, theology cannot accept the claims of a truth that does not know how to appropriate untruth. This is to say that according to our theory of theology, philosophical theology cannot accept either confessional theology or the factical possibilities it presents in the name of its warranting religion as factically absolutely true.

The two types of theology that have been sketched as being warranted from specific religions are both understood to be traditional in that they both concern themselves thematically with the tradition which warrants them. These two types of theology belong together in a way structurally analogous to how the two aspects of faith belong together. The key difference between them is philosophical theology's drive to revise the structure of significance-relationships in order to retain its warranting religion's adequacy in the event of authentic Dasein's projection of itself upon certain factical possibilities as mediated by the religious symbol system. These two types of theology are the only ones warranted from religion but they do not exhaust all of the possibilities of theology. There remain yet two genres of theology, or quasi-theology which are warranted from ideology. These ways of speaking are different in a number of ways from the two general theologies that are warranted from factical religion, but they are properly theological insofar as there can be any warranting of theology from ideology as quasi-religion. Max Myers, thinking ideology in the tradition of the Frankfurt School, writes, "The point is that ideologies may serve as proximate horizons within which human beings come to understand themselves, each other, and the world."[38] In certain moments of short-sightedness (read "falling"), proximate horizons may be as far as one can see; that is when ideology becomes virtually indistinguishable from religion.

Theology was analyzed above as being warranted from religion either to conserve and consolidate a world as mediated in a religious symbol system (by articulating its truth) or to reinterpret and augment existing categories in order to restore or preserve a religion's truth. The first step in entertaining the possibility of warranting theology from ideology consists in simply substituting the word "ideology" for "religion" in the descriptions of the two warrants we know about, and either accepting or rejecting the results.

Following this route, a preliminary projection of the quasi-theological counterpart of confessional theology that is warranted from an ideology will be: a mode of discourse which articulates the unity of what-is as mediated in an *ideological* symbol system. This genre of quasi-theology will be symmetrically construed as: the conserving and consolidating moment of an *ideology's* interpretation. The ontologically-determined ground of the warrant that founds ideology's counterpart to confessional theology must be, by analogy, ideology's truth. At this point, if the analogy is to survive, it appears that the understanding of the term "truth" that has been operating in connection with religion will have to be qualified, since "ideology" is categorically excluded from grammatically complementing "truth" in Heidegger's sense. The nature of the required qualification has already been suggested in the observation that in fallenness, untruth ontically comes to presence as truth. Ideology's truth is the public truth of the "they," which covers beings over and dissembles as the way things are.

Similarly, ideology's counterpart to philosophical theology can also be projected in a preliminary way. This other genre of quasi-theology will be warranted by the possibility of the apparent untruth of its ideology, that is, in this case, by the possibility of its ideology's actually coming to presence in its untruth, as it in fact ontologically is. Philosophical theology's ideological counterpart will also be expected to add categories of interpretation to an ideology's existing inventory in order to find and maintain an equilibrium. At this point these mechanical substitutions are justified more as hypotheses than as conclusions; although straightforward replacement of terms raises a few problems, the initial ease with which the resulting strings can be semantically analyzed suggests that the hypotheses are viable enough to justify calling these two modes of interpretation that are warranted out of ideology by the same general name as those warranted out of religion. Ontologically, all four entail some sort of attitude toward divinities which is decisive for their agendas.

Several aspects of religion and ideology are significant with regard to the hypothesized structural correspondence between the theologies warranted from religion and the (quasi-) theologies warranted from ideology. First, both religions and ideologies determine ways of being in the world. Second, both determine structures of significance-relationships, and ideology shares the quality of finite absoluteness with religion; within the respective domains of religion and ideology, all phenomena are intended to be construed and thus everything tends to be understood in the categories of the theologies, or as mediated by their symbol systems. Third, both grounds of theology, religion and ideology, stand in need of continual interpretation to place all phenomena in the world. Fourth, both may be ontically experienced in modes of truth and untruth. Fifth, and by no means least important, both religions and ideologies may factically be bases for communities of faith. These are the main similarities between religion and ideology in general that are significant here. There remains as difference, however, the ontological fact of falling which always distinguishes religion and ideology from each other.

Like religion, ideology also must have its "sacred texts," primary stories, explanations, and art works which may be orally transmitted, encoded in written documents, or otherwise inscribed such that they constitute the generally unchallenged basis of the symbol system, and around which a community of faith may grow up if the basis is explicit enough to be shared. For this reason, the understandings and decisions which occur under the sign of ideology must be as much subject to and needful of interpretation as those which emerge in the mode of religion. Originating in the structural resemblance between religions and ideologies is a theoretical justification for positing something like a theological mode of interpretation of ideology, since the faith that accompanies ideology and the faith that accompanies religion are structurally identical with regard to their respective bases; the structures of seeking and understanding are likewise related.

Given these formal similarities between religion and ideology, the kinds of interpretation involving the three elements of theology (faith, seeking, and understanding) that are warranted from the precincts of ideology cannot but appear as some sort of theology. These similarities, which touch on major features of the interpretation of religion and ideology, and not just trivial or incidental resemblances, strongly suggest that familiar, workable concepts that have informed traditional theology may admit of generalization to include the kinds of interpretation that are warranted from ideology.

The first conception of traditional theology that may be generalized from religion to ideology is the division of theology into the two established genres of confessional and philosophical theology. Though the genre names of the kinds of interpretation which are proper to ideology are meaningfully different from those proper to religion, and though there will be shown to be other, substantive, points of dissimilarity, two analogous genres of interpretation can be identified on the side of ideology. Analogous to the genre of confessional theology is a mode of discourse whose interpretations remain exclusively within the given categories of an ideology; as Nasr's essay did, this type of interpretation would use all available material for its own purpose of maintaining the absoluteness of the given categories of an ideology. Analogous to philosophical theology is a way of thinking which looks not only beyond its own ideology, but beyond ideology in general, though always with the intention of maintaining the influence of ideology. Phenomenally, the first sort of discourse often appears to be lexically conflated with the texts from which it originates and, as a result, the whole complex is placed under the rubric of "ideology"; there is an identifiable difference between the discourse of a fundamental text and that of an interpretation, however, that always needs to be recognized. The second type of ideologically warranted theology is susceptible to a different sort of confusion: it actually appears to be related to the religion of a traditional theology.

The first type of interpretation of ideology may go under the name of philosophy, and in two ways: one in a way that Quine indirectly suggests in "Ontology and Ideology Revisited" and the other in a way that Ayn Rand presents in the essay discussed below, "What Is Capitalism?" Quine's analysis does not say in so many words that the unreflective manifestations of ideology which show up as the language of daily affairs are themselves a type of philosophy, but it does imply that the elaborations of their meaning in analysis can be classed as philosophy. This sort of interpretation of ideology belongs to the linguistic analysis branch of philosophy, with which we are not concerned in this chapter.

An essay like Rand's, however, informed by positivistic presuppositions which engender totalistic (or logocentric) interpretations of what-is according to the logic of a specific ideological way of being in the world (rather than giving rise to linguistic philosophy's interpretations of statements about what-is), is also conventionally classed as philosophy. This categorization is problematical; in current usage, there is no recognizably adequate name for such discourse, which represents ideology's analogue to confessional theology. To call it political philosophy obscures its ontological agenda and to call it social commentary makes it appear that the day-to-day affairs of society are what is most important to it. If we are aware of ideology as technique of care, the deeper story is quite different, and the apparent terminological deficiency in the case of this genre of interpretation is not a mere oversight, but a useful lacuna which serves the interests of ideology.

The beginning of bringing this genre of interpretation to presence as the quasi-theology which it is comes with the giving of a name to it. Though it is true that a name acts to determine an analysis beforehand, the coercion is limited. On the basis of what is revealed in the analysis, it can always be determined after the fact if the name fits or not. Let us tentatively call ideology's analogue to confessional theology **secular theology**. The choice of this name is not purely arbitrary, but traces back to terminology adopted by Jacques Maritain in *Man and State*, in which he speaks of a "secular faith,"[39] which Michael Novak describes as " . . . adherence to . . . principles of practice . . . rooted in the practical nature of human beings."[40]

Interpretation of existence which informs understanding according to "secular faith" is secular theology. For reasons of our own, which are connected with the analysis of religion and ideology above, there is a basis for agreement with Novak's claim that secular faith is not religious faith; by extension, secular theology is not religious theology. In fact, secular theology is the only one of the four basic genres of theology catalogued here which functions virtually independently of religion.[41] The independence is only virtual, however, because the basic ontological unification in discord of religion and ideology never ceases. As the only genre of theology that functions virtually independently of religion, secular theology preserves its integrity by steadfastly maintaining the adequacy of its story as something of a first principle. There is no place for gods as determiners in secular theology, which right away frees secular theology from subservience to mythology (as Vahanian's Christian theology advocates on principle); in ideology, there is only a place for gods that can be determined by ideology, which is to say, no gods that are divinities as the term was developed in the first section. Thus, there is no place for divinities as harbingers of uncanniness or heralds of Being, and it is this exclusion which determines the essential limitation of the vision of secular theology.

In the traditional sense of "theology," what we are calling secular theology is a contradiction in terms, and in calling it a quasi-theology, a distance is established between secular and traditional theology. It is, however, important to see even this godless theology as a true phenomenon of human faithfulness. Secular theology is a faithful assertion of divine absence which is corollary to a faithful assertion of absolute human presence, and that, in turn, is grounded in a totalization of human presence, which can be seen in the explicit rejections of divinities as legitimating agents or determining influences in such diverse modern examples as Communist ideology, Skinnerian ideology, and the libertarian ideology of Ayn Rand.

It is as structured assertions of absolute presence that ideologies reveal themselves to be inherently metaphysical, which, it should be no surprise, is exactly what they always say they are *not* and exactly what they should be as manifestations of the Heideggerian existentiale of care. If the first interpretive principle of ideology were to be formalized from the standpoint of one ideology or another, which would also be a secular theology's own standpoint, there should be no disagreement among otherwise inimical ideologies about whether the semantic distinctive feature complex of secular theology is more properly represented as [+human] or [−god]. Ideology would understand itself as [+human] and there would be no question of god. From philosophical theology's standpoint, both features would be needed and signs could be decided theologically.

From looking at this issue, it becomes certain that secular theology and the ideology it represents are not to be confused with idolatry or with an (attempted) apotheosis of the human being. Theistic idolatry is excluded because it requires a god who meets specific needs of inadequate religious humanity, even if in a finite and ultimately untrue way. Further, Tillich's idea that idolatry consists in the mistaken ascription of ultimacy to a finite entity becomes problematical in the face of ideology's implicit assertion that ultimacy as "the beyond" is essentially nothingness, a stand which grows out of Dasein's finite temporalizing and presencing of what-is. The apotheosis of the human being, as essentially a location of the human in the place of the divine, cannot transpire when the divine has no place at all, not even a vacant one.

It is a common characteristic of ideology that humanity is conceived as "on its own" in a world of its own making, in the here and now. As Skinner writes,

> The evolution of human culture is in fact a kind of gigantic exercise in self-control. As the individual controls himself by manipulating the world in which he lives, so the human species has constructed an environment in which its members behave in a highly effective way. Mistakes have been made and we have no assurance that the environment man has constructed will continue to provide gains which outstrip losses, but man as we know him, for better or for worse, is what man has made of man.[42]

In terms of the problematic of religion and ideology, what is interesting is not the claim that culture exerts a causal influence on the behavior of human beings, but that Skinner is portraying that fact as virtually the whole story. It is just as the analysis of ideology in previous chapters would predict. There is simply no god *and* no place for one in this conception, and social behaviorism may be taken as typical of the ideological cast of mind.

There being no place for a god, the field is open for any attempt at the totalization of a worldview. Alasdair MacIntyre points out two characteristics of the conflicting versions of the truth that are bound to arise in this kind of situation: first, "conceptual incommensurability" and second, purporting " . . . to be *impersonal* rational arguments and as such . . . usually presented in a mode appropriate to that impersonality."[43] The practical result of the chaos is that a plethora of thinly-disguised projections of self-interest compete for the allegiance of fallen Dasein, which is always looking from place to place in search of the latest and best fascination.

The public play of ideological debate, reported at length and subjected to minute analysis, is perfectly suited to fallen Dasein's mode of Being. Fallen Dasein projects itself most energetically into the presence of the Present when public issues of apparently great moment are being decided and when anyone may have an opinion about the yes or the no, the right or the wrong. MacIntyre notices how ideology's ascendance in the technological age has affected ethics, the scene of the test of resoluteness:

> The most striking feature of contemporary moral utterance
> is that so much of it is used to express disagreements; and
> the most striking feature of the debates in which these
> disagreements are expressed is their interminable character.
> I do not mean by this just that such debates go on and
> on — although they do — but also that they apparently
> can find no terminus. There seems to be no rational way of
> securing moral agreement in our culture. [44]

MacIntyre has seen what has come to pass; he allows us to take the logic of the situation to its conclusion: there not only seems to be no rational way of securing moral agreement in our culture, there *is* no rational way of securing moral agreement in our culture or any other in which there is not already an agreement on what is *beyond reason*, namely, religion.

Godless as it is, secular theology is still faithful in an another important way: it is language being faithful to the possibility of theology itself in the carrying out of the sort of interpretations religion would warrant, even though true religion has been excluded. Moreover, secular theology educates human beings to the possibility *as such* of a world without gods, most especially the gods imagined in the condition of fallenness, which is being imagined here as an integral moment of religiosity. Just as it is emptiness which enables the form to stand out, or, in Lao Tzu's image, which makes the wheel a wheel, it is the exclusion of gods which makes the possibility of gods stand out. This exclusion comes to presence as a meaningful one only in the state-of-mind of anxiety; in fallenness, it must come to presence as a *pro forma* declaration, one which is, moreover, true for there are no real gods of the sort that fallen Dasein imagines. Phenomenally, ideology and secular theology may evidence the contrived (and ultimately spurious) emptiness of classical atheism or they may avoid that old pitfall and exclude divinities by constructing a closed system that works well enough without gods. Either way, the effect of preserving the form of theology without its traditional religious content is the same: even in the mode of fallenness, interpretation of the structure of significance-relations continues, but with the difference that the agenda is primarily social and ethical, rather than personal, since the person is taken for granted in the self-evidence of fallenness. This falling taking-for-granted and the concomitant oblivion of Being is precisely the possibility of deficiency that religion is designed to counter. As with the other two genres of theology that have been considered, a brief look at a representative sample of secular theology shows how these specifications are translated into practice.

Secular theology, because it partakes of ideology's unfailing encouragement of fallen Dasein's compulsive shifts of attention, does not have the same appearance of timelessness as confessional theology. Interspersed with discussions of principle will be the kind of topicality that can make an essay appear dated or peculiarly focused. It is necessary to look beyond these flashes of transitory relevance to see that secular theology is not just another kind of editorializing, but aims to be the propaedeutic for all editorializing; it proceeds logically, that is, by the logic of falling, which decrees that theory be brought into concrete, topical focus. This gives secular theology that feel of immediacy which allows it to snap interest away from previous fascinations and provoke discussion about what should be done in this or that situation. Let us recognize that not only the topicality of secular theology but also our impatience with the datedness or the apparent triviality of secular theological writings are all among the manifestations of fallenness, in which Dasein is always concerned to be *au courant*.

In its search for the debatability that fallen Dasein demands, secular theology is drawn to controversial topics and tends to open discussion using highly charged lexical items as banners to rally both sympathizers and adversaries alike. Fallen Dasein, we recall, cares only for its own existential tranquilization and that is largely satisfied by simply having something to do; actually winning disputes is an occasional secondary satisfaction, our ontology claims. "What Is Capitalism?" is the lead piece in a collection of Ayn Rand's essays that were assembled under the title *Capitalism: The Unknown Ideal*. "Capitalism" functions provocatively as one of the primary categories of interpretation in Ayn Rand's ideology, which she named "Objectivism" without a trace of irony. Objectivism was straightforwardly intended to be a practical ideology for right thinking and action, that is, thinking and action which conform to Rand's understanding of what is right. That understanding, whose content is less important for ontological purposes than its categories, we find reflected in her characterization of political ideology. As Rand theorizes:

> A political ideology is aimed at establishing or maintaining a certain social system; it is a program of long-range action, with the principles serving to unify and integrate particular steps into a consistent course. It is only by means of principles that men can project the future and choose their actions accordingly."[45]

There are several key words and phrases that reveal aspects of ideology at work in this passage. The first is "social system"; while it is both religion's and ideology's place to determine a system, it is only as care that Dasein projects itself into factically possible social systems. The actual determination of the systems themselves is not the task of inter-pretation, at least theoretically.[46] The system that is established need not be one based on a mechanical metaphor and need not be rationally constructed to satisfy the basic definitional requirements of symbol systems (as all systems arguably are), though it is a matter of record that Objectivism appreciates the first (i.e., mechanism) and demands the second (a rationally developed structure).

Relating to another aspect of secular theology is a second important word in Rand's ideological vocabulary: "program." The analogy of the computer program is *a propos* here. The specific characteristic of the computer program that attracts our attention is the appearance of a clear-cut separation of operational principles and content in the machine's system; ostensibly, the program provides a set of general principles that apply on a case-by-case basis to anything that comes their way. In practice, the program recognizes only those things which it and its interpreter are equipped in advance to recognize and its depth is limited to those aspects of things that it can process meaningfully and the kinds of relationships it is allowed to construct.

Ideology, like religion, always stands ready to dispose of all phe-nomena programmatically in language; the key difference between them lies in the tasks of the respective programs. Ideology's program seeks to capture and confine all phenomena within language, thus expanding its horizons of knowledge and reconstituting itself while essentially limiting understanding to what has been pre-established by the "they" as accept-able. It is characteristic of fallen, ideological Dasein to believe that it can succeed in this enterprise. Religion's program, on the other hand, may name and place entities but never imagines that in so doing an exhaus-tive understanding of every important aspect of their Being has already been achieved. For religion, this is just the beginning. Religion's program further demands openness to the unprecedented (which incidentally seems to be the key to the ontology of miracles).

The language of ideology is a closed system which obeys the rules of Wittgenstein's concept of the language game. To ideology, things are signifiers of words (and there is no freedom, or even consciousness, unless the totalized ideological structures are broken). To religion, on the other hand, words remain signifiers of things, pointing iconographically beyond themselves. Ideology's program is primarily concerned with adding more and more information as knowledge, of expanding the territory that lies within the field determined by program's operating parameters. Religion's program, in contrast, is more concerned with expanding awareness of the field that lies beyond knowledge and reflection. Religion's program tells the finger how to point at the moon.

Yet another feature of secular theology is suggested by a third significant term in Rand's proposed definition of political ideology. Ideology is especially fond of "principles," those asserted primes which are the bases of systems of privilege and prerequisites of program routines, generally speaking. Principles have the essential form of injunctions, or commands, not propositions, so there is no question of "true" or "false" principles. Obedience, or submission, as Islam points out by its name and theology in a context that is directly relevant to this problematic, is the only appropriate attitude. We also note in the above passage the words "unify and integrate"; these further relate the ideology that Rand conceives to religion as traditionally, not to mention ontologically, understood. It is important to the understanding of the difference between religion and ideology to bear in mind ideology's tendency to mimic religion in style while restricting any elements of the religious style that might undermine the existential serenity of wrestling with issues of policy and metaphysics.

It is likely that abstract understanding of an element of a set entails some understanding of whatever principles of inclusion govern the set. On her way to clarify the nature of political ideology, and her own project as well, Rand has laid out some of the major characteristics of ideology in general. This has not happened as a matter of course because not all ideology proclaims itself to be such as clearly as Objectivism does. Marx and Engels, for example, who deserve much of the credit for inventing the contemporary terms of ideology's presence-at-hand, claimed that Communism was itself not an ideology. In their view, ideology was the product of interested self-delusion. They saw ideology as a prop which is used to compensate for some inadequacy or imbalance by covering it over with a spurious story. In our Heideggerian critical theoretical framework, what we are calling "ideology" also covers over inadequacy but instead of locating this inadequacy in the concrete material-historical situation, as Marx and Engels did, our analysis locates it ontologically in Dasein's factical existential Situation, thereby making a differentiation that must appear specious and subjectivistic to material-ist onto-ideology.[47] Because our analysis does not accord to any individual or group a privileged position with respect to this inadequacy, there is no advantage in projecting it onto another; this tends to limit discussion in two ways: by eliminating incentives for use of the topic in a dynamic of domination and by making any discussion "personal."

Other clues to the nature of ideology show up in Rand's writing. One of them connects with Heidegger's mention in *Being and Time* of a disposition of the "they" to affect an attitude of "knowing everything." This disposition is analyzed as the proximate basis of ideology's sense of its own adequacy, and it is challenged, of course, by every true novelty that has the temerity not to fit the system. Rand deals with the problem directly, acknowledging that " . . . men are neither omniscient nor infallible . . . "[48] but she does not let this uncharacteristic show of modesty become an admission of ideological inadequacy. The real issue, she claims, is not a question of factual knowledge or a correspondence notion of correctness, but rather one of reason: " . . . the fact remains that reason is man's means of survival and that men prosper or fail, survive or perish in proportion to the degree of their rationality."[49] This is the position ideology must work from; it not only brings ideology's usefulness to the fore, but it also reflects ideology's drive to totalize itself by making rationality the measure of humanity. The logic is clear and invariant from ideology to ideology, and it brings us once again into the vicinity of Heidegger's critique of technology: if the human being is taken to be the measure of all things, and if rationality is the measure of human being, then reason must be the ultimate measure of all things.

The projection of reason as the measure of all things works toward restructuring one's sense of the world in a way that Rand or any secularist must want it to be. She writes:

> The *objective* theory holds that the good is neither an attribute of 'things in themselves' nor of man's emotional states, but *an evaluation* of the facts of reality by man's consciousness according to a rational standard of value. (Rational, in this context, means: derived from the facts of reality and validated by a process of reason.) [50]

Reason is thus presented in her writing as the adequate determiner of the good and, as the argument unfolds, as the adequate basis of all social systems. Speaking the hopes of fallen Dasein, Rand argues for reason's exclusive governance in the making of decisions, which is to say, for ideology's exclusive governance of reality. Ideology, as technique of care, clearly has a role to play in society, but if it closes off the non-rational, the full reality of Dasein can never happen. Dasein, as a choosing-move-ment-between, needs both religion and ideology. Augustine knows this as he affirms a differentiated structure of creation in the *Confessions*.

It is against the backdrop of an unequivocal advocacy of reason's prerogatives that Rand proposes to answer the question of what capital-ism is. She dispatches the task in one sentence: "Capitalism is a social system based on the recognition of individual rights, including property rights, in which all property is privately owned."[51] Her essay, nominally about capitalism, devotes the lion's share of its space and energy not to analysis of capitalism, but to a discourse on human nature. This is a good indication of where ideology's true interests are. In answering the ques-tion of what capitalism is, Rand does not hunt through history for examples that illustrate or approximate her idea of what capitalism is or should be. The reason is that hers is not an empirical description of history's capitalism; it is a description of her own ideology's "capital-ism." Having established that the essay under discussion is an ideologi-cal project, it is but a short step to see how it is a work of secular theology whose aim it is to clarify the categories of thinking such that the author will be able to bring them into line with her own ideology. It is no accident that she has chosen one of the key terms of her social context to re-work, for if she succeeds in re-defining capitalism, a major portion of Western society will then be following her ideology's line. It is appropri-ate to entertain the factor of the presence of futural rewards in a situation such as this, but as our ontology suggests, the greatest energy is being devoted to the animation of the present. Rand's way of re-defining capitalism is paradigmatic for ideological manipulation of categories; her technique is to re-define humanity itself so that capitalism is the only reasonable economic system, just as Skinner's was to re-define humanity to fit his idea of a "science of man." This impulse is not insignificant in gauging the working of ideology in history, especially in connection with the phenomenon of technology.

Rand's exposition is a classic of the type; like Nasr's it is distin-guished by its forthrightly polemical use of language. No ambivalences or hesitations mask the contours of Rand's and Nasr's prejudices. They share an exuberant confidence in their respective structures of decision and they forcefully project this confidence in their writings. Experience convinces them that their respective structures of decision are truthfully able to organize and unify phenomena, and they set themselves in service to this truth. They part company, however, on the focus of their attention.

While the confessional theologian is concentrating on problems of individual piety and understanding, the secular theologian is speaking of the crowd and to the crowd. Thus, in the example chosen, Rand is observed delivering up sweeping generalizations about history and human nature that are provocatively combined with analyses of current events whose attention to detail is eclectic, fascinating, and looks almost psychoanalytic, except that instead of bringing one to the truth of personal existence, this writing endeavors to bring one to the truth of social existence. Rand is not revealing social structures so that her readers may find their own ways to come to terms with them; following a theological agenda, she is preparing the way for the reader's theoretically rational acceptance of her position as the prerequisite of rational action in history. In Heideggerian terms, Dasein's attention is directed away from its own possibilities, that of its death especially, and toward the deathless flux of society. The way the attention is attracted and re-directed, as Ernest Becker mordantly observes in *The Denial of Death*, is such that the individual is seduced by the ideology into a heroic immortality-project which helps the they-self to perpetuate its repression of death; the dim intuition of the need for such a project eventuates in a faulty personal strategy which allows — no, demands — an evasion of the truth of one's own existence.[52] Rand puts her own "spin" on the Situation: "My philosophy, in essence, is the concept of man as a heroic being, with his own happiness as the moral purpose of his life, with productive achievement as his noblest activity, and reason as his absolute."[53] In this way, our fundamental ontology suggests, Dasein loses (sight of) itself, but never misses itself, being entertained and determined by the self-sufficient possibilities of the "they."

The "they" has an incessant craving for discussion or some other kind of presentation of themes with the glisten of heroism. When Rand takes capitalism as her nominal theme, she is calling attention to one kind of problem, the condition of capitalism, and covering up another, the human condition. Following the call of fallen Dasein for ever-greater images of self-importance, she writes in such a way that economics becomes the scene of the most fundamental issues of existence and reason's hegemony becomes the stakes. This is what makes her work ideological, not its essay format or its attention to theory of capitalism.

Reason proceeds at the explicit level by sequences of opposition and agreement and ideology elevates this feature to the status of an ultimate concern. Secular theology sells itself in part by setting up an opponent and then arguing that the important tension at the moment is between itself and its adversary. Whether the adversary is called secular humanism, apartheid, drugs, capitalist imperialism, fluoridation, or the destroyers of small animals does not matter *formally*; the effect is that Dasein is called away into novel involvements that may take on a life of their own, which is really a taking away of Dasein's life. If resolute Dasein chooses to take up a cause in authentic appropriation of a possibility thrown into circulation by the "they," it may factically advocate many of the same measures as fallen Dasein does; the visible difference will be interest in the Being of the adversary as well as the being of one's partisans. In Buddhism, this ideal appears to be included in the doctrine of right intention, in Christianity, by the teaching that one should love one's enemies. In every case, authentic Dasein's first loyalty in public affairs is to the shepherding of Being, yet it is always gripped by the contingencies of its situation and thus required to induce others to fall in some particular way by the logic of its own specific commitment. This is an important ontological fact for any Heideggerian ethics or psychology to consider. Authentic Dasein is double-bound by injunctions to belong with beings in their Being and to make its way in the world by appropriating certain initiatives of the "they," which always call Dasein away from authenticity. Inauthentic Dasein, by contrast, is untroubled by these considerations and thus free to devote itself to what is handed to it until the next fascination comes along.

It is against this ontological backdrop that we see another aspect of Rand's work, her unpopular vituperations against altruism. Given the importance of real or imagined altruism in the religious sensibilities of the culture she addresses, the frontal attack of ideology on religion is clearly evident. The fact of the attack is unremarkable but the construction of it is revealing of how ideology can move to include its opposition in its totalizing project. Whether by accident or by design, Rand has constructed a challenge that addresses both fallen and resolute Dasein. To fallen Dasein, she argues that altruism in society is like glue thrown into precision machinery; it perniciously dissipates the vital individual initiative that powers the engines of economic progress. To authentic Dasein, she argues in effect that altruism is an inauthentic taking up of the possibilities of others which conceals the realities of existence from them and implies a low valuation of one's own projects. The extended sermon by John Galt in *Atlas Shrugged*, itself as long as many short novels, can be read as an appeal to resolute Dasein. It is not intended to be a gospel of mean-spiritedness, according to Rand, but a reminder of where one's interests lie and an exhortation not to waver. In this, it is not so far removed from the words of the Koran, "And let not pity . . . withhold you from obedience to Allah . . . ."[54] The difference is that the

Koran focuses Dasein's attention on the inscrutable Allah while ideology focuses Dasein's attention in an intermittent way on the shifting absolutes of the finite, comprehensible community. To the ideal Moslem who lives in the light of the Koran, existence is uncanny; to the ideal Objectivist who lives within a totalized ideology, existence at its most difficult is merely complicated.

The complexity of existence, including hidden forces at work, is emphasized by ideology for its own purposes. If Dasein is always distracted by an internalized imperative to understand everything, it will avoid confrontation with the fact of its own Being-unto-death and excuse itself to do important work in the community. Thus the community is placed formally prior to the individual in falling. In her writing, Rand parts company with the majority of ideologues in that she does not explicitly elevate the community to a privileged position over the individual, and in fact, she occasionally rails at those who grant the community many prerogatives. This should not diminish the importance of the community to the human being she intends to create, though, for without the economic community, scene of the realization of Objectivist ideology's ideals, there is nothing there to give life meaning for her people. Her ideology is not alone in this, of course; the community has the same instrumental importance in Communism, though the expression of it is different and the way for people to realize it most fully in their lives is different. For ideology in general, the community is the ultimate concern and the source of the standards by which things are valued. It is important for Dasein that this is so.

Ideology as such (meaning not as religion) appears to be salutary to Dasein's realization of itself as Mitsein, which factically occurs for the most part as participation in communities and sub-cultures. When religion tries to expropriate major responsibility for community standards and practices from ideology, the results can be extreme: the Aztecs with their rivers of blood, the inconvenient cattle of India, the sexual segregation of Mount Athos, the burning of witches at Salem, the venomous anti-Western hysteria of present-day Iran, the choir system of the eighteenth-century Moravians, the celibacy of the Shakers, the Kool-Aid nightmare of Jonestown. When ideology sets itself up as religion, as Tillich observed that it easily could, the results are no better, of course: Hitler's genocide and Mao's attempted decapitation of China are just two examples.

The purpose of these observations is to help avoid seeing ideology as something that is either eradicable or undesirable. Whether the ideas of Ayn Rand or Karl Marx or other ideologues are attractive or not is ontologically beside the point; they are already a part of human reality as expressions of Dasein's existentiale of falling. The important question now is how they actually belong, given the fundamental ontology we have provisionally accepted. It has become clear that ideological initiatives cannot be regarded as simple lapses from a true religious faith, for they possess positive as well as negative attributes. It has also become clear how Vahanian can write that " . . . today secularization attacks the very heart of faith."[55] We see it attacking especially in the mode of quasi-religion's quasi-theologies.

Secular theology is but one of the two quasi-theologies that is indicated by our interpretation of the tradition in light of the ontological considerations of the previous chapters. To look at the second, we interrogate another work originating in the precincts of ideology and taking capitalism as its nominal theme, Michael Novak's already-cited *The Spirit of Democratic Capitalism*. Much as Rand's work corresponds to confessional theology, *The Spirit of Democratic Capitalism* corresponds to philosophical theology. In recognition of the true theme of its discourse and for want of an existing term, we shall refer to pieces of the type exemplified by *The Spirit of Democratic Capitalism* as **theologistics**. This type of theology stands in a pivotal place in a community of faith, since it negatively represents certain of the claims of religion as they they are lodged in moments of ideology's factical insufficiency as quasi-religion. In other words, theologistics is a reluctant response in the language of the they-self to the call of authenticity.

A number of thorny questions accompany the general project of theologistics and they have been made all the more compelling by circumstances attending the rise of technology; these questions insure that of the four genres of theology that have been typed, theologistics (if present in the Present) is determined in advance to receive the most attention as a phenomenon in the culture. It presents highly cathected novelties in ways that are exciting, but existentially non-threatening. It takes care always to guide discussion away from the borders of anxiety and uncanniness, and back into self-assurance. This feature of theologistics is of more than incidental interest; it has implications for the relationship of theologies of all types to the communities of faith which are their reason for being.

Theologistic discourse walks the tightrope of public opinion without a net and is always pre-determined to fall. It is not blood-lust that keeps fallen Dasein interested in the presentations of theologistics, though, but the hoping against hope that each new venture to domesticate the first term of the "religion and society" problematic will succeed where all others have failed. Novak's choice of title is the first indication that this book, which he describes as "a *general* theology of economics,"[56] originates outside of religion and has a different theme. From the beginning of the book the agenda appears to be other than theological even though the tone is at times religious. The reader of this book and any other theologistic text is confronted with a difficult decision early on: is the material at hand a work of religion or is it one of ideology? Much depends on being able to see the difference, and it is in the presence of discourse such as one finds in apparently liberal documents like *The Spirit of Democratic Capitalism* and the addresses of many religious fundamentalists that the possibility of generic confusion is highest. The fact of the matter is that outward appearance tells little about whether the origins of a piece are factically religious or ideological; all one can determine is from what basis or bases the discourse is warranted and what its implications are. The state-of-Being of the speaker remains opaque.

The opacity of the Being of the speaker in theologistic discourse is maintained in part by a generic requirement to exclude oneself from suspicion of producing the kind of illegitimate proof-texting that arises when fallen Dasein employs the language of religion as a tool of the they-self for ideology's purposes. While theologistics is in one sense a calculated attempt to salvage a troubled ideology, it does contain within itself the power to transform the language of the ideology and thus the ideology itself. Novak's own language is a case-in-point of the use of a religious idiom in close association with an agenda that looks ideological, often even political. The religious language looks out of place, but perhaps not so much more out of place than the language of technology looks in Vahanian's philosophical theology. Both philosophical theology and theologistics run the risk of using offensive language. In his theologistic project Novak may avoid the fundamentalist error but one is still left with questions about the ontological status of this ideological use of religious language and others resembling it in important details. The first question is from whence their warrants issue.

Upon stepping into the tangle of squirming categories that characterizes theologistics, one is called upon to recognize the genre, to see that the text at hand is more a work of ideology than of religion and to bear in mind why this is so. Early in *The Spirit of Democratic Capitalism*, for example, Novak quotes Jacques Maritain's observation that the social system which is currently being discussed under the rubric "democratic capitalism" lacked an adequate ideology.[57] The need to address a specific constituency, fallingly occupied with timely issues, demands a certain clarity of agenda; that clarity is a hallmark of ideology's counterpart to philosophical theology.

While the issues grasped for the moment as important by an ideology undeniably constitute an important component of theologistic discourse, what shifts theologistics from mere topicality into being a compelling object of concern for traditional and non-traditional religious theologians is that something resembling religion is also set forth as important. Acknowledgement of religion's importance does not become meaningful until it is made clear *what* about religion is important. In the example we have chosen, religion's importance is tied to the ideological intent of the discussion. This is exactly how fallen Dasein must grasp religion. If one were to assume that there are no principles of relationship among ideology, religion, and theology except principles of exclusion, a work such as this would appear schizophrenic. If, on the other hand, there is imagined to obtain an inclusive relationship among them, then theologistic essays possess the legitimacy of a genre of theology insofar as they respect their warrant.

Of the four genres of theology described in our attempt at a critical theory, theologistics appears to present the greatest difficulties in determining what the proper task is and what language is appropriate. Even Novak's early experience in religious theology seems not to have been able to guide him in establishing genre lines clearly enough to prevent the mixing of confessional language into the ideological text of this work (unless, of course, the mixing is intentional), and the warrant for the general discussion seems to have been obscure. Novak's reflection on his own task takes us part of the way toward a picture of the nature of theologistics and a description of the meaning of its warrant.

At one point Novak writes that he intends to discuss the " . . . theological presuppositions, values, and systemic intentions . . . "[58] of the spirit of democratic capitalism. Let us suggest that the spirit of democratic capitalism (a social system) is ideological in a way very much akin to how the spirit of Roman Catholicism is religious. In the analysis of Ayn Rand's work, we recall, it was noted that "community" was the pre-eminent underlying category in ideology, i.e. that without which the discourse of its theologies had no material to work on; the community must be the object of attention and primary issue for ideology so that Dasein can lose itself in daily or theoretical affairs. Community comes up again as the issue, this time in the genre of theologistics, when Novak writes concerning the philosophy of democratic capitalism, which is emerging even as he discusses it, "The ideology of individualism, too much stressed by some proponents and some opponents alike, disguises the essential communitarian character of its system."[59] A system that is *essentially communitarian*, as capitalism is, *originates in ideology*. While it is not necessary that a work which takes capitalism as its nominal theme originate in ideology, that is the case if the work emulates the example we have selected in seeing itself as a theology of economics or some other social endeavor, uses religious language in ways explicitly subordinate to the constructions of a warranting ideology, and sets itself to tasks that intend to bring religion into the service of ideologically-determined manipulations of presence.

Yet another aspect of theologistic discourse which may serve as an indication of the ideological origin of the work is the role of the concept of theory. Fallen Dasein, in its drive to master the order of reality, has a high regard for theory. The example at hand mentions moral theory at several points. In apposition with the idea of moral theory in this book is the idea of a theory about the life of the spirit. Moral theories conventionally deal with social relations and, whether they clearly originate in ideology or not, they always have to do with ideology. Theories about the life of the spirit are fundamentally different from moral theories because the life of the spirit is the *raison d'etre* of religion while morality is a superficial concern of ideology. The placement of ideas within theoretical (in the general sense Heidegger gives the term) frameworks is the main function of ideology, and one of the things ideology would like to do most is co-opt religion by defining the life of the spirit. Novak's concept of theory in this book is ideology's concept of theory; by including the life of the spirit among the things that theory claims competence to deal with, Novak supports ideology's sweetest fantasy by circumscribing spirit's possibilities to what ideological common sense (in the guise of theory) will allow, thus reducing the life of the spirit to a projection of common sense and eliminating both the autonomy of the theologies warranted by religion and the possibility of utopianism in religion.

One of fallen Dasein's most intense commitments is to management of the situation. Throughout *The Spirit of Democratic Capitalism*, morality consistently receives a heavy emphasis, as one would expect in a work of ideology. The concrete historical situation of the book, appearing as it did at a time when capitalism had frequently been under attack on moral grounds, may offer facts that help explain why morality is a timely topic, but the situation is not so transparent with respect to an explanation of why morality and the life of the spirit should be linked so closely as *The Spirit of Democratic Capitalism* suggests. *Being and Time* offers an ontological clarification. In the critical theory we have developed out of its framework, the kind of outward-directed vision required for moral theory as a component of social theory is a phenomenon associated with falling. This fall does not feel like a fall, though, because falling never does feel that way as it occurs. Heidegger writes, "But this plunge remains hidden from Dasein by the way things have been publicly interpreted, so much so, indeed, that it gets interpreted as a way of 'ascending' and 'living concretely.' "[60] In the case of morality, the fact of falling and the difference it makes to exist fallingly are especially obscured because of the obvious factical benefits that can accrue to the society as a result of its success. It is in character for ideology to give attention to morality as the way of right living, but out of character for ideology to call attention to the problematical basis of morality. For purposes of ideology, morality must appear as unquestionably and objectively real. We are reminded of the difficulty Kant had in the thinking of the basis of religion and morality.

Fallen Dasein maintains itself whenever possible with evidence that "all's well." In the universe of capitalist ideology this disposition often shows up in the publicizing of a contrast between the relative success of this era's capitalist economies and the relative failure of others, most notably the socialistic economies. The success of capitalism is correlated with the realism of capitalistic ideology and the morality it entails, and with the accuracy of its understanding of humanity and world. The sense of having discovered a higher truth which is more attuned to a posited given concrete reality appears often in the pages of *The Spirit of Democratic Capitalism* and corroborates Heidegger's observation that falling feels like a greater awareness. This sense of greater awareness is part of what perpetuates the public antagonism of religion and ideology.

To investigate this tension further let us consider an excerpt from an encyclical of Pope Paul VI stating the church's position with respect to certain contemporary economic arrangements.

> The liberal ideology . . . asserts itself in the name of eco-
> nomic efficiency for the defense of the individual against the
> increasingly overwhelming hold of organizations, and as a
> reaction against the totalitarian tendencies of political
> powers. Certainly, personal initiative must be maintained
> and developed. But do not Christians who take this path
> tend to idealize liberalism in their turn . . . while easily
> forgetting that at the very root of philosophical liberalism is
> an erroneous affirmation of the autonomy of the individual
> in his activity, his motivation and the exercise of his
> liberty?[61]

The Pope's remarks are noteworthy for several reasons.

First, the fact that the Pope chose to call the body of ideas he was criticizing an "ideology" at approximately the time Maritain was saying capitalism lacked an ideology shows the perspicacity of the Pope in discerning a way of being in the world that is somehow at odds with religion as well as showing Maritain's perception of the incompleteness of that ideology's self-understanding, even in its own terms. The Pope missed a significant generalization, though, in not implicating all other ideologies, perhaps because the concrete historical situation of the church is not so obviously threatened at the spiritual level by the less overtly individualistic ideologies or, perhaps, as Novak has suggested, because of personal ideological bias. Unlike Novak and also Marcuse, the Pope was not able to see the tight communitarian structure of capitalism through the fiction of individualism, but he was able to name something like what is being called democratic capitalism as an outgrowth of ideology.

The second element of interest in the Pope's remarks is the assertion in the concluding sentence that the basis of the ideology he castigates is "an erroneous affirmation of the autonomy of the individual." In these words, there comes to the surface a recognition of the sense of adequacy that informs ideology and it is designated as erroneous. Here is a concrete case of dynamics of decision sketched in the first section in which one structure of decision is seen marking all deviations of a certain type as error, specifically, those deviations which assert autonomy of the individual in precisely the way that ideology does: "in his activity, his motivation and the exercise of his liberty." It is almost preordained that capitalism, representing the interests of every ideology and fallen Dasein in general, will want to take issue with the church, representing religion, though this conflict in the arena of public discourse must be understood against the backdrop of Rome's historical opposition to any instantiation of ideological consciousness that either threatens the institutional church's influence in the world directly (as Communist atheism does) or indirectly (as democratic capitalism does).

Sooner or later, our critical theory projects, a church's agenda will be incompatible with that of any ideology, except insofar as the church's leadership falls into it, and a church's leadership (being human) must always be in danger of falling somewhere, most especially where the church involves itself in social issues. This implication of the Heideggerian ontology seems to support historically recurrent bans among the world's religions on certain kinds of political activity among the clergy, most especially holding public office. Religious institutions may be required to become involved with issues of religion and ideology, both practically and theoretically, but their answers are always suspect. The tensions represented in the Christian Realism of Reinhold Niebuhr might be recalled in this context. It is, moreover, no attack on the church for a theologian to raise the possibility of error in questions involving ideology, since falling into ideology is ontologically given through falling for Dasein and is constitutive of its truth.

The history of the church's involvement with ideology helps illustrate two aspects of a crucial point about falling that Heidegger's writings treat only indirectly. The problem has to do with coming to understandings of specific ideologies and formulating public judgements about them. It appears to be the case that only from the kind of ideological standpoint that falling opens up for Dasein can the ideological components of previous moods be recognized as such and isolated from components of the current mood as elements in significant conflict; moreover, it is in the moment of vision that the terms of ideology are first meaningfully transcended (even though they remain in play for all concerned). It is only when authentic vision allows Dasein to recognize itself as having-fallen and being always in-anticipation-of-falling that the sense of factical distinctions among ideologies transcends partisan sentimentalities and transforms ideological differences into existential issues. This radical transformation of the terms of existence is the most compelling justification for ecclesiastical involvement in politics and it is the only possibility for the language of authentic religion to find its way into the political arena and into the dynamics of managed misunderstanding, that is, education. There are, our ontology suggests, unavoidable tensions attendant upon interpreting the relationship of *logos* and *ethos*.

Among the problems that arise when resoluteness breaks the surface of fallen Dasein's world of involvements is the question about the realism of ideals, which in the present framework is a non-question whose only aim is to assert the primacy of the familiar in the face of resolute Dasein's radical incommensurability. Ideological Dasein is always determined by care to fabricate a workable and defensible account of the reality of its involvements, but at no time is the need more urgent than when traces of resoluteness cast the sufficiency of those involvements into question. And at no time is the motivation higher than when a new fascination has just presented itself as a pretext for the latest shift of attention, fallen Dasein's mass-produced equivalent of religious conversion. To one who has just shifted attention and fallen into a different way of being, the old structure of decision (authentic or not) must feel hopelessly out of touch with reality while the new one feels invigoratingly attuned to the pulse of the world and fresh with the promise of undiscovered possibilities. It is this kind of existential movement which incessantly calls theologians to pack up their language and cross the line from theology into theologistics.

Note that it is not mere disaffection with one's own tradition that precipitates such a move. In Vahanian's books, for example, an intense disaffection with the state of contemporary Christianity fairly leaps from the pages even while Vahanian, the theologian, labors on for its radical revitalization. He is candid about the present situation of his faith as he sees it.

> Admittedly, Christianity today seems to have dried up at its source. It does not quench the thirst for spiritual instauration and for social and cultural iconoclasm after which the contemporary world yearns. And its impotence is even more alarming when it is overwhelmed by the automization of nature or the robotization of ethics.[62]

Confronted by an ideal that does not work, the theologian who maintains resoluteness experiences the challenge that comes with the debilitation of the old while avoiding the temptation to preserve momentum by speaking a theology that is solicitous of fallen Dasein. The theologian *in extremis* may, as Vahanian does, engage in a thoroughgoing attempt to remain true to the warranting religion or may pursue the most primitive and the most advanced activity of theology, the production of "unwarranted" propaedeutics and reflections of resoluteness that are ontologically prior to theologies of structured traditions. Both philosophical theology and theologistics are bound to propose changes in religious traditions on grounds that something is not working, but they do so for very different purposes. Philosophical theology wants to fix a broken tool; theologistics wants to put the broken tool to a different use, one in which its brokenness will cease to be problematical and become in fact desirable. Both genres of theology understand themselves to be working in advance of the general understanding on the assumption that the connections they propose will be made sooner or later; theologistics hopes to hasten the day when its ideology is securely totalized while philosophical theology struggles to maintain the openness to Being that is the antithesis of death, existentially understood.

For philosophical theology, a revivifying reform of the warranting tradition is the central concern, while for theologistics the reform of any ideologically appropriated tradition is sketched according to the present exigencies of its warranting ideology's strategic situation. In the examples chosen, Vahanian, in his concern for Christianity (explicitly as church, though not in its institutional aspect), reaches beyond the traditionally given inventory of categories to grasp technology, which had previously been an *object of* interpretation, and turns it convincingly into a *matrix for* interpretation which, it happens, coheres with Heidegger's thinking. Also challenging existing understandings, Novak has made a different switch. The Roman Catholic religion, which was originally his matrix for interpretation, becomes an object of interpretation in *The Spirit of Democratic Capitalism*. In both cases, we see, the origin of the discourse becomes the *subject* of interpretation, not a phenomenal *object* of interpretation.

As subjects of interpretation, neither Christianity nor democratic capitalism is examined phenomenologically or scientifically after the fact in its theology. Rather, both come to be what they are through predications made in the languages of philosophical theology and theologistics. Though both of these types of theology contain descriptions of events, situations, and beings, they are not essentially descriptive genres. In this, an important commonality of philosophical theology and theologistics, and one that is not shared with either confessional or secular theology, is revealed. Existentially-ontologically, it means that in moments of indecision, Dasein must make its own way. Only by the light of philosophical theology can there occur a decision that is an *Ent-scheidung*, because theologistics closes off the regions of consciousness that are capacious enough receive this possibility of Being.

Both confessional and secular theologies are bound to the categories they inherit in such a way that even in the most energetic interpretation, the categories resist every alteration. In their respective domains, they constitute an inflexible grid, and the interpretive assignments of phenomena to locations within this grid are accomplished by linear extrapolations from an existing corpus which itself is never in question in any important way. This is the basis of all orthodoxy and the reason why pluralism is so foreign to religions and ideologies alike. It contributes to our understanding of why resolute Dasein, once it has taken up an ideology, argues strenuously for it; it is a matter of survival.

As theologians have generally agreed, interpretations that do not "toe the line" of linear extrapolation from the sacred text do not belong in the world of the religious or ideological faithful and they are excluded categorically from the field of discourse. This is because in both confessional theology and secular theology, an implicit sufficiency of the warranting basis reigns and a standard of truth as correspondence epistemologically governs all interpretation which must make sense in public discourse. When truth as correspondence governs, legalism is not far off; legalism is the sign of religion fallen into ideology. Gerhard Ebeling seeks to explain the dynamics of Dasein's fascination with the imagined certainties of law:

And in so far as it can be said that the law provides
knowledge, it is not a case of knowledge of the good, but of
knowledge of sin; not knowledge of what ought to happen,
but knowledge of what has already happened; not knowledge of possibilities that are open, but knowledge of possibilities that are excluded and lost. But now, that implies
that the law, taken on its own, is always law that is misused
and therefore also law whose true nature is not perceived.
What makes its impotence into power is the fact that it
determines the structure of human existence. Whether Jew,
or sinner, or Gentile, whether pious or godless, every mode
of existence despite all the differences is the same as all the
others in that all are existence under the law. Every religion
or world-view, including an atheistic one, but also the
Christianity that has been perverted from faith into a religious ideology — all have the common structure of the law.
They are all one against faith. [63]

From the thought that faith is the essence of religion, the opposition of
religion and ideology is overdetermined through the opposition of law
and its calculated strucures of correspondence against faith.

This is not to say, however, that a standard of truth as correspondence necessarily governs the Being of the religion or ideology whose
decisions are being interpreted, only that theological statements which
the thinker presents are always subject to falsification based solely upon
their agreement or disagreement with the primary principles of the
religion or ideology. In the language of semantic theory, the discourse of
both confessional and secular theologies is categorized as constative[64]
with respect to its originating structures of decision and performative
with respect to the phenomena they interpret, including especially
humanity. That is, their statements may be found true or false depending upon agreement with the principles of the original religious or
ideological matrix, but not on the basis of supposed agreement with
other, differently-warranted statements about the same phenomena.
Superficial appearances of either agreement or disagreement among
symbol systems mean nothing until they have been interpreted according
to the logic of some specific system. Since the categories given by primary
texts are not open to reinterpretation by confessional or secular theology,
the logics of different texts are likely to be incommensurate. When there
is a possibility of engineering an agreement between systems, as occurs in
philosophical theology and theologistics, differences may retreat from
prominence or may be amplified, but this is a function of Dasein's
mood; it points up the fact that when we speak of incommensurate logic

of texts, we are really speaking of incommensurate readings and incommensurate inscriptions of texts.

Because the normative statements of confessional and secular theologies primarily refer back to the originating matrix, it is the originating matrix which is responsible for the existential sufficiency of their interpretations once the propositions they contain have been determined to be true. Statements of empirical fact or of scientific theory are never substantively included in the warrants of these theologies, and they depart from their programs if they attempt to propagate or incorporate such statements of fact or theory and bind themselves in a relationship of contingency to any other frameworks of interpretation. Traditional theologies already have a history of looking for and trying to use the apparent factical corroborations of their interpretations that are generated in science; this history is a scandal to theology as it arises out of an impulse inherent in theology to hold sway over the widest field possible, but which ironically yields only a succession of episodes in which theology violates its own truth in the Present and vitiates itself for the future.

The cases of philosophical theology and theologistics are somewhat different with respect to their primary texts from those of confessional and secular theology. In both of these genres, the categories themselves are at stake. The nominal originating matrix is itself problematical for them. Thus, Vahanian is seen revising Christian theology at the same time as he is writing Christian theology in an ensemble of categories which are all decisively altered by addition of the category of "technology." Novak also adds a category, "spirit," to his originating matrix, democratic capitalism. Before Vahanian, technology was a term of the opposition to Christianity just as before Novak, spirit was a term foreign to capitalism. The innovations that bring these terms into religious and ideological matrices are only imaginable because these terms are not foreign to Dasein in moments of indecision. As these two examples of recent categorial innovation show, philosophical theology and theologistics set themselves to the task of redefining their themes. The redefinition comes when Dasein is at loose ends. In the midst of such projects of redefinition, it would be absurd to apply the criteria of constative utterance to qualify questionable statements "about" the nominal originating matrix. With respect to that matrix, both philosophical theology and theologistics should be construed as employing performative language such that by their acts of saying, the nominal originating matrix is changed to a greater or lesser degree. The changes do not occur haphazardly.

In order to maintain the unity that must characterize primary structures of decision, which both Christianity and democratic capitalism are in their own ways, a principle of coherence is necessary. Creative interpretation of a new category is the basic contribution that each of these genres of theology makes. Vahanian thus introduces a new "technology" and then proceeds to develop an understanding of Christianity that comes back again and again to the notion of "technique of the human." It appears that he wants there to be no mistaking the essential integrity of this addition he is proposing to the central vocabulary of Christianity. Novak similarly introduces a new "spirit" and proceeds to change the face of capitalism. In neither case do the categorial changes that are introduced result in an unrecognizable or deracinated version of the original structure of significance-relationships. There appears to be a condition on the categorial changes that can be made on a structure of decision, a condition that is best thought of as *naturalness*: the structure must appear to be engendering its own logical transformation.[65] Both philosophical theology and theologistics can be seen in their discourse to portray the newly added category which they import and then use as an orienting base, as somehow belonging with the primary structure of decision that is in question. There is coherence from the outset; a new order is already in place as the old is transcended. In both genres, the nature of the change is such that nostalgia for the old structure would appear to be nothing less than perverse.

The reason why a natural principle of coherence is important has to do with the legitimacy of the performative utterances that constitute the essence of philosophical theology and theologistics. Performative utterances structurally presuppose the power of the speaker to effect the performance, to make the change the language announces. An individual's bare opinion, however enthusiastically presented, can not be sufficient grounds for restructuring the understanding of a religion, especially in view of religion's built-in assumption of human inadequacy. A natural basis is instrumental in providing authority for the philosophical theologian. Vahanian, for example, not only raises the point that Christianity and technology share a historical relationship, he also forcefully reminds Christianity that its complex relationship with technology continues, and on terms that are only dimly understood.

> The task itself ("the quest for cultural identity") is such that it entails the responsibility of Christianity in an inalienable — if perhaps partial — manner. Whether partial or not, as a matter of fact it is for this reason that today Christianity is tempted to assume this responsibility even at the price of its own identity, and to the point of losing sight of that which is at stake in the current crisis. Indeed, what will remain of the Christian faith if, under the pretext of

living up to the secularity it calls for, it must dissolve into
secularism? [66]

Vahanian's philosophical theology brings pressure to bear on two levels,
history and doctrine.

In the case of theologistics, arising as it does out of ideology, the
opinion of the individual, especially a well-reasoned opinion, has far
more weight. A provocatively presented opinion which has staying
power can legitimately alter the conception of the structure of decision
since ideology values provocation to sustain the flow of meaning and
acknowledges the adequacy of reason from the beginning. It is in
implicit recognition of the power of reason in the realm of ideology that
Novak writes, "The first of all moral obligations is to think clearly.
Societies are not like the weather, merely given, since human beings are
responsible for them. Social forms are constructs of the human spirit."[67]
Given this high estimation of reason, the performative utterances of
theologistics are destined to meet a threshold of resistance that is lower in
principle than what philosophical theology has to contend with, but the
need for coherence ensures that naturalness will play at least as large a
part in the discourse of theologistics as it does in philosophical theology.
For religion, it is necessary that the way beyond presence not be interrupted. For ideology, it is necessary to maintain existential tranquility.

Naturalness is closely related to unity of vision. What is natural is
what fits into an existing order without jumping out to transcend it,
disturb it, default from it, or restructure it. Both religion and ideology
have been described as structures of decision that unify experience and
therefore already carry criteria of naturalness within themselves.
Nonetheless, in *The Spirit of Democratic Capitalism*, Novak straightforwardly denies that capitalism represents a unifying vision. "Democratic
capitalism is not a system aimed at defining the whole of life,"[68] he
writes. This is shown, Novak claims, by the pluralism built into it. The
claim is not valid, however, since democratic capitalism still wants to
define the phenomena that it pluralistically allows in its own categories.
Its definitions need not be exhaustive to be absolute, only sufficiently
determinative for its own purposes. The point can be illustrated
concretely.

Let us digress from our ontological agenda for a moment to look
again at the two major competing social-economic ideologies, democratic
capitalism and Communism, and look at what they do with a phenomenon, in this case religion. Novak's overt religious terminology notwithstanding, it is clear that practical religion is essentially external to
understanding in democratic capitalism. The same is true of Commun-

ism. Both systems place the *idea* of religion similarly. The difference between them shows up in their definitions of the phenomenon of religion. Democratic capitalism does not pursue the definition of religion to great depth except when religion appears either as a limit or when it functions to direct the process of economic development, which is territory that democratic capitalism has explicitly staked out for itself. The intrusion of the alien Being of authentic Dasein upsets commerce; enmeshed and encapsulated in the terms of ideology, Dasein's vision is limited so that only as a viable economic factor does religion appear as a recognizable challenge to democratic capitalism's (ideological) absoluteness. Novak's book may be taken as a manifestation of exactly this dynamic. He writes that religion " . . . judges each and every system and finds each gravely wanting."[69] While it looks as though the judgement of religion is being taken to heart, one does well to recall that it appears within a text whose major premise is the judgement that *democratic capitalism has found religion wanting*. No religion can ever do more than superficially agree with an ideology and when the fact is discovered, the ideology will move to define the religion into impotence as quickly as possible. The main difference between pluralistic systems and overtly totalitarian ones is that the overtly totalitarian ideologies discover the problem sooner and act more directly in response.

Communism not only places religion within its horizons, as any ideology would, it also monotheistically demands an impossible congruence of religion's absoluteness with its own. An overtly totalitarian ideology must find that any living religion is unacceptable within the arrangement it determines. The intense hostility of Communism to religion can be explained both in terms of the social dynamics of competing centers of power and in terms of differences between religion and ideology. As a diffraction of the momentum of the material basis, religion in its aspect of competing power center presents a strategic problem. As an alternative way of understanding, religion injects unwanted differences into the system and thus creates unintended syntheses. The smooth flow of public discourse is put at risk. The broad outlines of the logic of intolerance that rules totalitarian systems are not difficult to discern. On the other hand, the contrasting tolerance in apparently looser systems, such as democratic capitalism, is less transparently justified. It returns us to the structural relationship between religion and ideology.

Religion, knowing human inadequacy, must posit Dasein's inadequate self-understanding as kind of epistemological entailment. One of the consequences of this inadequate self-understanding can be delusions of adequacy. Religious Dasein, always having recovered from falling, knows the ways of falling and can place the phenomena of falling within its horizons of understanding through confessional theology. Ideology, on the other hand, operating with a sense of adequacy, has a characteristic attitude toward religion: religion is essentially irrelevant as long as it does not interfere with the ideological program. We recall Novak's taking Pope Paul VI to task for an encyclical that faithfully represents the standpoint of religion in that it calls the faithful away from ideology in general and which, more important for Novak's immediate project, is especially inimical to democratic capitalism.

Both religious and ideological genres of discourse encounter pressures to accommodate differing perspectives. Pressure on ideology from either inside or outside must be dealt with intellectually, by calculation, if ideology is to maintain itself as viable by its own lights. Religion deals with pressure by warranting philosophical theology to appropriate faithfully, if at all possible, any threat to religion's enrouting sufficiency. Symmetrically, ideology can warrant theologistics to keep itself up to date. The existence of these two modes of theology points to a shared recognition on the parts of religion and ideology: that sometimes changing is the only way to "stay the same." The meaning of "the same" in this context is essentially identical with "absolute," and the purpose of introducing major changes for either religion or ideology is to include and neutralize potentially destructive interests within the structure of decision. The question of self-maintenance is more interesting in the case of relatively sophisticated ideological phenomena such as democratic capitalism, since they are not internally mechanistically bound to engage in the inevitable superficial skirmishes with religion that a totalitarian system would be. Democratic capitalism has a choice of attempting the inclusion of religious initiatives by coercion (either the violent type or the honeyed type which has won democratic capitalism a following enthused by the prospect of more positive reinforcement through a flow of material rewards) or by rational persuasion. It is in an ideology's attempt to persuade that the relationship between religion and ideology is most clearly displayed outside of explicit theory; as the imperative of rational presentation leads ideological discourse to press for global consistency, sufficient information is given that not only is ideology's intended public construction brought into view for critical and uncritical audiences alike, but also, to critical eyes, traces of some of the concealments entailed in the ideology's presuppositional substrate. The aim of theologistics is to show, in terms an uncritically reasonable person could accept, that a given ideology can do more to realize the ideals of a particular religious tradition than any of the competing ideologies are likely to do.

Knowing the strength of this point if it can be made, theologistics emphatically argues that these must be the terms in which the choice for or against its warranting ideology is to be made. The more fundamental possibility of choosing between religion and ideology is excluded right away in this appeal to the interests of resolute Dasein. If resolute Dasein must make use of the possibilities of the "they," theologistics says in effect, it should be circumspect enough to know where the choice is best. *Being and Time*, in asserting care and falling as existentiales of Dasein, lays the ontological groundwork for the structure of choice that theologistics factically advocates. Thus it is that theologistics subtly invites *homo religiosus* to fall into its warranting ideology rather than one of the alternatives. It becomes a matter of which ideology offers a religion the best deal. For fallen Dasein as well as for resolute Dasein, this is not an inconsequential decision. Theologistics comes to appear as one of those increasingly familiar "pharmacological" phenomena that can have both salutary and deleterious effects.

In its most honest realizations, theologistics will not minimize the effect on religion of Dasein's falling into its warranting ideology or into one of the less desirable alternatives. It knows pre-ontologically that Dasein has no choice but to contract to participate in an economy and, if it follows good business practice, will not play games about the terms of the contract it offers. Given that theologistics speaks from within the absolute totalization of its warranting ideology, there is no self-consciousness which would leads theologistics to want to conceal the fact that within any ideological structure of decision, the place of religion is always already decided. And it is decided that religion shall be understood as one of many competing kinds of symbol systems, a move that denies religion its Being as a totalized way whose purpose is to gather all things and renew the world. Under any ideology, religion becomes something like a feeling. Without its radical possibility, any religion becomes just one more irrational (thus, defective) ideology. Once that happens, "religion" is easily displaced by some other ideology.

Ideology knows this. Novak, in our example, shows little difficulty in generalizing the (economic) pluralism of democratic capitalism to the world of ideas and then placing religions on these terms within the world of ideas where they become fair game in the intellectual marketplace. In effect, we are brought back to Anthony Flew's absurd requirement that religious language must be philosophically defensible. The beginning of the end for a religion is being placed in a different position, according to the specifications of any ideology, than it would place itself, and the sealing of the end of the possibility of a factical religion would be acceptance or even the silent countenancing of any such proposal within the community of faith.

The idea that one chooses religious ideas and symbols as one chooses an ideological system (or a suit of clothes, for that matter) presumes the very sense of adequacy to make such choices that is the condition of ideology and the *absence* of which is the condition of religion. Expression of this idea, however, does not unilaterally strengthen ideology. On the one hand, critics of literally impossible discourse do religion proper a service by ruling out every possibility of manifestations of ideology opportunistically masquerading as religion; in this way, the focus on the presence of religion theoretically removes from play one of the most mischievous forces history has known. On the other hand, what is left of religion after a theologistic renovation is only a simulation of its Being as we have glimpsed it. In the end, no ideological expression of respect, reverence, or concern for the energies of religion can do more than paper over the irreconcilable difference between religion and ideology.

An ideology may warrant a form of theology to attempt the impossible task of subordinating a larger vision to a narrower one, but the result, like Anselm's theology, will only be satisfactory to those who are already convinced. It is clear by now that the subordination must always be argued from the standpoint of ideology, if the task of theologistics is even to be begun. Ideology's tolerance of even a deracinated subversive also has its limits, however, and when these limits are encountered, ideology's powerful instinct for self-preservation determines in advance that every functional transcendence of its terms be discarded or discredited. It should not be imagined that addition of new categories opens up an ideology in the way that the same formal move affects religion.

Our analysis has suggested that the relationship of any religion with any ideology — a kind of relationship which must come to pass whenever any religion factically obtains in the world — will always be deeply problematical. No system which places religion anywhere other than where religion places itself can ever be at peace with religion or enjoy anything like its approval, and no ideology can ever accommodate religion to that extent. Why, then, is it legitimate for ideology to warrant theologistics, which can attempt to co-opt religion as well as other ideologies? In terms of our analysis, it is that ideology understands itself as competent to place all phenomena and *must* persist in this attitude to prevent the dialectic in which Dasein exists from collapsing.

Any ideology is bound to attempt reasoned manipulations both of religion in general and of all other competing ideologies. Vahanian can see ideology on this basis as " . . . a critique of uncritically endorsed ideas . . . ."[70] This critical impetus which leads ideology on is responsible, as Vahanian analyzes it, for ideology's being a "self-styled dissenter"[71] which, moreover, is always destined to become "totalitarian."[72] According to our analysis, ideology is ontologically determined to aim for absoluteness, but the example of *The Spirit of Democratic Capitalism*, if we are correct in analyzing it as a theology warranted by an ideology, indicates that totalitarianism in the usual sense only represents one extreme in the spectrum of possibility. Totalitarianism, in the sense of a pervasive domination of culture, as the term is used by Marcuse, however, is not an extreme, but the norm. The dissent-character of ideology propels it toward some variety of totalitarianism, it is true, since religion, the structural foil for ideology, is already itself essentially totalitarian. But, as Novak's example shows, an ideology may also choose to draw its own explicit *ontological* horizons comparatively closely. By excluding issues, rather than meeting them point-by-point, the sense of adequacy we find essential to ideology is the more easily maintained in falling consensuality and the system's sufficiency is the more readily demonstrated.

Both the theologies warranted out of religion and those originating in ideology as quasi-religion have a stake in the issue of sufficiency. Confessional theology's task is to demonstrate the sufficiency of a religion's categories to the faithful while secular theology rationally argues the sufficiency of an ideology's categories in the attempt to remake the audience. At the interface, philosophical theology reaches from religion into the world of the public consensus to expand or enhance the language of religion, while theologistics reaches from ideology into the language of religion to expand the power of the consensus. Each of the four genres is warranted by a structure of decision according to the logic of that structure and for a specific purpose. The combination of these conflicting purposes and the different modes of existence they bring to presence gives Dasein's existence its distinctive structure and kaleidoscopic character.

Notes

[1] Bernard J.F. Lonergan, S.J., *Philosophy of God, and Theology*. London: Darton, Longman and Todd, 1973, p. 15.

[2] SZ, p. 343; BT, p. 393.

[3] SZ, p. 298; BT, p. 344.

[4] Ibid.

[5] SZ, p. 169; BT, p. 213.

[6] SZ, pp. 169-170; BT, ibid.

[7] SZ, p. 298; BT, p. 345.

[8] SZ, p. 306; BT, p. 354. See also the following three pages for more on relationship of resoluteness, death and anxiety.

[9] Tillich, *Systematic Theology*, Vol. 1. p. 24.

[10] SZ, p. 299; BT, p. 345.

[11] Ibid.

[12] Seyyed Hossein Nasr, "The Quran — the Word of God, the source of knowledge and action," *Ideals and Realities of Islam*. Boston: Beacon Press, 1966, p. 47; henceforward QWG.

[13] QWG, p. 50.

[14] SZ, p. 33; BT, p. 56.

[15] Martin Heidegger, "Logos," *Early Greek Thinking*, tr. D.F. Krell and F. Capuzzi. New York: Harper and Row, 1975, p. 76.

[16] SZ. p. 33; BT, p. 56.

[17] Martin Heidegger, "The Nature of Language," *On the Way to Language*, tr. P. Hertz. New York: Harper and Row, 1971, pp. 87-88; "Das Wesen der Sprache," *Unterwegs zur Sprache*. Pfullingen: Neske, 1959, p. 193.

[18] QWG, p. 55.

[19] Ibid.

[20] Ibid.

[21] Carl Raschke, "The Deconstruction of God," *Deconstruction and Theology*, ed. C. Raschke. New York: Crossroad, 1982, p. 14.

[22] QWG, p. 46.

[23] SZ, p. 218; BT, p. 261.

[24] Ibid.

[25] SZ, p. 220; BT, p. 263.

[26] SZ, p. 256; BT, p. 300.

[27] SZ, p. 220; BT, p. 263.

[28] SZ, p. 222; BT, p. 264.

[29] SZ, p. 223; BT, p. 265

[30] SZ, p. 299; BT, p. 345.

[31] SZ, p. 298; BT, p. 345.

[32] SZ, p. 299; BT, p. 346.

[33] GU, p. xv.

[34] GU, p. 27.

[35] GU, p. xxiii.

[36] GU, p. 43.

[37] GU, p. xi.

[38] Max Myers, " 'Ideology' and 'Legitimation' As Necessary Concepts for Christian Ethics," *Journal of the American Academy of Religion*, Vol. XLIX, No. 2, p. 202.

[39] Jacques Maritain, *Man and State*. Chicago: University of Chicago Press, 1951, p. 111. The term also appears in Ernest van den Haag's "An Open Letter to Sidney Hook: A defense of religious faith," in Hook, op cit., p. 103.

[40] Michael Novak, *The Spirit of Democaratic Capitalism*. New York: American Enterprise Institute/Simon and Schuster, 1982, p. 65. (Henceforward SDC.)

[41] Vahanian's analysis of ideology as critique would place secular theology in an ultimately dependent relationship with religion, whereas the relationship seems to be more one of co-dependence within our ontological framework, since the analysis of ideology proposed in these pages proposes that religion and ideology are ontologically equiprimordial.

[42] B.F. Skinner, *Beyond Freedom and Dignity*. New York: Alfred A. Knopf, 1971, p. 206.

[43] Alasdair MacIntyre, *After Virtue*. Notre Dame, IN: Notre Dame Univ. Press, 1981, p. 88.

[44] Op. cit., p. 6.

[45] Ayn Rand, "The Wreckage of the Consensus," *Capitalism: The Unknown Ideal*. New York: The New American Library, 1967, p. 222. We note parenthetically that this passage concerning ideology occurs in one of the two essays in the collection containing the word "consensus" in the title. For Rand, "consensus" denotes the political and economic compromise of the individual — a meaning which is somewhat removed from those occurrences of the word above in connection with falling. Still, the basic structural relationships between the consensus and the individual in Rand and as suggested above are similar in that the individual is co-opted by the group.

[46] Thus the point that systematic theology attends to its warranting system and does not attempt to build a system of its own.

[47] See Karl Marx and Friedrich Engels, *Selected Correspondence*. New York: International Publishers, Inc., 1936, p. 51, and Emile Burns, *A Handbook of Marxism*. New York: International Publishers, Inc., 1935, pp. 118-119.

[48] Rand, "What is Capitalism?" op. cit., p. 17.

[49] Ibid.

[50] Op. cit., p. 22.

[51] Op. cit., p. 19.

[52] See Ernest Becker, *The Denial of Death*. New York: Macmillan, 1973, especially chapters 6 and 11.

[53] Ayn Rand, "About the Author," *Atlas Shrugged*. New York: New American Library, 1957, p. 1085. Compare this with the view from a distant band of the ideological spectrum by Herbert Marcuse, who says of contemporary industrial society, " . . . its sweeping rationality, which propels efficiency and growth, is itself irrational." (*One-Dimensional Man*, p. xiii) The charge of irrationality is the most damning of all for ideology.

[54] *The Meaning of the Glorious Koran*, tr. and ed. M.M. Pickthall. New York: Mentor, n.d., XXIV:2. It may be a coincidence or it may belong essentially to resoluteness that there is an appearance of heartlessness in these examples. We recall in this connection the story of Bashō's treatment of the waif and a line of the *Tao Te Ching*, "The wise are ruthless." (Lao-tzu, *Tao Te Ching*, tr. Gia-Fu Feng and J. English. New York: Vintage, 1972, Ch. 5.)

[55] GU, p. xi.

[56] SDC, p. 240; Novak's italics.

[57] SDC, p. 18.

[58] SDC, p. 14.

[59] SDC, p. 94.

[60] SZ, p. 178; BT, p. 223.

[61] Pope Paul VI, *Octogesima Adveniens*, in SDC, p.128.

[62] GU, p. xv.

[63] Gerhard Ebeling, *Word and Faith*, tr. J.C.B. Mohr and P. Siebert. Philadelphia: Fortress Press, 1963, p. 279.

[64] John Lyons, in *Semantics* (Cambridge: Cambridge Univ. Press, 1977), Vol. 2, p. 726, writes, "Constative utterances are statements: their function is to describe some event, process or state of affairs, and they (or the propositions expressed) have the property of being either true or false. Performative utterances, by contrast, have no truth value: they are used to do something, rather than say that something is or is not the case." This distinction remains to be thought with reference to the mythology/technology issue. Thomas Olshewsky makes a beginning when he writes, "The performative character of myth is what gives it normative force." ("Between Science and Religion," *The Journal of Religion*, Vol. 62, No. 3 [July 1982], p. 248.) Olshewsky contrasts myth's inherent performativity with the language of science, which he characterizes as predictive. In light of the Heideggerian critique of technology, it appears that technological science functions performatively also.

[65] Vahanian, introducing the category of "technology," begins his revision of the interpretive possibilities of Christianity with the familiar integrating observation that "Christianity . . . is . . . implicated in the rise of the technological phenomenon." (GU, p. 1.)

[66] GU, p. 2.

[67] SDC, p. 20.

[68] SDC, p. 65.

[69] SDC, p. 335.

[70] GU, p. 32.

[71] GU, p. 33.

[72] Ibid.

X. At Cross-Purposes: Religion, Ideology, Theology

The tension between religion and ideology is productive, and not just for theology, but for existence in general. According to our rudimentary Heideggerian critical theory, it is not necessary that the tension be made explicit for the results of its productivity to emerge into being as *being human*. Even though human existence appears able to find ways to integrate the tension between religion and ideology that do not depend upon a theoretically explicated mechanism, these integrations frequently have been scenes of clumsy and profligate attempts to "live an exemplary life" or "set the world aright," attempts that historically have often been accompanied by extremes of violence, as personal or social absolutisms have striven to extinguish all trace of deviance from their own imagined ideals. Every attempt to come to terms with existence entails a theoretical grasp of reality, whether the theory is an explicit one or not; the great advantage in having an explicit theory is that formerly inchoate compulsions are brought into some kind of light. Thus begins the dialectic of enlightenment, a technological development.

History is replete with fictional dilemmas that have been posed by projections of a need to choose between imagined dichotomous possibilities within a single ideology or between "religion" and "the world." The theory under development has tried for a number of reasons to make explicit an ontological basis of these kinds of tensions; in addition to the obvious (but remote) possibility of reducing pain and suffering by demystifying and thus de-energizing the agents of totalization, the most important reasons for trying to explicate the ontology of religion and ideology are to contribute to the hermeneutics of public discourse and to contribute to an ethics which begins its analysis with the non-substantialistic thinking of the Being of human beings.

To do this, we tried first to break free of the impulse to define religion and ideology clearly in advance, in order to see how an informal understanding might work itself to clarity in conversation with the fairly formal ontology of Heidegger's existential analytic. In this respect, the discussion departed from its technological program, but only in order to return to it more fully at a later time. The departure was occasioned by a need to develop understandings of religion and ideology that are technologically viable, that is, which have the appearance of independent motivation. This we did by researching *Being and Time*. Even though the formal ontology of *Being and Time* was incomplete and incapable of communicating very much about Being itself, it at least raised the question of Being at the scene of beings and encouraged the attempt to imagine religion and ideology critically-theoretically as classes of ontical possibilities with an ontological basis.

Religion and ideology also did not need to be defined in advance because in an important sense they had come into the discussion already defined by their historical Being and presence-at-hand. Presence-at-hand was seen to be a property of tools in *Being and Time* and, in a step beyond that text, tools were defined to include symbol systems, including religions and ideologies. With the hindsight granted by the analysis of technology, it became evident how symbol systems as tools can become mechanisms for the technological manipulation of understanding. We have not renounced this possibility, since it seems to be part of the task of the university in society to realize this possibility of consciousness and, with some measure of hermeneutical maturity, *to be conscious of doing so.*

The presence-at-hand of religion and ideology in general was established by the fact of so much discussion. Through the analysis of *Being and Time*, it was defined that things become present-at-hand when they pose a problem or present some kind of challenge; after working through the problem of religion's presence-at-hand with reference to *Being and Time*'s concept of falling, our conclusion was that the presence-at-hand of religion and ideology does not appear to be beneficially construed as a sign of malaise. On the contrary, by opening up understanding to technological development, the presence-at-hand of religion and ideology creates new possibilities of consciousness that supercede and transcend the old. This is not an expression of naive modernism. To gain perspective on the current presence-at-hand of religion and ideology and to provide something of a frame of reference for the critical theory, a reading of the history of religion's presence-at-hand was proposed which culminated in Heidegger's effective re-introduction to Western philosophy of the possibility of religious human beings who were not simply fearful primitives or calculating opportunists.

The presence-at-hand of religion and ideology was still being viewed primarily as an ontical phenomenon until the notion of falling was formally introduced as that aspect of the Being of Dasein which produced involvement with the presence of the Present. Falling was schematized as the way from religion to ideology, as religion was corre-lated with authenticity and ideology, with inauthenticity. Through the thinking of falling and the interest in the social world that Heidegger derived from it, a picture emerged of a mode of Being that could be recognized as a basis for ideological consciousness. This consciousness is such that that it would strive to develop an all-inclusive view of the world; logically, it would deny the validity of all other interpretations, thereby determining that its own sense of reality should remain supreme in an undisputed totalization. Failing that, the consciousness that stands behind ideology would be driven single-mindedly to provoke ceaseless disputation with manifestations of every other construction of self and world visible within its horizons of understanding.

The public commotion of ideological conflict and the flow of meaning generated as ideologies maintain themselves are well-suited to the preservation of fallenness for good or ill. The only way for one to live authentically in this situation, according to the early Heidegger, was through resoluteness. Resolute existence entailed holding oneself back from total involvement in the world of the "they" in order to live one's own life and not get caught up in society's idealized, reductionistc representations of life. In later years, Heidegger developed the idea of releasement toward things, which, we argued, was the successor concept to *Being and Time*'s "resoluteness." It preserved *Being and Time*'s location of humanity's authentic possibilities among the presentations of the inauthentic by keeping the consciousness of Being within the world of beings. Through this concept, it became possible to see in technology something other than a demonic distortion and occlusion of the Being of beings, though that possibility is never dismissed.

Technology's danger and its relation to ideology could come clear after the existential origins of these concepts in falling were outlined. The promise of technology was not evident, however, until religion came to be seen as a true liberation from the dangers of technological thinking. There was no way to grasp religion solely through the account of falling, even though religion was plainly cast as the existential-semantic opposite of ideology. Further, religion could not be conceived as a simple negation of ideology without turning into autism; its positive nature needed to be laid out. This was done in the course of thinking through a collection of Heidegger's remarks on divinities. In order to keep from lapsing into the defunct patterns of general, essentialistic metaphysics, divinities were imagined in terms of existential categories and the logic of an existential metaphysics. From this thinking, religion could be presented as relation to a divinity and the institutionalization of an understanding of perduring absence and imperfection in existence. Once that had been accomplished, the difference between religion and ideology appeared as different modes of totalization. Religion functioned in the wider context, and iconoclastically.

In early chapters, the discussion was claimed to be motivated by the question of why we should distinguish between religion and ideology. To pursue that question ontologically, it was necessary to bring both religion and ideology into view in their Being, and that in turn called for bringing them into view as ontical manifestations of the related existentialia of authentic and inauthentic existence. Because authentic and inauthentic existence are joined in the ontology through the concept of falling, religion and ideology were determined to belong together. The picture was not adequate to answer the question of why religion and ideology should be distinguished until it included the phenomenon of theology. Theology was shown to possess at least four genres, and with their explication, the difference between religion and ideology could be seen in both theoretical and practical aspects. Dividing up the phenomena of religion, ideology, and theology this way also served to divide up the question of why we should want to distinguish between them.

From the precincts of ideology came the assertion that religion and ideology really should not be distinguished. This conflation is in ideology's own interest, of course, since ideology determines the factical content of common sense and thus dominates the arena of public discourse. Ideology's distinction between religion and ideology is not real because it does not recognize any Being of religion that cannot be determined by ideological metaphysics. In ideology's view, religion is a competing species of symbol system that retreats into mystification at the first sign of difficulty. Since religion has shown itself more than willing to involve itself in issues of public policy, the ideologue is bound to argue, it should be held accountable by the same rules as ideological participants. In that view, religious discourse and ideological discourse are collapsed into public discourse. It was shown to be almost inevitable that theologians themselves would not always be precise in making the distinction between religion and ideology and it is for this reason that one can understand why ideological discourse has often enough issued from the churches; problems arise, however, when factical (ontical) confusions are interpreted as indications of theoretical homogeneity. We come back to the law of form which says that distinctions are drawn because contents are seen to differ in value; any theory is thus constrained to take seriously the pre-ontologically grasped difference between religion and ideology, instead of trying to obliterate it.

It was seen that religion and ideology understand beings and world essentially differently. From these differences, it is inevitable that their structures of significance-relationships will be different, meaning that the semantics of religious discourse and the semantics of ideological discourse will be decidedly dissimilar. Something of the semantics of religious discourse could be glimpsed in the brief account of Nasr's essay and confessional theology in general. When religious discourse enters the public arena, it is likely to have an air of unreality about it if it goes beyond mere pronouncements and its logic comes into view; Reinhold Niebuhr's essays laying out the theology behind Christian Realism illustrate the point. If the views of ideology carry, then theologians who disagree with the experts who construct ideological-technological reality are no more than ideologues without the proper education to teach them the difference between dreams and reality. If religion prevails, ideologues who disregard the way are relegated to the ranks of the unwashed, waiting as ever for grace to understand the faith.

With the many possibilities for misunderstanding, there is good reason for one to have some sense of how religious and ideological constructions function in discourse and to be able to bring that recognition to language. Care is needed not to mistake the one for the other. Yet it is care (think circumspection) that brings people into the region of involvements where ideology holds sway. Once in this region, resolute Dasein gains nothing by the jealous guarding of a pious mood. Only in the conscious plunge of releasement toward things can one preserve the attention to Being that is central to religion at the same time as one enters the domain of public interpretation that is home to ideology. Without religion, the totalizations of ideology, which deny in every way the Being of beings, take over.

The logic of religion, grounded in authenticity as a state of having-chosen, determines that religion in its essence does and does not determine human existence alone. In the light of Being, the revelation of the Holy on the way beyond presence, the belonging together of beings in their Being, is reality. But in factical moments of religion's "not," when ideology determines consciousness, the way to Being is not just compromised, it is lost, which is to say beings are lost. Being underway, the reality of being human, is the reason to distinguish between religion and ideology.

235

Bibliography

Ayer, A.J. *Language, Truth and Logic*. New York: Dover, (n.d.).

Barth, Karl. *Anselm: Fides Quaerens Intellectum*, tr. I.W. Robinson. Richmond, Va.: John Knox Press, 1960.

Becker, Ernest. *The Denial of Death*. New York: Macmillan, 1973.

Bennett, Jonathan F. *Kant's Dialectic*. Cambridge: Cambridge University Press, 1974.

Berger, Peter. "Capitalism and Socialism: Ethical Assessment," *Capitalism and Socialism*, ed. Michael Novak. Washington, D.C.: American Enterprise Institute, 1979.

Bloch, Ernst. *Man on His Own*, tr. E.B. Ashton. New York: Herder and Herder, 1971.

Burns, Emile. *A Handbook of Marxism*. New York: International Publishers, Inc., 1935.

Camus, Albert. *The Rebel: An Essay on Man in Revolt*, tr. A. Bower. New York: Knopf, 1957.

Comstock, Richard. "Toward Open Definitions of Religion," *Journal of the American Academy of Religion*. 52:3, pp. 499-517.

Cox, Harvey. "Beyond Bonhoeffer? The Future of Religionless Christianity," *The Secular City Debate*, ed. D. Callahan. New York: Macmillan, 1966.

Destutt de Tracy, Antoine Louis Claude. *Treatise on Political Economy, to which is Prefixed a Supplement to a Preceding Work on the Understanding, or, Elements of Ideology*, tr. Thomas Jefferson, in John M. Dorsey, *Psychology of Political Science. Detroit, MI: Center for Health Education, 1973*.

Ebeling, Gerhard. *Word and Faith*, tr. J.C.B. Mohr and P. Siebert. Philadelphia: Fortress Press, 1963.

Eliade, Mircea. *The Sacred and the Profane*, tr. W.R. Trask. New York: Harcourt, Brace and World, 1959.

Ellul, Jacques. *The Technological Society*, tr. John Wilkinson. New York: Alfred A. Knopf, 1964.

Flew, Anthony. "Theology and Falsification," *New Essays in Philosophical Theology*, ed. A. Flew and A. MacIntyre. New York: SCM Press, 1969.

Germino, Dante. *Beyond Ideology*. New York: Harper and Row, 1967.

Geuss, Raymond. *The Idea of Critical Theory*. Cambridge: Cambridge University Press, 1981.

Gilkey, Langdon. "Is Religious Faith Possible in an Age of Science?" *Society and the Sacred: Toward a Theology of Culture in Decline*. New York: Crossroad, 1981.

Greene, Theodore M. "The Historical Context and Religious Significance of Kant's *Religion*," *Religion within the Limits of Reason alone*, tr. T.M. Greene and H.H. Hudson. New York: Harper and Row, 1960.

Heidegger, Martin. *The Basic Problems of Phenomenology*, tr. Albert Hofstadter. Bloomington: Indiana University Press, 1982.

———. "Brief über den Humanismus," *Wegmarken*, Frankfurt/M.: Klostermann, 1978.

———. "Das Ding," *Vorträge und Aufsätze*, Vol. 2. Pfullingen: Neske, 1954. ("The Thing," *Poetry, Language, Thought*, tr. A. Hofstadter. New York: Harper and Row, 1971.)

———. "Logos," *Early Greek Thinking*, tr. D.F. Krell and F. Capuzzi. New York: Harper and Row, 1975.

———. *Einführung in die Metaphysik*. Tübingen: Niemeyer, 1953.

———. "Die Frage nach der Technik," *Vorträge und Aufsätze*, Vol. 1. Pfullingen: Neske, 1954. ("The Question Concerning Technology," *The Question Concerning Technology and Other Essays*, tr. W. Lovitt. New York: Harper and Row, 1977.)

———. "Memorial Address," *Discourse on Thinking*, tr. J.M. Anderson and E.H. Freund. New York: Harper and Row, 1966.

———. "Nachwort zu: Was ist Metaphysik?" *Wegmarken*. Frankfurt/M.: Klostermann, 1978. ("What Is Metaphysics?" *Existence and Being*, tr. R.F.C. Hull and Alan Crick. South Bend, Indiana: Gateway, 1949.)

———. "Die onto-theo-logische Verfassung der Metaphysik" ("The Onto-theo-logical Constitution of Metaphysics"), *Identity and Difference*, tr. Joan Stambaugh. New York: Harper and Row, 1969.

———. "Phänomenologie und Theologie," *Wegmarken*, Frankfurt/M.: Klostermann, 1978.

———. *Sein und Zeit*. Tübingen: Neomarius, 1927. (*Being and Time*, tr. J. Macquarrie and E. Robinson. New York: Harper and Row, 1962.)

_____. "The Turning," *The Question Concerning Technology and other Essays*, tr. W. Lovitt. New York: Harper and Row, 1977.

_____. "Der Ursprung des Kunstwerkes," *Holzwege*. Frankfurt/M.: Klostermann, 1972. ("The Origin of the Work of Art," *Poetry, Language, Thought*, tr. A. Hofstadter. New York: Harper and Row, 1971.)

_____. "Vom Wesen der Wahrheit," *Wegmarken*. Frankfurt/M.: Klostermann, 1978.

_____. "Das Wesen der Sprache," *Unterwegs zur Sprache*. Pfullingen: Neske, 1975. ("The Nature of Language," *On the Way to Language*, tr. P. Hertz and J. Stambaugh. New York: Harper and Row, 1971.)

_____. *What Is Called Thinking?* tr. J. Glenn Gray. New York: Harper and Row, 1968.

_____. "Wozu Dichter?" *Holzwege*. Frankfurt/M.: Klostermann, 1972. ("What Are Poets For?" *Poetry, Language, Thought*, tr. A. Hofstadter. New York: Harper and Row, 1975.)

_____. "Zur Erörterung der Gelassenheit," *Gelassenheit*. Pfullingen: Neske, 1959. ("Conversation on a Country Path About Thinking," *Discourse on Thinking*, tr. J.M. Anderson and E.H. Freund. New York: Harper and Row, 1966.)

Heraclitus, "Heraclitus," *The Presocratics*, tr. and ed. P. Wheelwright. New York: Odyssey press, 1966.

Hook, Sidney. *The Quest for Being*. New York: Delta, 1934-1961.

James, William. *Varieties of Religious Experience*. New York: New American Library, 1958.

John Paul II. "Man has a thirst for a higher being," *China Post*, 31:11605 (Oct. 4, 1983), p. 3.

Jung, Hwa Yol. *The Crisis of Political Understanding: A Phenomenological Perspective in the Conduct of Political Inquiry*. Pittsburgh: Duquesne University Press, 1979.

_____. "The Orphic Voice and Ecology." MS

Kant, Immanuel. *Lectures on Philosophical Theology*, tr. A.W. Wood and G.M. Clark. Ithaca, N.Y.: Cornell University Press, 1978.

_____. *Prolegomena to Any Future Metaphysics*, tr. P. Carus. Indianapolis: Bobbs-Merrill, 1950.

_____. *Religion within the Limits of Reason alone*, tr. T.M. Greene and H.H. Hudson. New York: Harper and Row, 1960.

Kaufmann, Walter, *Critique of Religion and Philosophy*, Garden City, N.Y.: Anchor/Doubleday, 1958.

Kuhn, Thomas. *The Structure of Scientific Revolutions*, 2nd ed. Chicago: University of Chicago Press, 1970.

Lao Tzu. *Tao Te Ching*, tr. Gia-Fu Feng and J. English. New York: Vintage, 1972.

Law, William. *A Serious Call to a Devout and Holy Life*. Grand Rapids, Mich.: Wm. B. Eerdmans, 1966.

Lonergan, Bernard J.F. *Philosophy of God, and Theology*. London: Darton, Longman and Todd, 1973.

Löwith, Karl. *Heidegger: Denker in dürftiger Zeit*. Göttingen: Vanderhoeck and Ruprecht, 1965.

Lucretius (Titus Lucretius Carus). *Of the Nature of Things*, tr. W.E. Leonard. New York: E.P. Dutton & Co., 1921.

Lyons, John. *Semantics*, Vol. 2. Cambridge: Cambridge University Press, 1977.

MacIntyre, Alasdair. *After Virtue*. Notre Dame, Indiana: Notre Dame University Press, 1981.

Manuel, Frank. *The Changing of the Gods*. Hanover, N.H.: University Press of New England/Brown University Press, 1983.

Marcuse, Herbert. "The Concept of Essence," *Negations: Essays in Critical Theory*, tr. J.J. Shapiro. Boston: Beacon Press, 1968.
_____. *One-Dimensional Man*. Boston: Beacon Press, 1964.

Maritain, Jacques. *Man and State*. Chicago: University of Chicago Press, 1951.

Marx, Karl. *The German Ideology*. New York: International Publishers, 1970.
_____ and Friedrich Engels. *Selected Correspondence*. New York: International Publishers, Inc., 1936.

Marx, Werner. *Heidegger and the Tradition*, tr. T. Kisiel and M. Greene. Evanston, Illinois: Northwestern University Press, 1971.

Meaning of the Glorious Koran, The, ed. M.M. Pickthall. New York: Mentor, n.d.

Mumford, Lewis. *Technics and Civilization*. New York: Harcourt, Brace and World, 1934.

Myers, Max. " 'Ideology' and 'Legitimation' As Necessary Concepts for Christian Ethics," *Journal of the American Academy of Religion*, 49:2, pp. 187-207.

Nasr, Seyyed Hossein. "The Quran — the Word of God, the source of knowledge and action," *Ideals and Realities of Islam*. Boston: Beacon Press, 1966.

Neville, Robert C. *The Tao and the Daimon: Segments of a Religious Inquiry*. Albany, N.Y.: State University of New York Press, 1982.

New English Bible, The. New York: Cambridge University Press, 1961.

Niebuhr, Richard R. *Schleiermacher on Christ and Religion*. New York: C. Scribner's Sons, 1964.

Nietzsche, Friedrich. *The Will to Power*, tr. W. Kaufmann and R.J. Hollingdale. New York: Vintage Books, 1967.

Novak, Michael, ed. *The Corporation: A Theological Inquiry*. Washington, D.C.: American Enterprise Institute, 1980.

_____. *The Spirit of Democratic Capitalism*. New York: American Enterprise Institute/Simon and Schuster, 1982.

O'Keeffe, Terence M. "Ideology and the Protestant Principle," *Journal of the American Academy of Religion*. 51:2 (June 1983). pp. 305.

Olshewsky, Thomas. "Between Science and Religion," *The Journal of Religion*. 62:3, pp. 242-260.

Otto, Rudolf. *The Idea of the Holy*, tr. J. W. Harvey. London: Oxford University Press, 1928.

Paul VI. *Octogesima Adveniens*

Quine, Willard. "The Scope and Language of Science," *Ways of Paradox and Other Essays*. New York: Random House, 1966.

_____. "Ontology and Ideology Revisited," *The Journal of Philosophy*, 80:9 (Sept. 1983), pp. 499-502.

Rand, Ayn. *Atlas Shrugged*. New York: New American Library, 1957.

_____. "The Wreckage of the Consensus," *Capitalism: The Unknown Ideal*. New York: The New American Library, 1967.

Rank, Otto. *The Myth of the Birth of the Hero*, tr. C.F. Atkinson. New York: Vintage, 1932 (1959).

Raschke, Carl. "The Deconstruction of God," *Deconstruction and Theology*, ed. C. Raschke. New York: The Crossroad Publishing Co., 1982.

Rawls, John. *A Theory of Justice*. Cambridge, Mass.: Harvard University Press, 1971.

Reichel, Jörn, *Dichtungstheorie und Sprache bei Zinzendorf*. Bad Homburg, Germany: Gehlen, 1969.

Richardson, William. *Heidegger: Through Phenomenology to Thought*. The Hague: Martinus Nijhoff, 1974.

Ritschl, Dietrich, "Johann Salomo Semler: The Rise of the Historical-Critical Method in Eighteenth-Century Theology on the Continent,"

Introduction to Modernity, ed. R. Mollenauer. Austin, Texas: University of Texas Press, 1965.

Ryle, Gilbert. "Dispositions and Occurrences," *Dispositions*, ed. Raimo Tuomela. Dordrecht, Holland: D. Reidel, 1978.

Scharlemann, Robert P. "The Being of God When God Is Not Being God," *Deconstruction and Theology*, ed. Carl A. Raschke. New York: The Crossroad Publishing Co., 1982.

Schleiermacher, Friedrich. *On Religion: Speeches to its Cultured Despisers*, tr. J. Oman. New York: Harper and Row, 1958
_____. *The Christian Faith*, Vol. 1, ed. and tr. H.R. Mackintosh and J.S. Stewart. New York: Harper and Row, 1963.

Schneidermann, Stuart. *Jacques Lacan: The Death of an Intellectual Hero*. Cambridge, Mass.: Harvard University Press, 1983.

Skinner, B.F. *Beyond Freedom and Dignity*. New York: Alfred A. Knopf, 1971.

Smart, Ninian. *Beyond Ideology: Religion and the Future of Western Civilization*. San Francisco: Harper and Row, 1981.

Smith, Huston. *The Religions of Man*. New York: Harper and Row, 1958.

Solmsen, Friedrich. *Plato's Theology*. Ithaca, N.Y.: Cornell University Press, 1942.

Spencer-Brown, G. *Laws of Form*. New York: Julian Press, 1972.

Szasz, Thomas. *The Myth of Mental Illness: Foundations of a Theory of Personal Conduct* (rev. ed.). New York: Harper and Row, 1974.

Thompson, William I. *Passages About Earth: An Exploration of the New Planetary Culture*. New York: Harper and Row, 1974.
_____. *The Time Falling Bodies Take to Light*. New York: St. Martin's Press, 1981.

Tillich, Paul. *Dynamics of Faith*. New York: Harper and Row, 1957.
_____. *Systematic Theology*, Vol. 2. Chicago: University of Chicago Press, 1951.
_____. *Ultimate Concern: Tillich in Dialogue*, ed. D. Mackenzie Brown. New York: Harper and Row, 1965.

Vahanian, Gabriel. *The Death of God*. New York: Braziller, 1957.
_____. *God and Utopia*, tr. P. Lachance, P. Schwartz, R.D. Kozak, and author. New York: Seabury, 1977.

Warren, Mark. "Neitzsche's Concept of Ideology," *Theory and Society*, 13:4 (July 1984), pp. 541-565.

Wiggins, James B. "Within and Without Stories," *Religion as Story*, ed. J.B. Wiggins. New York: Harper and Row, 1975.

Wittgenstein, Ludwig. *Tractatus Logico-Philosophicus*, tr. D.F. Pears and B.F. McGuiness. London: Routledge and Kegan Paul, 1961.

Wood, Allen W. *Kant's Rational Philosophy*. Ithaca, N.Y.: Cornell University Press, 1978.

DATE DUE

MR21 '94			

DEMCO 38-297